TO HELL WITH THE DEVIL

By the Same Author:

JESUS OF NAZARETH, A DELUDED MESSIAH
THE END OF CHRISTIANITY
WHO, WHERE, AND WHAT IS GOD?
THE GOSPELS EXPLAINED

Albrecht Dürer: St Michael Overcoming the Devil

ALBERTUS PRETORIUS

TO HELL WITH THE DEVIL

AN ANALYSIS OF THE SCRIPTURES' TEACHINGS ABOUT SATAN

RESOURCE *Publications* • Eugene, Oregon

TO HELL WITH THE DEVIL
An Analysis of the Scriptures' Teachings about Satan

Resource Publications
An Imprint of Wipf and Stock Publishers
199 W. 8th Ave., Suite 3
Eugene, OR 97401

www.wipfandstock.com

PAPERBACK ISBN: 979-8-3852-1930-8
HARDCOVER ISBN: 979-8-3852-1931-5
EBOOK ISBN: 979-8-3852-1932-2

CONTENTS

CHAPTER	PAGE
FOREWORD	vii
1. INTRODUCTION: WHO THE DEVIL IS THE DEVIL?	1
2. CONVENTIONAL VIEWS ABOUT THE DEVIL	3
3. THE ANCIENT WORLD-VIEW	32
4. THE PROGRESS OF SCIENCE	84
5. READING AND UNDERSTANDING THE SCRIPTURES	103
6. SATAN IN THE HEBREW SCRIPTURES	115
7. SATAN IN THE CHRISTIAN SCRIPTURES	157
8. SATAN IN THE MUSLIM SCRIPTURES	247
9. DEDUCTIONS AND INTERPRETATIONS	255
BIBLIOGRAPHY	282
LIST OF ILLUSTRATIONS	291

Abbreviations Used:

APA	American Psychiatric Association
Cath Enc	Catholic Encyclopedia
Enc Brit	Encyclopaedia Britannica
Enc com	Encyclopedia.com
Jewish Enc	Jewish Encyclopedia
NW Enc	New World Encyclopedia

Albrecht Dürer: St Michael and his Angels Fight the Dragon

FOREWORD

Most of my adult life was spent in the ministry of the Dutch Reformed Church in South Africa. After studying at the Theological Seminary in the university town of Stellenbosch, I spent more than two years studying in Europe and helping in two congregations as a part-time pastor.

During my time as minister of religion in three congregations in South Africa, I continued my studies. In the end, I attained two doctorates and other qualifications. My motive was to be the best pastor and preacher I could hope to be.

When preparing a sermon, I always relied on my knowledge of ancient Hebrew and ancient Greek to analyze the biblical text I used for my message to my congregation. During my studies in South Africa and Europe, I was trained in the art of exegesis, the discipline of interpreting old texts. I was fortunate to lecture theology at two universities in South Africa. I intend using those skills and experience in writing this book to find out what the Scriptures can tell us about the devil and his demonic deputies.

I am confident that I am well qualified to tackle this controversial and challenging subject, namely whether or not there is sufficient proof for the belief of believers in the reality of Satan and other evil spirits.

During all the years I have spent in the ministry, I often encountered people who were confused regarding the teachings of the Bible about the devil and demons. Some of them ascribed the strange and often unacceptable behavior of others as cases of demonic possession. Cases of alcoholism or drug dependency were, for instance, attributed to the incursion of a demon into that person, with the result that the expulsion of this demon would lead to a cure.

Others lived in constant fear of being contaminated by anything that may have been associated with pagan idols, such as ceremonial masks from Africa or images of the Buddha, and the invisible demons lurking and hiding somewhere inside these objects.

After having written a number of books on biblical subjects, it dawned upon me that I ought to make a thorough study of what the Bible, as well as the Qur'an, teaches us about Satan. This book is the result. The attentive reader will note that I have included some paragraphs and passages from previous books of mine at appropriate spots.

This book is written from the perspective of a retired minister of religion who cannot forget that he spent most of his adult life in the service of the church, but who also wants to know as much as possible about the world in which we live.

Albertus Pretorius, South Africa, March 2024

Chapter 1
INTRODUCTION: WHO THE DEVIL IS THE DEVIL?

The devil is not an unfamiliar figure and we know him under various names and nicknames: Satan, Beelzebul, Old Nick, Mephistopheles, Lucifer, the Fiend, the Prince of Darkness, the Ruler of the Demons and Evil Spirits, the Evil One, Azazel, the Deuce, the Deceiver, the Old Serpent, and so forth.

But who is he really? Does he indeed exist? Or is he only a personification of all that is abdominal, bad, criminal, detestable, evil, frightening, horrible, indecent, and wrong? Many Jews, Christians, and Muslims do seem to think that he is a real spiritual personage, trying to lure people into bad and wrong actions, as well as the source of all calamities, chaos, and catastrophes. This figure is often encountered in the holy Scriptures of these religions and most believers take it for granted that the descriptions of Satan in their Scriptures can be relied upon.

He is usually regarded as a spiritual and non-material figure who is able to read people's minds and infect their thoughts with bad intentions and wishes and lead them into wrong and bad deeds by his temptations and tricks and telepathic messages. Children are often warned not to allow the devil a place in their lives. But, apart from that, he remains a shadowy, spooky, sinister, and surreal figure.

In our age, where we are surrounded by technological marvels and where knowledge about scientific break-throughs is common, more and more people seem to regard him as a piece of mythology, fiction, and/or part of fairy tales, in the same league as

Father Christmas, the Easter Bunny, the Loch Ness Monster, or the Tooth Mouse. One may, therefore, ask: Who the devil is the devil? Does the devil still have the right to exist and make life miserable for people?

The Scriptures also describe lesser little devils, called evil or unclean spirits and demons. They are popularly regarded as Satan's helpers, his fighters who do all the dirty work – more or less as Darth Vader served the "Dark Side".

The object of this book is to analyze what the Bible, as well as the Qur'an, can teach us about this cruel, dark, evil, invisible, naughty, and seemingly powerful figure, the adversary of God – and how we must understand him.

This study explores the official stances of Protestant Churches and the Catholic Church regarding the devil, as formulated in their confessional creeds and other official documents. It may be assumed that believers from the Orthodox Churches harbor similar ideas.

Thereafter, it will be explained how the authors of the different books of the Bible described the world in which we live and how we must understand and interpret those descriptions against the background of the insights gained by credible scientists about the world. The appearances of Satan in the Old Testament, the New

Testament, and the Qur'an are explored and placed in perspective. The findings and conclusions of this investigation will be summarized in a final chapter.

It is, therefore, necessary to describe the pre-scientific and mythological world-view as found in the Scriptures, as well as how educated people of our age understand the world in which we live, due to all the scientific and technological advances of our age.

The devil became a rather controversial figure in the Dutch Reformed Church in South Africa during recent years. The general synod of this denomination adopted reports in 2007 in which it was left to members to decide for themselves whether to believe or not to believe in the existence of this figure.

Many conservatively-minded members and congregations of this church protested against this stance, because they were convinced that the existence of Satan and demons is clearly and explicitly taught in the Bible. A conservative reformed theologian such as Professor Flip Buys of the Reformed Theological Faculty at Potchefstroom University ascribed this position as the outcome of a liberal theology that had gained a foothold in many mainstream churches.[1] This book is an effort to bring more clarity on this topic.

In this book, the proper name of Satan will be written with a capital "S", while the designation "devil", as an indication of what type of entity or being we are dealing with, will be spelt with a lowercase "d".

[1] Buys, "The Relevance of Reformed Perspectives".

Chapter 2
CONVENTIONAL VIEWS ABOUT THE DEVIL

Before we can declare, "to hell with the devil", it is necessary to determine what Christians usually understand when they talk, think, and are troubled about the devil. For that purpose, four confessional creeds of Protestant churches must be scrutinized, namely he Augsburg Confession, the Belgic Confession, the Heidelberg Catechism, and the Westminster Confession.

The practice of exorcism of the Roman Catholic Church will also be dealt with.

THE AUGSBURG CONFESSION

This confession was formulated by the reformer, Philip Melanchton, and was submitted to His Imperial Majesty Charles V of the Holy Roman Empire at the Diet of Augsburg in 1530. It is accepted by Lutheran churches world-wide as an expression of their faith.

This document contains 24 articles, of which Article 23 is the longest and in which certain superstitions, erroneous beliefs, and abuses of the Roman Catholic Church of the sixteenth century are rejected. The other articles describe the doctrines accepted by Protestants. The articles in which the devil is mentioned are discussed below:

Article III: Of the Son of God

> He also descended into hell, and truly rose again the third day; afterward He ascended into heaven that He might sit on the right

> hand of the Father, and forever reign and have dominion over all creatures, and sanctify them that believe in Him, by sending the Holy Ghost into their hearts, to rule, comfort, and quicken them, and to defend them against the devil and the power of sin.

The existence of the devil is taken for granted and it assumed that everybody would know who or what is meant by this word. The point that this article wishes to make is that Jesus Christ, who experienced hell when he was crucified and who was resurrected and ascended to heaven, protects those who believe in him against the onslaughts of the devil. No details of these onslaughts are given, but they presumably consist of temptations to commit sins and disobey God.

Article XVII: Of Christ's Return to Judgment

> Also they teach that at the Consummation of the World Christ will appear for judgment, and will raise up all the dead; He will give to the godly and elect eternal life and everlasting joys, but ungodly men and the devils He will condemn to be tormented without end.
> They condemn the Anabaptists, who think that there will be an end to the punishments of condemned men and devils. They condemn also others who are now spreading certain Jewish opinions, that before the resurrection of the dead the godly shall take possession of the kingdom of the world, the ungodly being everywhere suppressed.

This article mentions "devils" in the plural. This is clearly a reference to demons or evil spirits. They will be banished to everlasting punishment in hell on Judgment Day when Christ returns to the earth.

The doctrine of chiliasm or postmillennialism is also rejected.

Article XIX: Of the Cause of Sin.

> Of the Cause of Sin they teach that, although God does create and preserve nature, yet the cause of sin is the will of the wicked, that is, of the devil and ungodly men; which will, unaided of God, turns itself from God, as Christ says John 8, 44: "When he speaketh a lie, he speaketh of his own."

The sins committed by the devil and ungodly people cannot be ascribed to God who created the world but is due to their own choices and decisions.

Article XX: Of Good Works.

> Men are also admonished that here the term "faith" does not signify merely the knowledge of the history, such as is in the ungodly and in the *devil*, but signifies a faith which believes, not merely the history, but also the effect of the history—namely, this article: the forgiveness of sins, to wit, that we have grace, righteousness, and forgiveness of sins through Christ. Now he that knows that he has a Father gracious to him through Christ, truly knows God; he knows also that God cares for him, and calls upon God; in a word, he is not without God, as the heathen. For devils and the ungodly are not able to believe this article: the forgiveness of sins. Hence, they hate God as an enemy, call not upon Him, and expect no good from Him.
> Furthermore, it is taught on our part that it is necessary to do good works, not that we should trust to merit grace by them, but because it is the will of God. It is only by faith that forgiveness of sins is apprehended, and that, for nothing. And because through faith the Holy Ghost is received, hearts are renewed and endowed with new affections, so as to be able to bring forth good works. For Ambrose

says: Faith is the mother of a good will and right doing. For man's powers without the Holy Ghost are full of ungodly affections, and are too weak to do works which are good in God's sight. Besides, they are in the power of the devil who impels men to divers sins, to ungodly opinions, to open crimes. This we may see in the philosophers, who, although they endeavored to live an honest life could not succeed, but were defiled with many open crimes. Such is the feebleness of man when he is without faith and without the Holy Ghost, and governs himself only by human strength.

The devil is mentioned on three occasions in this article. Although the devil and ungodly men may be familiar with the history described in the Bible, that does not amount to a genuine faith and does not lead to good works on account of the forgiveness of sins.

Article XXIII: Of the Marriage of Priests

But while the commandment of God is in force, while the custom of the Church is well known, while impure celibacy causes many scandals, adulteries, and other crimes deserving the punishments of just magistrates, yet it is a marvelous thing that in nothing is more cruelty exercised than against the marriage of priests. God has given commandment to honor marriage. By the laws of all well-ordered commonwealths, even among the heathen, marriage is most highly honored. But now men, and that, priests, are cruelly put to death, contrary to the intent of the Canons, for no other cause than marriage. Paul, in 1 Tim. 4, 3, calls that a doctrine of devils which forbids marriage. This may now be readily understood when the law against marriage is maintained by such penalties.

The practice of the Roman Catholic Church to expect of priests to stay celibate and never to marry, is called a doctrine of the devil. It may be assumed that all doctrines that do not agree with the Bible may be deemed to have originated with the devil.

Article XXVI: Of the Distinction of Meats

Col. 2, 16: "Let no man, therefore, judge you in meat, or in drink, or in respect of a holy-day, or of the Sabbath-day"; also: "If ye be dead with Christ from the rudiments of the world, why, as though living in the world, are ye subject to ordinances: Touch not, taste not, handle not!" And Peter says, Acts 15, 10: "Why tempt ye God to put a yoke upon the neck of the disciples, which neither our fathers nor we were able to bear? But we believe that through the grace of the Lord Jesus Christ we shall be saved, even as they." Here Peter forbids to burden the consciences with many rites, either of Moses or of others. And in 1 Tim. 4, 1. 3 Paul calls the prohibition of meats "a doctrine of *devils*"; for it is against the Gospel to institute or to do such works that by them we may merit grace, or as though Christianity could not exist without such service of God.

The custom of the Roman Catholic Church to force its members to adhere to certain dietary prescriptions, which run counter to the Bible, is called a doctrine of the devil.

Article XXVIII: Of Ecclesiastical Power

If bishops have the right to burden churches with infinite traditions, and to ensnare consciences, why does Scripture so often prohibit to make, and to listen to, traditions? Why does it call them "doctrines of *devils*"? 1 Tim. 4, 1. Did the Holy Ghost in vain forewarn of these things?

The reliance of the Catholic Church on tradition – alongside the teachings of Scripture and even contradicted by Scripture – must be rejected as a doctrine inspired by the devil.

THE BELGIC CONFESSION

The website of the Christian Reformed Church in the USA describes this document as follows:

> "The oldest of the doctrinal standards of the Christian Reformed Church is the Confession of Faith, popularly known as the Belgic Confession, following the seventeenth-century Latin designation 'Confessio Belgica.' 'Belgica' referred to the whole of the Netherlands, both north and south, which today is divided into the Netherlands and Belgium. The confession's chief author was Guido de Bräs, a preacher of the Reformed churches of the Netherlands, who died a martyr to the faith in the year 1567. (…)
>
> "De Bräs prepared this confession in the year 1561. In the following year a copy was sent to King Philip II [of Spain, who also ruled over the Netherlands], together with an address in which the petitioners declared that they were ready to obey the government in all lawful things, but that they would 'offer their backs to stripes, their tongues to knives, their mouths to gags, and their whole bodies to the fire,' rather than deny the truth expressed in this confession."

This confession teaches the following regarding the devil:

Article 12: The Creation of All Things

We believe that the Father, when it seemed good to him, created heaven and earth and all other creatures from nothing, by the Word — that is to say, by the Son. God has given all creatures their being, form, and appearance and their various functions for serving their Creator. Even now God also sustains and governs them all, according to his eternal providence and by his infinite power, that they may serve humanity, in order that humanity may serve God. God has also created the angels good, that they might be messengers of God and serve the elect. Some of them have fallen from the excellence in which God created them into eternal perdition; and the others have persisted and remained in their original state, by the grace of God. The devils and evil spirits are so corrupt that they are enemies of God and of everything good. They lie in wait for the church and every member of it like thieves, with all their power, to destroy and spoil everything by their deceptions. So then, by their own wickedness they are condemned to everlasting damnation, daily awaiting their torments. For that reason, we detest the error of the Sadducees, who deny that there are spirits and angels, and also the error of the Manicheans, who say that the devils originated by themselves, being evil by nature, without having been corrupted.

God created everything and still rules his creation. He also created the angels, spiritual beings, to serve Him and mankind. Some of them rebelled against God and became devils and evil spirits. They lure people to commit sins and they are the source of all that is bad and wrong. They will all be sentenced to everlasting damnation as their deserved punishment.

Article 13: The Doctrine of God's Providence

We believe that this good God, after he created all things, did not abandon them to chance or fortune but leads and governs them according to his holy will, in such a way that nothing happens in this world without his orderly arrangement.

Yet God is not the author of, nor can he be charged with, the sin that occurs. For his power and goodness are so great and incomepre-

hensible that he arranges and does his work very well and justly even when the devils and wicked men act unjustly.
We do not wish to inquire with undue curiosity into what he does that surpasses human understanding and is beyond our ability to comprehend. But in all humility and reverence we adore the just judgments of God, which are hidden from us, being content to be Christ's disciples, so as to learn only what he shows us in his Word, without going beyond those limits.
This doctrine gives us unspeakable comfort since it teaches us that nothing can happen to us by chance but only by the arrangement of our gracious heavenly Father. He watches over us with fatherly care, keeping all creatures under his control, so that not one of the hairs on our heads (for they are all numbered) nor even a little bird can fall to the ground without the will of our Father.
In this thought we rest, knowing that he holds in check the devils and all our enemies, who cannot hurt us without his permission and will. For that reason we reject the damnable error of the Epicureans, who say that God involves himself in nothing and leaves everything to chance.

This article teaches that God, as creator, rules his creation with the result that nothing just happens by chance, but must be seen as the acts of God. Believers are assured that God will protect them against the onslaughts of the devils and evil spirits. Although nothing happens without God's will, He cannot be seen as the author of evil.

Article 14: The Creation and Fall of Man

We believe that God created man from the dust of the earth and made and formed him in his image and likeness-- good, just, and holy; able by his own will to conform in all things to the will of God.
But when he was in honor he did not understand it and did not

> recognize his excellence. But he subjected himself willingly to sin and consequently, to death and the curse, lending his ear to the word of the devil.
> For he transgressed the commandment of life, which he had received, and by his sin he separated himself from God, who was his true life, having corrupted his entire nature.
> So he made himself guilty and subject to physical and spiritual death, having become wicked, perverse, and corrupt in all his ways. He lost all his excellent gifts which he had received from God, and he retained none of them except for small traces which are enough to make him inexcusable. (…)

Although the idea of human free will is rejected – which means that all our actions are being determined by God – man, nevertheless, decided to listen to the devil and fell into sin. The result is that man became bad and godless, is guilty in the eyes of God, and his transgressions are "inexcusable".

Article 34: The Sacrament of Baptism

This article, which deals with baptism, mentions the devil in passing and equates him with Pharaoh, from whom the Israelites fled out of Egypt and through the Red Sea, which is a symbol of baptism.

Article 37: The Last Judgment

> (…) The evil ones will be convicted by the witness of their own consciences, and shall be made immortal-- but only to be tormented in the everlasting fire prepared for the devil and his angels. (…)

This single sentence from a much longer passage declares that "the evil ones" – the unrepentant sinners – will share "the everlasting fire" in hell with the chief devil and his followers, the demons, evil spirits, or fallen angels.

This means that the devil is not at present residing in hell. That will only be his fate on Judgment Day.

THE HEIDELBERG CATECHISM

According to the website of the Christian Reformed Church in the USA, this creed can be described as follows:

> "This catechism, or instruction in the Christian faith, received its name from the place of its origin, Heidelberg, Germany, the capital of the Electorate of the Palatinate. That the Reformed faith might be taught and maintained in his domain, the godly elector Frederick III commissioned Zacharias Ursinus, professor at the Heidelberg University, and Caspar Olevianus, court preacher, to prepare a manual for instructing the youth and guiding pastors and teachers in the basic doctrines of the Christian faith. Prepared with the advice and cooperation of the entire theological faculty, heartily approved by the Elector himself, and sanctioned by the Synodical gathering of prominent Reformed preachers and theologians, it was first published in Heidelberg with a preface dated January 19, 1563."

Preamble

Question 1: What is your only comfort in life and in death?
Answer: That I, body and soul, both in life and in death,1 am not my own, but belong to my faithful Savior Jesus Christ, who with His precious blood has fully satisfied for all my sins, and redeemed me from all the power of the devil; and so preserves me that without the

will of my Father in heaven not a hair can fall from my head; indeed, that all things must work together for my salvation. Wherefore, by His Holy Spirit, He also assures me of eternal life, and makes me heartily willing and ready from now on to live unto Him.

This preamble contains a short summary of the beliefs of Christians of Reformed persuasion. It states, inter alia, that believers are confident that they were redeemed from the power of the devil by Christ.

The existence and origin of the devil is not explained and it is accepted that the readers would know who or what the devil is.

The Fall of Man

Question 9: Does not God, then, do injustice to man by requiring of him in His Law that which he cannot perform?
Answer: No, for God so made man that he could perform it;1 but man, through the instigation of the devil, by willful disobedience deprived himself and all his descendants of those divine gifts.

This portion declares that man freely chose to disobey God after having been tempted by the devil.

Anointed Christians

Question 32: But why are you called a Christian?
Answer: Because by faith I am a member of Christ1 and thus a partaker of His anointing, in order that I also may confess His Name, may present myself a living sacrifice of thankfulness to Him, and with a free conscience may fight against sin and the devil in this life, and hereafter in eternity reign with Him over all creatures.

Believers who partake in the anointment of Christ have the duty to fight against sin and the devil.

Bought by the Blood of Christ

Question 34: Why do you call Him "our Lord"?
Answer: Because not with silver or gold, but with His precious blood, He has redeemed and purchased us, body and soul, from sin and from all the power of the *devil*, to be His own.

Christ is the Lord of a believer's life, because he was bought by Christ's blood from the power of the devil.

The Commandment to be Truthful

Question 112: What does the ninth commandment require?
Answer: That I bear false witness against no one,1 twist no one's words, be no backbiter or slanderer,3 join in condemning no one unheard or rashly; but that on pain of God's heavy wrath, I avoid all lying and deceit as the very works of the devil; and that in matters of judgment and justice and in all other affairs, I love, speak honestly, and confess the truth; also, insofar as I can, defend and promote my neighbor's good name.

It is expected of Christians to always speak the truth since deceit and lying are the works of the devil.

The Kingdom of God

Question 123: What is the second petition?
Answer: "Your kingdom come;" that is, so govern us by Your Word and Spirit, that we submit ourselves to You always more and more;1 preserve and increase Your Church; destroy the works of the devil, every power that exalts itself against You, and all wicked devices formed against Your Holy Word, until the fullness of Your kingdom come, wherein You shall be all in all.

It is expected of Christians to pray for the coming of God's kingdom, which will become visible where people accept God's authority and where the works of the devil and all other ungodly powers are destroyed. The kingdom will be only totally realized on Judgment Day when the devil will be finally vanquished.

Deliverance from the Evil One

Queston 127: What is the sixth petition?
Answer: "And do not lead us into temptation, but deliver us from the evil one;" that is, since we are so weak in ourselves that we cannot stand a moment,1 and besides, our deadly enemies, the devil, the world, and our own flesh, assail us without ceasing, be pleased to preserve and strengthen us by the power of Your Holy Spirit, that we may make firm stand against them and not be overcome in this spiritual warfare, until finally complete victory is ours.

When Christians pray to be delivered from the evil one, the devil, they acknowledge their lack of power to take a firm stand against the devil, the world, and their own weak flesh, and that they need the help of God.

THE WESTMINSTER CONFESSION OF FAITH

The Westminster Confession of Faith is an expression of the beliefs of English-speaking Presbyterians. It was written on behalf of the Westminster Assembly, which was called together by the Long Parliament in 1643, during the English Civil War. This assembly met regularly in Westminster Abbey until 1649. The document was completed in 1646 and presented to Parliament for approval in June 1648 after some revisions.

When the English monarchy was restored in 1660, the episcopal form of church government was reinstated, and the

Presbyterian confession lost its official status in England. It was, though, adopted by the Church of Scotland in 1647. Various Presbyterian churches in other countries regard it as authoritative, as well. Some Congregationalists and Baptists also adopted this confession.[2]

Chapter I

Of the Holy Scripture

I. Although the light of nature, and the works of creation and providence, do so far manifest the goodness, wisdom, and power of God, as to leave men inexcusable; yet are they not sufficient to give that knowledge of God, and of his will, which is necessary unto salvation; therefore it pleased the Lord, at sundry times, and in divers manners, to reveal himself, and to declare that his will unto his Church; and afterwards for the better preserving and propagating of the truth, and for the more sure establishment and comfort of the Church against the corruption of the flesh, and the malice of Satan and of the world, to commit the same wholly unto writing; which maketh the holy Scripture to be most necessary; those former ways of God's revealing his will unto his people being now ceased.

It was necessary for God to reveal his will for mankind in writing in the holy Scriptures to counter "the malice of Satan". The existence and identity of Satan is regarded as an established fact.

Chapter V

Of Providence

VI. As for those wicked and ungodly men whom God, as a righteous judge, for former sins, doth blind and harden; from

[2] Enc Brit, "Westminster Confession".

> them he not only withholdeth his grace, whereby they might have been enlightened in their understandings, and wrought upon their hearts; but sometimes also withdraweth the gifts which they had; and exposeth them to such objects as their corruption makes occasion of sin; and withal, gives them over to their own lusts, the temptations of the world, and the power of Satan; whereby it comes to pass that they harden themselves, even under those means which God useth for the softening of others.

God allows wicked people to give in to their lusts, the temptations of the world, and the power of Satan, although He will condemn them for their sins.

Chapter VI

Of the Fall of Man, of Sin, and of the Punishment thereof

> I. Our first parents, begin seduced by the subtlety and temptations of Satan, sinned in eating the forbidden fruit. This their sin God was pleased, according to his wise and holy counsel, to permit, having purposed to order it to his own glory.

God permitted man to fall into sin after being seduced by the temptations of Satan.

Chapter XVII

Of The Perseverance of the Saints

> III. Nevertheless they may, through the temptations of Satan and of the world, the prevalancy of corruption remaining in them, and the neglect of the means of their perseverance, fall into grievous sins; ad for a time continue therein: whereby they

> incur God's displeasure, and grieve his Holy Spirit; come to be deprived of some measure of their graces and comforts; have their hearts hardened, and their consciences wounded; hurt and prevalancy others, and bring temporal judgments upon themselves.

It is possible that the saints, the believers, may succumb to the temptations of the world and Satan and commit serious sins. That will, however, not cause them to forfeit God's grace.

Chapter XX

Of Christian Liberty, and Liberty of Conscience

> I. The liberty which Christ hath purchased for believers under the gospel consists in their freedom from the guilt of sin, the condemning wrath of God, the curse of the moral law; and in their being delivered from this present evil world, bondage to Satan, and dominion of sin, from the evil of afflictions, the sting of death, the victory of the grave, and everlasting damnation; as also in their free access to God, and their yielding obedience unto him, not out of slavish fear, but a childlike love, and a willing mind. All which were common also to believers under the law; but under the New Testament the liberty of Christians is further enlarged in their freedom from the yoke of the ceremonial law, to which the Jewish Church was subjected; and in greater boldness of access to the throne of grace, and in fuller communications of the free Spirit of God, than believers under the law did ordinarily partake of.

Sinners who are caught in "bondage to Satan" are liberated by Christ when they believe.

Chapter XXI

Of Religious Worship and the Sabbath-day

I. The light of nature showeth that there is a God, who hath lordship and sovereignty over all; is good, and doeth good unto all; and is therefore to be feared, loved, praised, called upon, trusted in, and served with all the hearth, and with all the soul, and with all the might. But the acceptable way of worshipping the true God is instituted by himself, and so limited by his own revealed will, that he may not be worshipped according to the imaginations and devices of men, or the suggestions of Satan, under any visible representation or any other way not prescribed in the holy Scripture.

God must be worshipped according to his prescriptions, and not according to the "suggestions of Satan".

ROMAN CATHOLIC THEOLOGY

The position of the Roman Catholic Church regarding Satan is explained by the Catholic Encyclopedia as follows:

> "Mention is made of the Devil in many passages of the Old and New Testaments, but there is no full account given in any one place, and the Scripture teaching on this topic can only be ascertained by combining a number of scattered notices from Genesis to Apocalypse, and reading them in the light of patristic and theological tradition.
>
> "The authoritative teaching of the Church on this topic is set forth in the decrees of the Fourth Lateran Council (cap. i, 'Firmiter credimus'), wherein, after saying that God in the beginning had created together two crea-

> tures, the spiritual and the corporeal, that is to say the angelic and the earthly, and lastly man, who was made of both spirit and body, the council continues:
> 'Diabolus enim et alii dæmones a Deo quidem naturâ creati sunt boni, sed ipsi per se facti sunt mali.' ('The Devil and the other demons were created by God good in their nature but they by themselves have made themselves evil.')"

Kent remarks: "Here it is clearly taught that the Devil and the other demons are spiritual or angelic creatures created by God in a state of innocence, and that they became evil by their own act. It is added that man sinned by the suggestion of the Devil, and that in the next world the wicked shall suffer perpetual punishment with the Devil."[3]

The Catholic Encyclopedia provides the following definition of exorcism:

> "Exorcism is (1) the act of driving out, or warding off, demons, or evil spirits, from persons, places, or things, which are believed to be possessed or infested by them, or are liable to become victims or instruments of their malice; (2) the means employed for this purpose, especially the solemn and authoritative adjuration of the demon, in the name of God, or any of the higher power in which he is subject."

This definition presupposes the reality of evil spirits, which can inhabit people, places, and objects. They can be driven out by appropriate ceremonies and rituals.

---

[3] Kent, Đevil".

SUMMARY

The Augsburg Confession does not tell us much about the nature and origin of the devil. His existence is taken for granted and he is described as the origin of false doctrines that cannot be reconciled with the Bible. His sinful nature cannot be ascribed to God who created the world and rules it.

The Belgic Confession contains a little more information about the devil than the Augsburg Confession. The most important is that some angels rebelled against God and thereby became the devil and other evil spirits. The devil is the source of all that is evil, bad, and sinful, and he tries to trap people to fall into sin. He and the demons will receive their deserved punishment on Judgment Day when they will be banished to hell with its everlasting fire.

The Catechism regards the existence of the devil as given. Christians are saved from the clutches of the devil by Christ's blood on the cross and they can rely on God to aid them in their struggle against the devil and the temptations in the world. All deceit, lying, and other sins are the works of the devil. In contrast with the Belgic Confession, the Catechism declares that man chose freely to listen to the devil and become disobedient towards God.

Very little information about the devil or Satan is given in the Westminster Confession. He is merely mentioned as the seducer of man to fall into sin by causing man to succumb to temptations. Satan is the source of superstitions and sin. Believers are, though, freed from his grip by Christ who protects them against his onslaughts.

It transpired that the thinking in the Catholic tradition regarding the devil agrees largely with Protestant views. Exorcism or the expulsion of demons is practiced in this church.

Many popular Christian authors provide their readers with a similar overview. A good example is, for instance, the book by well-known evangelist Billy Graham: Angels, God's Secret Agents, which was reprinted several times. He explained that Satan or Lucifer is the leader of a group of angels who rejected God's authority and were banned or exiled from heaven.

All the confessions quoted above regard the existence of an evil spiritual being and a fallen angel, the devil or Satan, as a matter of fact. After all, the Bible, as the Word of God, often refers to him and his demons or evil spirits. He is described as the origin of sin and erroneous beliefs. He lured the first humans to eat of the forbidden fruit and become disobedient towards God. He can be regarded as the main opponent of God and his fate is sealed because he, his demons, and all godless people will be condemned to hell.

Pan – Greco-Roman Antioch Floor Mosaic, 3rd Century A.D. (Hatay Archaeology Museum, Antakya)

One can safely conclude that this presentation of the devil is still more or less the popular mental picture of many believers in our time. He is even represented in caricatures as a beast wit horns, a tail, and the legs of a goat – almost the same as the ancient god Pan.

Satan has been portrayed in a great number of works of art by artists through the centuries. He has appeared in many stories and films. The three most important literary works dealing with Satan are The Divine Comedy by Dante Alighieri, Paradise Lost by John Milton, and The Tragedy of Faust by Johann Wolfgang von Goethe.

THE INQUISITION AND DEVIL PHOBIA

Ecclesiastical Courts

The darkest chapter in the history of Christianity is certainly the story of the Holy Inquisition, a series of ecclesiastical courts that had to try people suspected of heresy and witchcraft. These courts were active between the twelfth and nineteenth centuries in Europe and the Americas. Witches had to be rooted out because they were allies or agents of Satan and heretics had to be removed from society because they got their evil and erroneous ideas from the devil.

The origin of the Inquisition can be traced to Pope Lucius III who ordered bishops in 1184 to root out all forms of heresy in their dioceses. Pope Gregory IX appointed special ecclesiastical judges as inquisitors, mostly from the ranks of the Dominican and Franciscan orders, and they had jurisdiction over all Christians, except for bishops and their officials. There was no central authority for these judges other than the Pope and his bureaucrats. The first manual for the conduct of inquiries onto heresy and how to deal with heretics was issued in 1248.[4]

The normal rules of justice were not followed during these inquiries and trials. Failure to appear at a trial was considered an admission of guilt. Formal charge sheets were mostly not issued to the suspects, they were usually not informed of who accused or denounced them, and they were not allowed legal representation. Confessions of guilt were often extracted through torture. No appeal against a finding of guilt was possible.

People found guilty were handed over to the civil authorities and they were often incarcerated for life in solitary confinement or burned at the stake. Thousands died in this way. For instance, in Andalusia, Spain, two thousand heretics and witches were burned in

[4] Enc Brit, "Inquisition".

1482 alone. Burning was the preferred method of execution because it did not entail the spilling of blood, which was deemed to be abhorrent to Catholic clerics. When mitigating circumstances were found, the victim was not burned but strangled. Those who confessed and renounced their heretical beliefs and the devil were usually punished less harshly, including imprisonment and confiscation of all their possessions, which left them destitute.

Even dead people could be subjected to a trial by the Inquisition. If anybody was accused of heresy after having died, his or her body or bones could be dug up, put on trial, and then consigned to the flames.

Needless to say, the excommunication that went with a verdict of guilt, with the authority of the Pope behind it, automatically meant that the soul of that person was sent directly to hell, even months or years after his or her death. The belongings of the condemned that were inherited by his or her heirs were also confiscated and the inquisitors could keep part of the proceeds for themselves; the rest went to the Pope.

No record exists of any accused who was found to be innocent. There were cases, however, where no proof of guilt could be found. Just to be on the safe side, the poor accused victim was locked up in a dungeon for the rest of his or her life.

The inquisitors, who were mostly bishops and priests, were naturally concerned about the salvation of the souls of those whom they tried, tortured, and tormented. It was thought that any method justified the end, that is, the salvation of the soul of the suspect. If that person confessed his sins and accepted the doctrines of the church, be it under duress, then that person was saved from eternal damnation in hell – which was, of course, much more important than living a life without persecution, pain, and punishment.

The members of the Inquisition were convinced that they

had biblical authority for doing what they did. After all, the apostle Paul emphatically called the condemnation of God upon all those who preached a Gospel that differed from his (Gal 1: 8–9). Various passages in the Old Testament called for the execution of those who were guilty of breaking the Sabbath, adultery, fornication, sodomy, sorcery, or idolatry.

Inquisitors had papal authority to absolve each other should it happen that they caused accidental deaths or unnecessary pain upon their unfortunate tortured victims.

Tomas de Torquemada

The most infamous inquisitor was the Spanish Dominican friar Tomas de Torquemada (1420–1498). During his reign of 15 years more than 114 000 people fell victim to his tender ministra-tions and 10 220 were consigned to the flames.

Moreover, the inquisitors had the promise of the Pope that their good deeds by rooting out heresy and witchcraft and fighting against Satan would guarantee them a place of honor in heaven.

The Inquisition's reign of terror rendered any resistance to this cruel institution ineffective. People were simply too afraid to speak out against these practices and they rather fled abroad if they thought that they stood a chance of being denounced or reported and prosecuted. Only after the Napoleonic wars, in 1818, were these barbaric practices abolished by the Roman Catholic Church.[5]

---

[5] Enc Brit, "Inquisition, Burning at the Stake and Heresy"; Martinez, "The Spanish Terror:, 64–75; De Rosa, *Vicars of Christ*, 102, 162–78.

In our age, we just cannot condone the actions of the Inquisition. We find these deeds to be cruel, sadistic, bad, tragically misguided, and totally wrong. But our judgment should perhaps not be too harsh – these people honestly believed that they were serving God and executed his will by getting rid of people who served the devil. They were convinced that they were doing their victims a favor by saving them from the horrors of hell if they repented as well as ridding the holy church of dangerous and despicable heretics and witches.

In the light of all this, the following evaluation of the inquisitors by the Catholic Encyclopedia is utterly incomprehensible: "Far from being inhuman, they were, as a rule, men of spotless character and sometimes of truly admirable sanctity, and not a few of them have been canonized by the Church. There is absolutely no reason to look on the medieval ecclesiastical judge as intellectually and morally inferior to the modern judge."

However, this encyclopedia does concede that torture was indeed applied: "Curiously enough, torture was not regarded as a mode of punishment, but purely as a means of eliciting the truth." The encyclopedia also had to admit: "Torture was applied only too frequently and too cruelly…"[6]

Protestants were also guilty of killing heretics. For instance, the Spanish theologian, Miguel Servet, was found guilty of heresy and burned alive on 27 October 1553 in the Protestant town of Geneva with the approval of the reformer John Calvin, although he preferred beheading instead of burning.[7]

Witch Hunts

During the past, but especially during the 14th to 18th centuries AD,

---

[6] Cath Enc, "Inquisition".

[7] Enc Brit, "Servetus, Michael".

when the lives of people were ruled by all sorts of superstitions, people were very easily suspected of witchery or sorcery if they displayed any type of eccentric behavior, suffered from a mental disorder, or looked different from their neighbors. Witches and sorcerers were seen as the allies and servants of Satan and, therefore, had to be exterminated. The church got biblical authority for these steps from Deut 18: 9–14, 2 Kgs 9: 22, 2 Chr 33: 6, Mic 5: 12, Gal 5: 20, and Rev 22: 14–15 where sorcery and witchcraft were condemned and the death penalty was ordered by God.

It was one of the tasks of the Inquisition to root out all witches and rid the earth of these instruments of the devil. Protestants, likewise, were guilty of hunting and killing suspected witches.

Since these wretched people were thought to be in cahoots with Satan, they had no rights whatsoever and they could be tortured and killed at will by ecclesiastic and secular courts. It is known that up to half of the populations of certain villages fell victim to this inhuman practice. The pleas for mercy and screams of their victims convinced the inquisitors and torturers that they were inflicting pain on Satan himself.

A manual for the treatment of witches was issued by the Inquisition, called the Malleus Maleficorum (Hammer of the Witches). It contained fantastic tales of sexual orgies, sexual intercourse with the devil, and satanic worship given by people under torture who said anything their tormentors wanted to hear. These tales were dished up as the holy truth, and Satan almost gained as much power over the credulous and superstitious clergy as the almighty God himself.[8]

It must be remarked that no case was ever recorded where a

---

[8] Enc Brit, "Witchcraft"; De Rosa, *Vicars of Christ,* 181–91.

single witch or sorcerer was able to use his or her supposed magical powers against the inquisitors or to free themselves from the torture chambers. In no single case did Satan aid any of his alleged followers to harm or stop the ecclesiastical and secular judges after they had been cursed by their victims. The evil powers ascribed to the so-called witches by the Inquisition were, therefore, purely a case of wishful or delusional thinking. The extreme obsessional interest of many inquisitors in the imagined sexual exploits of their victims must have been quite sick and pathological.[9]

Exorcism

The present author had the dubious privilege of witnessing ceremonies where exorcism was performed, usually in charismatic or Pentecostal groups. These practices are often executed in a church, but also in private homes. It usually amounts to great entertainment for the onlookers.

Those who regard themselves as having the gift of discerning the spirits, usually put up a great show. The poor person who was suspected of having been invaded by a demon, was made to sit or stand at a spot where the exorcist(s) could perform their rituals on him or her. These rituals usually consisted of prayers shouted at the top of the exorcist's voice, insults aimed at the demon, dancing, chants, the singing of hymns, repeating certain biblical texts or potent formulae, the laying on of hands, the handling of Bibles, crucifixes, and burning candles, and the sprinkling of olive oil or holy water.

The person suspected of harboring an evil spirit often went into convulsions as the suspected spirit struggled against the efforts of the exorcists. This person often started to sob, scream, or fall

---

9 De Rosa, *Vicars of Christ,* 189–90.

down in a swoon. Cases are known where victims were even assaulted to drive the demons away.

Buys, an expert on Christianity in Africa, reported that especially Pentecostal pastors in countries such as Nigeria or the Congo demand large amounts of money from parents to exorcise evil spirits from their vulnerable children with health problems.[10]

A former parishioner of the present author told him of his mother who had a demon phobia. She saw a demon in every and any mishap and she even tried to exorcise an evil spirit from her motor car in the name of Jesus when this vehicle refused to move any further. When he rushed to help his mother, it transpired that the fuel tank was empty.

Many mental disorders and diseases, like cancer, are often attacked in this manner – without any visible or permanent cure.

It must be pointed out that these exorcists, who do their best to drive demons from believers, forget the following remarks in the Bible:

- "Don`t you know that you are a temple of God, and that God`s Spirit lives in you?" (1 Cor 3: 16).
- "For you are a temple of the living God" (2 Cor 6:16).
- The same thought occurs in Rom 8: 11; 1 Cor 6:19; Eph 2:20; Hebr 3:6; 1 Peter 2:5.

One must ask: how is it possible for a demon to invade the body or the mind of a believer if that person is supposed to be a temple of God or the Holy Spirit? Will God or the Holy Spirit be willing to share that believer with an evil spirit? That does not seem possible and, therefore, the exorcism performed on fellow-Christians cannot be reconciled with teachings of the New Testament.

---

[10] Buys, "The Relevance of Reformed Perspectives".

Satanism

People who practiced magic and witchery through the centuries were accused of worshipping the devil. No real evidence of any organized devil-worship or satanism was, however, found.

During the eighties of the last century, conspiracy theorists in the English-speaking world caused a wide-spread scare by alleging that there were international satanistic organizations with bizarre rituals during which drug abuse and sexual perversity were rife and other scary practices were purportedly followed.

There were, at most, some ant-establishment youths who wore black clothes and black make-up to show off their hatred for society – without belonging to any organized underground groups. This scare has blown over since the start of the present century[11]

Personification?

Many educated people of the present age have some difficulty believing in this diabolical being and evil spiritual entities and they regard them as mere mythological creatures. The devil is held as a personification of all that is bad, wrong, detestable, uncouth, malevolent, immoral, and wretched. Their world-view has been shaped by both the Bible and the scientific insights of our age.

It is, therefore, necessary to investigate the knowledge and accepted theories that scientists of various disciplines have gained and have helped to shape our modern intellectual world. That must be compared with the primitive and pre-scientific world-view one finds in the Scriptures. That is the subject of the next chapter.

---

[11] White, "Satanism".

Chapter 3
THE ANCIENT WORLD-VIEW

THE COSMOLOGY OF THE ANCIENT WORLD

Greek Scholars

Although the ancient Greeks have made some notable scientific discoveries, science as a rigorous, methodical, and rational activity only took off during the late Renaissance of the sixteenth and seventeenth centuries. Before that time, people had no means to explore nature and the cosmos systematically and find explanations for phenomena, such as the weather, the seasons, how plants and animals develop and multiply, the movements of the planets, and diseases.

The ancients noticed certain regularities, such as the cycle of the moon, the seasons, and the movements of the planets. They could even predict lunar and solar eclipses[12], but they didn't have rational explanations for these occurrences. Their observations, therefore, did not amount to rigorous science as such.

Greek scholars achieved some noteworthy results. Archimedes was noted for his mathematical skills and engineering innovations.[13] Eratosthenes found that the earth is a globe and he even calculated the size of the earth.[14] Euclid discovered the axioms of geometry on a flat plane.[15] These achievements, however, did not

---

[12] Enc Brit, "Eclipse",

[13] Toomer, "Archimedes".

[14] Enc Brit, "Eratosthenes".

[15] Van den Warden, "Euclid".

have the exact and systematic pursuit of scientific knowledge as a result, although the ideas of these men found some practical applications in architecture, warfare, engineering, and commerce.

Before genuine scientific investigations started, mankind's understanding of the cosmos and natural processes were based on observations made with the naked and unaided eye, as well as supernatural and mythological explanations of observed phenomena. This primitive world-view is also found in the Bible and the Qur'an, albeit with some adaptations to cater for a monotheistic religious view, in contrast with the polytheism of other cultures.

God, Heaven, Angels, Hell, World, Stars, Spirits, and Souls

It is necessary to take a good look at how the authors of the Hebrew and Christian Scriptures conceptualized key religious concepts such as *God, heaven, angel, hell, world, star, spirit,* and *soul*. It amounts to an investigation into the cosmology of those times. It is also necessary to investigate how the Qur'an treats these concepts.

Believers of the twenty-first century easily assume that when they find these words and concepts in the Bible – or the Qur'an – that the authors of these Scriptures attached the same meanings to these expressions and had similar mental pictures of these concepts. An analysis of the ways in which these words were used in the Scriptures shows, however, that this is not the case. People in biblical times had very different ideas regarding these words and concepts. Their conceptions were unsophisticated, concrete, and pre-scientific. One must understand why the ancients had these ideas, which differ widely from ours. They just did not have the tools and methods to investigate, explain, and understand the world and natural processes as we do today.

The religious documents of Israel, called the Old Testament by Christians, clearly show the influence of the views of their neighboring nations, especially the Babylonians and Persians.

The Babylonian Cosmos

Most of the Hebrew Scriptures were created or finalized only after the Babylonian exile and the Hebrew Bible only got its ultimate form in the second century BC with the inclusion of the book of Daniel.[16] During this exile, which formally ended in 538 BC, the elite of the Judeans were exposed to the most advanced civilization of the day and that exerted a profound influence on their religious views as expressed in their Scriptures.[17]

The Babylonians and their Mesopotamian predecessors, the Sumerians and the Chaldeans, were the first people to observe the skies systematically and to leave records of their observations of the stars and the weather patterns. They found that there were seven moving bodies across the skies, which they called planets, namely the sun, the moon, Mercury, Venus, Mars, Jupiter, and Saturn (to use their current Latin/English names). They dedicated a separate day to each of these planets and thereby created the seven-day week – which was taken over by the Jews and which is still in use today. We still name the days of the week after these planets and we can recognize names such as Sunday, Mo(o)nday and Satur(n)day.

These celestial bodies were deemed to be gods and were worshipped as such. The astronomers/astrologers of Mesopotamia were also priests since observing the skies – and the gods – was primarily a religious activity.[18] The current Latin/English names of the five outer planets are translations of Greek, Egyptian, and Mesopotamian names and are also the names of ancient deities.

The planets were seen to move against the background of the so-called fixed stars. These fixed stars were grouped into constellations and they represented personages, animals, and

[16] Armstrong, *The Bible,* 31–43.

[17] Enc Brit, "Babylonian Exile".

[18] Thiel, *And then there was Light,* 35; Malina, *On the Genre and Message of Revelation*, 2–10.

inanimate objects. We still use the Greek and Latin names for these constellations. Some were supposed to depict divine beings like Perseus, Orion, the Twins (Gemini – Castor and Pollux), and Hercules. Others were seen as celestial personages, such as Virgo (the Virgin), Ophiuchus (the Snake Catcher), Aquarius (the Water Carrier), Cepheus (the king of Aithiopia), Andromeda (the daughter of Cepheus) and Boötes (the Ploughman).

Other mythological figures were: Pegasus (the Winged Horse), Cetus (the Sea Monster), Centaurus (the Centaur or a being with the upper body of a man and the lower body of a horse) and Sagittarius (the Archer – also in the form of a centaur). Other animals are Leo (the Lion), Aquila (the Eagle), Capricornus (the Goat with a fish tail), Ursa Major (the Big Bear), Scorpius (the Scorpion), Serpens (the Serpent) and Pisces (the Fishes). Inanimate objects included Scutum (the Shield), Ara (the Altar), Eridanus (the Celestial River) and Crater (the Chalice). These stars and constellations were deemed to be unchanging and eternal.

The Mesopotamians found that the sun moved through twelve of these constellations in a year's time and, therefore, these constellations received special attention. They form the so-called Zodiac – meaning the circle of living beings – and they divided the year into twelve months. Each month coincided more or less with the period between two successive new moons. The Jews adopted the Mesopotamian year of twelve months (moons) and today we still divide the year into twelve portions.[19]

JEWISH VIEWS OF THE COSMOS

Adoption of Babylonian System by the Jews

---

[19] Gauquelin, *Astrology and Science,* 101–03; Hengel, *Judentum und Hellenismus*, 432–33; McGregor and Purdy, *Jew and Greek,* 291–92; Peters, *The Harvest of Hellenism*, 437–39; Thiel, *And then there was Light,* 43–44.

The Jews adopted the Babylonian celestial constellations and regarded them as real entities. In Job 9: 9 and 38: 31–32 we read of the Zodiac (Hebrew: מַזָּרוֹת – *Mazzarot* – a word derived from "sunrise"), the Bear (Ursa Major), Orion (the Hunter) and the Pleiades (the Seven Sisters), a star cluster inside Taurus (the Bull). Orion and the Pleiades are also mentioned in Amos 5: 8. The "fleeing serpent" in "the heavens" is mentioned in Job 26: 13, and with that the constellation of Serpens (the Serpent) is meant. Serpens was traditionally associated with the snake of Genesis 3, the serpent that tricked Adam and Eve into eating the forbidden fruit.[20]

Jeremiah 44: 17–19 mentions the "queen of the sky". It is not quite sure what this means – it may well refer to the moon or to the planet Venus, that is, Astarte of the Israelites' pagan neighbors. In Second Kings 17: 30 a pagan deity "Nergal" is mentioned; this was the Mesopotamian name for the constellation of Sagittarius.[21]

The people who hid the so-called Dead Sea Scrolls in a series of caves near Qumran in Palestine during the Jewish war against the Romans of AD 66–70 adopted and adapted the Babylonian astrology. They had, among others, an astrological calendar naming the twelve constellations in the Zodiac by their Hebrew or Aramaic names. This document was dated to the last decades of the first century BC. They removed the pagan elements from the names and the descriptions of these constellations to avoid any form of pagan idolatry.[22]

The Jews still adhered to the Babylonian Zodiac a few centuries into the Christian era. Archaeologists have found mosaic floors of ancient synagogues in the country of Israel depicting the Zodiac,

---

[20] Allen, *Star Names,* 375.

[21] Allen, *Star Names,* 354.

[22] Jacobus, "The Zodiac Sign Names".

with Hebrew names for the different constellations. The mosaic in the Beit Alpha synagogue (sixth century AD) is the best known and best preserved.[23]

The Beit Alpha mosaic with Hebrew names for the different constellations of the Zodiac. The seasons are depicted on the corners.

The Babylonians had extensive creation myths and the biblical authors adopted those myths, albeit with some significant alterations. The best-known creation myth in the Bible is to be found in Genesis 1. Where the Babylonians regarded the sun, moon, planets and stars as gods, the Hebrew Bible stressed the view that their God, YHWH, created all these bodies.

[23] Dennis, "Jewish Myth".

The Jews thought that the planets, stars, and constellations were angels and cherubs, instead of gods – which amounts to pretty much the same. In Job 38: 4–8 we are told that when the foundations of the earth were laid by God, "the morning stars sang together, and all the sons of God shouted for joy." The "sons of God" are, of course, the angels – and they are equated with the stars.

Ps 148: 2–3 contains this call: "Praise him, all his angels! Praise him, all his host! Praise him, sun and moon! Praise him, all you shining stars!" That means that the angels, the host of heaven and the astrological bodies were seen to be the same entities. Nehemiah 9: 6 assures us that God created everything, including the "host" of stars and that "the host of heaven" worships God.

Influence of the Stars

The Sumerian, Chaldean and Babylonian priests and astrologers studied the skies to find out what the intentions of the gods in the sky were regarding the fate of kingdoms, kings, and other important people. They drew up horoscopes in which the positions of the sun and other planets against the constellations of the Zodiac and the horizon were plotted. That helped important people to make decisions regarding auspicious days on which to start new ventures and how to avoid potential dangers.[24]

The Hebrew Scriptures seem to hold the same view. In Job 38: 33, this question is asked: "Do you know the laws of the heavens? Can you establish the dominion of it over the earth?" This question presupposes the view of ancient pagan astrology that events on earth are being influenced by the stars. Jeremiah 31: 35 mentions "the ordinances of the moon and of the stars", which were given by God. We also read of God's "ordinances of heaven and

[24] Malina, *On the Genre and Message of Revelation*, 2–20.

earth" in Jer 33: 25. These expressions suggest the rules according to which the ancient astrologers interpreted the divine intentions.

Hebrew View of Heaven and Earth

The Hebrew word for *heaven* is הַשָּׁמַיִם (ha-*shamayim*). This word was used in more than one way and has more than one meaning, namely the sky (containing the atmosphere and the clouds), the starry heaven, and the abode of God. It has to be pointed out that this word is used only in the plural form and, therefore, it should actually be translated as 'heavens' – encompassing the firmament, the stars in heaven, and the home of God. It will become clear that the authors of the Old Testament regarded these different meanings as synonyms. For them the sky filled with clouds was essentially the same space as the starry heaven and the dwelling place of God beyond the stars.

Together with the Mesopotamians, the Judeans thought of the sky or the heaven as a vault above the earth. God created the "expanse" or vault of heaven to divide the waters above and below the earth (Gen 1: 6). The author of the book of Job informs us in 22: 14 that God "walks on the vault of the sky"; that means that He was to be found immediately beyond the dome surrounding the earth and onto which the planets and the other stars are affixed. Isaiah 40: 22 tells us that God "sits above the circle of the earth, and the inhabitants of it are as grasshoppers…" The Hebrew word for "circle" (חוּג – *chug*) may also be translated as "vault" or "dome".

In various texts the idea is to be found that God spread the sky or the heavens like a sheet or a curtain over the earth (Job 9: 8; Ps 104: 2; Isa 40: 22; Isa 42: 5; Isa 44: 24; Isa 45: 12–13; Zech 12: 1). We also find the notion that God dwells between the stars: "Isn`t God in the heights of heaven? See the height of the stars, how high they are!" (Job 22: 12). Ps 19: 4 calls the firmament "a tent for the sun" behind which he hides at night and comes forth in the morning "as a bridegroom coming out of his chamber". This firmament rests on pillars that are planted on earth (Job 26: 11).

The following question is posed in Isa 40: 12 – "Who has measured the waters in the hollow of his hand, and meted out the sky [alternative: heavens] with the span, and comprehended the dust of the earth in a measure, and weighed the mountains in scales, and the hills in a balance?"

The answer to this question is, of course: God. The result of all this is that the heavens as the abode of God are part of the same space occupied by the earth and other celestial bodies. After all, Isa 66: 1 proclaims: "Thus says YHVH, heaven is my throne, and the earth is my footstool." There is, therefore, continuity between heaven and earth and the cosmos is a closed system, containing God's heaven, the stars, and earth.

The ancient peoples usually thought of their gods as living on a high mountain, somewhere in the north. The Sumerians thought that the throne of Anu, the god of the heavens, was situated on a high mountain or at the northern celestial pole. The Greeks saw Mount Olympus, in northern Greece and the highest mountain in Greece, as the home of their gods and the throne of Zeus, the father of the gods.[25]

Similar ideas are to be found in the Hebrew Scriptures. The king of Babylon is addressed in Isa 14: 13 –

> "You said in your heart, I will ascend into heaven, I will exalt my throne above the stars of God; and I will sit on the mountain of congregation, in the uttermost parts of the north ..."

In Job 37: 22 it is written: "Out of the north comes golden splendour;

---

[25] Cornelius, *Geistesgeschichte der Frühzeit*, 13, 35–36; Visser, *De Openbaring aan Johannes*, 57–58.

with God is awesome majesty" (see also: Ps 11: 4; 1 Kgs 11: 19; Isa 6; Ezek 1: 4).

Isaiah 11: 9, Isa 65: 25 and Ezek 28: 14 mention God's "holy mountain" (see also Ps 48: 2–3) and Isa 2: 2 affirms that God's house is on a high mountain. We are informed by 1 Kgs 22: 19 – "I saw YHVH sitting on his throne, and all the host of heaven standing by him on his right hand and on his left." In other words: the throne of God was thought of as situated between the stars to the north.

This identification of the throne of God with the northern celestial pole makes sense from the viewpoint of the ancient cosmology, since everything in the sky, the sun, the moon, the other planets, and all the stars seemed to revolve around that central point.

Genesis 1: 1 reminds us that the heavens and earth were created together and at the same time, "in the beginning". Psalm 148: 4 tells us of "waters that are above the heavens". These must be regarded as the storage places of the rain and, therefore, the heaven and the sky had to have windows through which this water could be poured down upon the earth (Gen 7: 11; Gen 8: 2; 2 Kgs 7: 2; Mal 3: 10).

Various texts contain the thought that God is observing the earth and the people on the earth from the vantage point of heaven where he resides – and that is the reason why he is able to see and know everything (Gen 21: 17; Ps 14: 2; Ps 33: 13–14; Ps 102: 19).

The weather was experienced as the result of the direct intervention of God. Thunder was regarded as God's voice (2 Sam 22: 14; Job 37: 4–5; Ps 104: 7), clouds were deemed to be his clothes (Job 22: 14), rain fell when he commanded it (Ps 147: 8) and hail stones fell when he hurled them from heaven (Jos 10: 11). Ps 104: 3 declares: "He makes the clouds his chariot. He walks on the wings of the wind."

All these texts make it clear that the Judeans thought of the heaven in a very concrete way. For them the sky, the atmosphere, the starry skies, and the heaven as the home of God were parts of one and the same system or space. The people who built the Tower of Babel even thought that they could erect a structure "whose top reaches to the sky" (or heavens) (Gen 11: 4). The contemporary idea that God's heaven must be somewhere outside the universe, probably in another dimension, would have been incomprehensible to the authors and original readers of the Old Testament books.

To summarize: there was, according to ancient Israel, no real difference between the sky with its clouds, the vault from which the stars were hanging and the dwelling place of God. For that reason, they used only one word, **הַשָּׁמַיִם** (ha-*shamayim*), to name the *sky*, the *starry heavens* and the *heaven* as dwelling place of God.

The world was thought to be a flat disc that floated upon the primeval ocean (Exod 20: 4) and as such it had boundaries or an edge (Ps 74: 17). Proverbs 30: 4 mentions "all the ends of the earth" – in other words: the world had a limit or an edge where it ended. It was thought that there was water below the earth – most probably the source of the water that flowed from fountains (Deut 4: 19). Psalm 136: 6 says that God "spread out the earth above the waters." Proverbs 8: 28 mentions "the springs of the deep".

The world rests upon pillars or foundations (Ps 82: 5; Prov 8: 29; Jer 31: 37; Zech 12: 1). In 1 Sam 2: 8 we are informed: "For the pillars of the earth are YHWH's, He has set the world on them." Psalm 104: 5 adds: "He laid the foundations of the earth, that it should not be moved forever." Psalm 93: 1 and Ps 96: 10 both declare: "The world is also established. It can`t be moved." On the other hand, the earth was deemed to be hanging in the void and Job 26: 7 says that God "stretches out the north over empty space, and hangs the earth on nothing."

Hebrew View of the Underworld

The Old Testament gave very little attention to the afterlife and it is only the late book of Daniel that contains a promise that the faithful will be resurrected at the end of time and inherit life everlasting with God in heaven. We read in Dan 12: 2–3 –

> "Many of those who sleep in the dust of the earth shall awake, some to everlasting life, and some to shame and everlasting contempt. Those who are wise shall shine as the brightness of the expanse; and those who turn many to righteousness as the stars forever and ever."

In other words: Daniel expected the deceased faithful to gain places in the starry skies.

For the rest, the Israelites merely expected to go to the underworld (Hebrew: שְׁאוֹל – *Sheol*) after they had died where they would experience a shadowy existence (Gen 37: 35; Gen 42: 38; Gen 29: 31; Ps 55: 16; Ezek 31: 15 *etcetera*). This realm of the dead was thought to be below the surface of the flat earth. Ps 63: 9 locates it in "the lower parts of the earth". Amos 9: 2 thought that it was even possible to "dig into Sheol". Whenever the Old Testament mentioned Sheol, it was made clear that the dead had to "descend" into this underworld.

In Num 16: 31–34 we read of a remarkable incident:

> "It happened, as he [Moses] made an end of speaking all these words, that the ground split apart that was under them [the rebels]; and the earth opened its mouth, and swallowed them up, and their households, and all the men who appertained to Korah [the leader of the rebel group], and all their goods. So they, and all that appertained to them, went

> down alive into Sheol: and the earth closed on them, and they perished from among the assembly. All Israel that were round about them fled at the cry of them; for they said, lest the earth swallow us up."

This is, no doubt, a description of a sinkhole, a case where the earth's surface suddenly caved in and dropped into a cave or hollow space below the surface. The author of this report interpreted this hole as an opening into Sheol, the abode of the dead under the earth's surface.

We read in 1 Sam 28: 7–25 how King Saul of Israel consulted an oracle of the dead, the witch of En-dor, and requested her to raise the prophet Samuel from the dead. The woman reported to Saul: "I see a god coming up out of the earth" (vs 13). The spirit of Samuel then asked Saul: "Why have you disquieted me, to bring me up?" (vs 15). The report of this episode confirms the conclusion that the Old Testament thought of Sheol as being somewhere below the earth's surface. It was, therefore, a real physical locality.

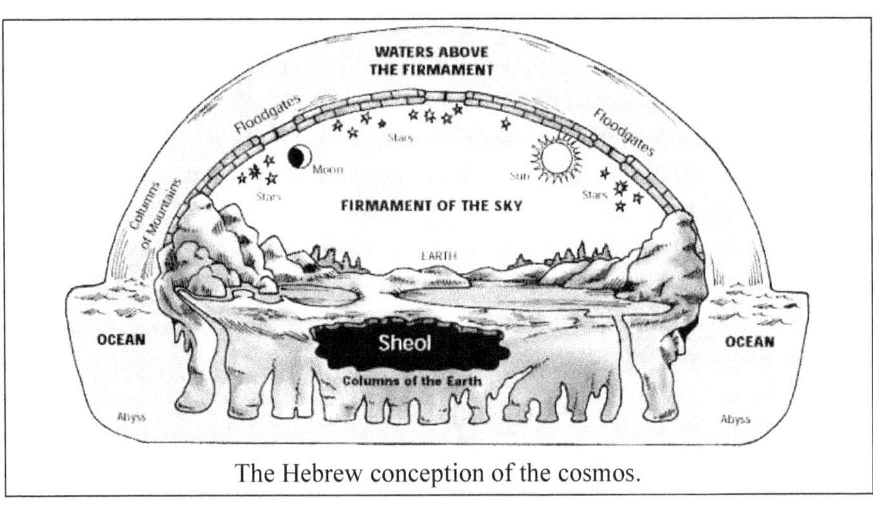

The Hebrew conception of the cosmos.

Below the surface of the earth there was also supposed to be a deep abyss, called תְּהוֹם (*tehom* – Gen 1: 2; Prov 8: 27–28). This word has many meanings: "deep, depths, deep places, abyss, the deep, deep of subterranean waters, primeval ocean, the grave. This abyss encompassed the whole of the underworld".

The illustration (above) provides a simplified view of how the cosmos – the heavens, earth, the netherworld and the ocean under the earth – was conceptualized by the authors of the Old Testament.

Hebrew View of God

The Hebrew Scriptures often mention that God is somehow associated with fire and light.

The evil cities of Sodom and Gomorrah were destroyed when it "rained on Sodom …. sulfur and fire from YHWH out of the sky" (Gen 19: 24). Moses encountered God in "a flame of fire out of the midst of a bush" while tending the flocks of his father-in-law (Exod 3: 2). When the Israelites escaped from slavery in Egypt, "YHWH went before them by day in a pillar of cloud, to lead them on their way, and by night in a pillar of fire, to give them light, that they might go by day and by night" (Exod 13: 21). When Moses received the Ten Commandments from God, "Mount Sinai, the whole of it, smoked, because YHWH descended on it in fire; and its smoke ascended like the smoke of a furnace" (Exod 19: 19). Num 16: 35 relates how "fire came forth from YHWH, and devoured the two hundred-and-fifty men who offered the incense."

The sun is even seen as a sign of God's presence: "For YHWH God is a sun and a shield" (Ps 84: 11). Malachi has a similar thought: "But to you who fear my name shall the sun of righteousness arise with healing in its wings" (Mal 4: 2).

In Deut 4: 12 and 36 the Israelites were reminded: "YHWH spoke to you out of the midst of the fire: you heard the voice of words, but you saw no form; only [you heard] a voice. (….) Out of heaven he made you to hear his voice, that he might instruct you: and on earth he made you to see his great fire; and you heard his words out of the midst of the fire". We are told in Judg 13: 20 that "the angel of YHWH ascended in the flame of the altar".

Second Samuel 22: 9 contains the following description of God: "There went up a smoke out of his nostrils, fire out of his mouth devoured: Coals were kindled by it."

The prophet Elijah and the prophets of Baal held a contest to determine whose deity was the real God. The prophets of Baal tried their best but got no response from Baal. Elijah prayed and "the fire of YHWH fell, and consumed the burnt offering, and the wood, and the stones, and the dust, and licked up the water that was in the trench" (1 Kgs 18: 1–38). When Elijah was taken up into heaven by God, it happened in "a chariot of fire, and horses of fire, which parted them both apart; and Elijah went up by a whirlwind into heaven" (2 Kgs 2: 11).

Daniel described Judgment Day as follows:

> "I saw until thrones were placed, and one who was ancient of days sat: his clothing was white as snow, and the hair of his head like pure wool; his throne was fiery flames, [and] the wheels of it burning fire. A fiery stream issued and came forth from before him: thousands of thousands ministered to him, and ten thousand times ten thousand stood before him: the judgment was set, and the books were opened." (Dan 7: 9–10).

Job 36: 30 informs us about God: "Behold, he spreads his light around him". The following prayer is voiced in Ps 4: 7 – "YHWH, let the light of your face shine on us." The poet of Ps 27: 1 confirms: "YHWH is my light and my salvation". Psalm 36: 10 assures us: "In your light shall we see light." In Ps 89: 15 we are taught: "Blessed are the people who learn to acclaim you. They walk in the light of your presence, YHWH." In Ps 104: 2 we read about God: "He covers himself with light as with a garment." Isaiah 2: 5 encourages us: "House of Jacob, come, and let us walk in the light of YHWH."

All these pronouncements make it clear that the Hebrew conception of God was very concrete. Just as heaven as the residence of God was seen as part of the cosmos, so God was also deemed to be an entity within the cosmos – often associated with fire, flames, and light. After all, the author of the book of Job informs us in 22: 14 that God "walks on the vault of the sky" – which means that he is an entity within the cosmos as a whole, although he is also the creator of the cosmos.

We are also told that the Israelite leader, Joshua, prayed to God to make the sun and the moon stop their progress across the sky to get more daylight during a battle the Israelites were on the verge of winning (Josh 10: 12–13). In other words, God was seen as having the power to stop the movements of the heavenly bodies.

The Old Testament often mentions God's eyes, ears, face, arms, hands, or voice, as well as his love, anger, sorrow, and disappointment – as if he had a human form and a human mind with human emotions. Biblical scholars tend to ascribe this usage to the literary construct of "anthropomorphism", the tendency to make God more intelligible by ascribing human attributes to him. These scholars also see this as figurative or metaphoric speech. It is clear in the light of all the quotations from the Old Testament that the Israelites thought of heaven as God's domicile and of God himself in physical and concrete – and even (super)human – terms.

Hebrew View of Angels

The Old Testament uses two words for angelic beings: מַלְאָךְ (*mal'ak*), which literally means a "messenger" and is mostly translated with *angel*, but we also read of *cherubs* or cherubim (Hebrew: כרובים – *keroubim*), heavenly beings who form the entourage of God in heaven. It has already been shown that the Hebrew Scriptures identified the stars with angels (Job 38: 4–8; Ps 148: 2–3; Neh 9: 6).

The Old Testament refers numerous times to God as "YHWH of Hosts" (for instance, Ps 24: 10, Isa 54: 5, and Hos 12: 5). The word for *hosts* (צְבָאוֹת– *tsebaot*) was used of the army of angels at God's disposal, but equally to the myriads of stars in the heaven where God lives (Gen 2: 1; Deut 4: 19; 2 Kgs 7: 16; Jer 19: 13).

It seems as if the angels were also equated with the wind and with fire. Ps 104: 4 declares of God: "He makes his messengers [angels] winds; His servants flames of fire." Ezekiel 1: 13–14 gives the following description of angels:

> "As for the likeness of the living creatures, their appearance was like burning coals of fire, like the appearance of torches: [the fire] went up and down among the living creatures; and the fire was bright, and out of the fire went forth lightning. The living creatures ran and returned as the appearance of a flash of lightning."

We are also told: "These are the four winds of the sky, which go forth from standing before the Lord of all the earth." (Zech 6: 5).

God is often referred to as "YHWH of Hosts who sits [above] the cherubim" (1 Sam 4: 4; 2 Sam 6: 2; 2 Kgs 19: 15; Ps 80: 1). Therefore, his *hosts* or army of angels/cherubs – actually, the stars –

support him. We are also told: "He rode on a cherub, and did fly; yes, he was seen on the wings of the wind" (2 Sam 22: 11).

On occasion, mortals had conversations with heavenly beings that appeared in human form. Abraham and Lot received heavenly visitors (Gen 18: 2–15; 19: 1–22). Jacob wrestled with one (Gen 28: 12). Gideon was called by a heavenly being to become the leader of his people (Judg 6: 11–24). An angel announced to Manoah that his son, Samson, would be dedicated to the Lord's service (Judg 13: 6–21). The prophet Ezekiel had various encounters with heavenly beings and Daniel saw a "son of man" (Dan 7: 13; 10: 16).

The way the Old Testament conceptualized of angels and cherubs demonstrates that these beings were regarded in a concrete way. They were equated with the stars, with the wind and with flames. They were not seen as "spiritual", supernatural or non-material beings; they were visible and tangible inhabitants of the same cosmos in which humans also live.

The parts of the Hebrew Scriptures mentioned above were mostly written after the Babylonian exile. It may be assumed that the identification of angels with the stars was copied from the Babylonian astrology where the stars and celestial constellations were seen as deities.

Hebrew View of Stars

The starry heavens were very visible to the people of the ancient Middle East with its clear skies at night. It is, therefore, no surprise that the Mesopotamians initiated the systematic study of the celestial bodies. It has already been pointed out that the Israelites were familiar with Mesopotamian star lore.

The Old Testament repeatedly stresses that God created the stars (Gen 1: 16; Gen 2: 1; 1 Sam 40: 26; Neh 9: 6; Ps 33: 6). The "hosts" of the heaven – consisting of the stars and the angels – were seen as living and intelligent beings and they had the task of singing God's praise (Ps 148: 1–4; Neh 9: 6). The reason for the creation of the bodies in the heavens was to be "lights in the expanse of sky to divide the day from the night; and let them be for signs, and for seasons, and for days and years" (Gen 1: 14). Thus, God intended them to be time keepers, as well as "signs" or warnings and omens, presumably of his intentions.

The starry skies have the task of proclaiming God's glory. Ps 19: 1–4 announces:

> "The heavens declare the glory of God. The expanse shows his handiwork. Day after day they pour forth speech, and night after night they display know-ledge. There is no speech nor language, where their voice is not heard. Their voice has gone out through all the earth, their words to the end of the world."

In other words: the heavens, with all that is contained in them, are able to speak and must, therefore, be living and intelligent beings.

According to Dan 12: 2–3, the deceased "wise" people would receive eternal life and "shall shine as the brightness of the expanse; and those who turn many to righteousness as the stars forever and ever." In other words: God's faithful could expect to become shining stars in the sky after Judgment Day.

Hebrew View of the Spirit

The Hebrew word for *spirit* is רוּחַ (*ruach*) and it has a wide range of meanings: "wind, air, breath, mind, heart, spirit". It is also used of the "Spirit of God". In the light of the finding that the Old Testament envisaged God, heaven, and angels in a very concrete way, it seems likely that all these meanings of the word *spirit* were actually synonyms and that the spirit was not regarded as a non-material entity, but something composed of air or wind and equated with the breath of man. An analysis of the use of this word in the Old Testament confirms this expectation.

The whole human being is regarded as a spiritual being (Ex. 35: 21; Ezek. 18: 31). God created the spirit in man (Zech 12: 1).

The following pronouncements in the Old Testament clearly use the words *spirit* and *breath* or *wind* as synonyms:

- "But there is a spirit in man, and the breath of the Almighty gives them understanding" (Job 32: 8).
- "Thus says God YHWH, he who created the heavens, and stretched them forth; he who spread abroad the earth and that which comes out of it; he who gives breath to the people on it, and spirit to those who walk therein" (Isa 42: 5).
- "Then said he to me, Prophesy to the wind, prophesy, son of man, and tell the wind, Thus says the Lord YHWH: Come from the four winds, breath, and breathe on these slain, that they may live. So I prophesied as he commanded me, and the breath came into them, and they lived, and stood up on their feet, an exceeding great army" (Ezek 37: 9–10).
- "Woe to him who says to the wood, 'Awake!' or to the mute stone, 'Arise!' Shall this teach? Behold, it is overlaid with gold and silver, and there is no breath at all in the midst of it" (Hab 2: 19).

The finding that the words "spirit" and "breath" must be regarded as synonyms is, no doubt, due to the fact that many people breathe out a last breath with a sigh the moment they die. This las breath was, therefore, seen as the spirit leaving the dying person.

The human mind and heart as seat of emotions is also often called "spirit":

- “When my spirit was overwhelmed within me” (Ps 142: 3).
- “Therefore my spirit is overwhelmed within me” (Ps 143: 4).
- “My spirit fails” (Ps 143: 7).
- “A glad heart makes a cheerful face; but an aching heart breaks the spirit” (Prov 15: 13)
- “A cheerful heart makes good medicine, but a crushed spirit dries up the bones” (Prov 17: 22).
- “Nebuchadnezzar dreamed dreams; and his spirit was troubled, and his sleep went from him” (Dan 2: 1).

The human spirit is also seen as the seat of the mind and thoughts:

- “The spirit of my understanding answers me” (Job 20: 3).
- “My spirit diligently inquires: Will the Lord reject us forever?” (Ps 77: 6–7).

The spirit is seen as the source of desires:

> “With my soul have I desired you in the night; yes, with my spirit within me will I seek you earnestly” (Is 26: 9).

The following text says that the spirit of man survives death:

> “And the dust returns to the earth as it was, and the spirit returns to God who gave it” (Eccl 12: 7).

There is, though, also the idea that the spirit disappears at death:

> “His spirit departs, and he returns to the earth. In that very day, his thoughts perish” (Ps 146: 4).

From the preceding it may be concluded that the human spirit was not seen as an invisible part of man but that it often stood for the whole person, his thoughts, emotions, and breath.

The Old Testament often mentions the *Spirit of God* (Gen 1: 2; Judg 3: 10; Jud 14: 6; 1 Sam 10: 10; 1 Sam 19: 23; Ps 139: 7 *etcetera*). Christians are tempted to see in these texts references to the Holy Spirit, the third Person in the divine Trinity. That was, however, never the intention of the Old Testament authors. With the expression *Spirit of God* they simply meant God's mind or God himself, God who is capable of acting, thinking, talking, and having emotions. The *Spirit* of God was never seen as a separate personage or entity from God. We may even translate this expression as the *breath* or *wind of God.*

Hebrew View of the Soul

In the Old Testament we repeatedly find references to the *soul* of man. The Hebrew word is נֶפֶשׁ (*nephesh*) and it has multiple meanings: "soul, self, life, creature, person, appetite, mind, living being, desire, emotion, passion, throat, and breath. It could even be used for a dead body".

This word denotes the life force of a person. At the creation of man (Gen. 2: 7), God gave him his breath, his soul, his life force. At times the soul of a human is identified with his blood because when a person has lost enough blood after being wounded he cannot live any longer (Gen. 9: 4; Lev. 17: 11, 14; Deut. 12: 23).

The soul is also the seat of human emotions (Ps. 35: 9–10; 1 Sam. 20: 17; Ps. 42: 2). The soul is, however, never depicted as a "spiritual", supernatural or immaterial object. We read about a hungry soul (Ps. 107: 9) or a thirsty soul (Pr. 25: 25). The *soul* often represents the whole human being (Gen. 2: 7, Lev. 21: 1; Num. 5: 2). For this reason, many Bible translations sometimes translate the word for *soul* with *life*.

It is, therefore, safe to conclude that the Hebrew view of the soul amounted to a very concrete concept. The *soul* was not regarded as something separate from the human body; it was only the less visible aspects of the human being – his mind, his emotions, his needs, and his life force as represented by his blood, even his (invisible) breath.

It is clear that the concepts of *spirit* and *soul* are somehow connected. In Isa 26: 9 they are even used as synonyms: "With my soul have I desired you in the night; yes, with my spirit within me will I seek you earnestly."

Summary

The preceding explanation of the Hebrew cosmology boils down to the following:

- The heavens filled with clouds and stars, and the home of God, the flat earth below it, and the netherworld containing the abode of the dead, were seen as a single system, filling a continuous space.
- God was conceptualized as associated with light and fire. His throne was to be found between the stars, at the northern celestial pole.
- The angels were equated with the stars and they were the servants and messengers of God.
- There was no real difference between a spirit or a soul and the wind or a person's breath.

THE EARLY CHRISTIAN VIEW OF THE COSMOS

Astrology in the Ancient Greek World

The world in which the first Christians lived differed in important respects from the Old Testament world. These Christians lived in the Roman Empire and they were ruled from Rome in Italy.

Greek became the dominant language in the countries of the eastern Mediterranean, including Greece, Asia Minor, Syria, Mesopotamia, Palestine, and Egypt, after the Macedonian king, Alexander the Great, created a vast empire within a short period during the fourth century BC, encompassing all these regions and absorbing the Egyptian and Persian empires. After his death, his empire was divided between his generals who became kings. This part of the civilized world became Hellenized, and that is the reason why the New Testament was written in Greek. Even the educated Romans spoke Greek and that is why Paul wrote his letter to the Christians in Rome in Greek instead of in Latin – which he, as a Roman citizen, would have known (Acts 22: 25–29; Acts 23: 27).

The intellectual, religious, and philosophical world around the eastern Mediterranean from the fourth century BC onwards was based on a mixture of Greek and Babylonian ideas. The Babylonian or Chaldean cosmology with its emphasis on astrology became widespread and the dominant intellectual paradigm. Taylor and Hay remarked regarding the city of Alexandria in northern Egypt, the intellectual and academic center of the world in those days, that "in this city, astral symbolism was built into its very nomenclature". They also concluded "that astrology was one of the most important 'Chaldean' cultural imports into Alexandria".[26]

Peters found: "For nearly five centuries, from the mid-second century before Christ to the triumph of Christianity, the ancient world was in the almost unchallenged grip of this half-religious, half-scientific phenomenon" of astrology.[27]

The Greeks were aware of the fact that the world is a globe and not a flat disk. Eratosthenes of Cyrene (276–194 BC) was the

---

[26] Taylor and Hay, "Astrology in Philo of Alexandria's De Vita Contemplativa", 1, 18.

[27] Peters, *The Harvest of Hellenism*, 438.

first person to measure the size of the earth.[28] For the Greeks, the round earth was the stationary center of the universe and it was surrounded by the heavens containing the winds, the clouds, the planets and the fixed stars. The stars were hanging onto a huge dome or vault surrounding the earth.[29]

It is doubtful, though, whether the first Christians absorbed this insight. In all probability, they adhered to the Old Testament notion of a cosmos with three stories – the heavens above, a flat earth in the middle and the netherworld below.

In addition to Chaldean astrology, the intellectual life of the Hellenized world was influenced by the ideas of Greek philosophers.

Greek Philosophers

The two most influential ancient Greek philosophers were Plato (428–348 BC) and Aristotle (384–322 BC). They based their philosophies and ideas regarding the nature of the cosmos partly on the work of their predecessors, Empedocles and Democritus.

Empedocles (490–430 BC) taught that all matter was composed of four essential ingredients or elements, namely fire, air, water, and earth, and that nothing either comes into being or is destroyed but that things are merely transformed, depending on the shape and ratio of these basic substances to one another. The soul is, according to him, also material in nature and, therefore, indestructible. Those who have sinned must wander for thousands of seasons through many mortal bodies and be tossed from one of the four elements to another. Escape from this fate required purification.[30]

---

[28] Enc Brit, "Eratosthenes of Cyrene".

[29] Malina, *On the Genre and Message of Revelation*, 4.

[30] Enc Brit, "Empedocles".

Democritus (460–370 BC) visualized space, or the Void, as a vacuum, an infinite space in which an infinite number of atoms moved that made up the physical world. These atoms are indestructible and invisible; absolutely small, so small that they cannot be divided into anything smaller. Such a particle was, therefore, called an atom (Greek: ἄτομον – *atomon*: that which cannot be cut up). Atoms differ only from each other in shape, arrangement, position, and size.[31]

Plato is remembered today especially for two intellectual constructs: the realm of ideas or forms and the division of the person into two separate substances, body and soul. The realm of ideas or forms existed in an invisible part of the universe and contained ideal "prototypes" of all attributes, qualities, and essences of everything encountered in the real world. In this realm one could also find the ideal forms of virtues such as bravery, piety, and friendship, of qualities such as colors and geometrical shapes, but also of material objects such as trees, animals, and furniture. This realm found its unity and culmination in the Idea of the Good or of the One.

The soul existed before it was united with a certain body to form a particular person. This soul pre-existed in the realm of ideas and forms and all knowledge attained throughout life amounted to recollections of the ideas or forms.[32]

Plato's ideas regarding the cosmos were explicated in his book, the Timaeus, and the influence of Empedocles and Democritus is clear. He wrote, for instance:

> "Wherefore also God in the beginning of creation made the body of the universe to consist of fire and earth. But two things cannot be rightly put together without a third; there

[31] Enc Brit, "Atom".

[32] Barnes, "Plato".

> must be some bond of union between them. (. . .) God placed water and air in the mean between fire and earth, and made them to have the same proportion so far as was possible (as fire is to air so is air to water, and as air is to water so is water to earth); and thus he bound and put together a visible and tangible heaven. And for these reasons, and out of such elements which are in number four, the body of the world was created, and it was harmonized by proportion, and therefore has the spirit of friendship; and having been reconciled to itself, it was indissoluble by the hand of any other than the framer."[33]

He continued that time and the heavens came into being at the same instant, patterned on the templates of the eternal ideas or forms:

> "Such was the mind and thought of God in the creation of time. The sun and moon and five other stars, which are called the planets, were created by him in order to distinguish and preserve the numbers of time; and when he had made their several bodies, he placed them in the orbits in which the circle of the other was revolving-in seven orbits, seven stars. First, there was the moon in the orbit nearest the earth, and next the sun, in the second orbit above the earth; then came the morning star and the star sacred to Hermes [Mercury], moving in orbits which have an equal swiftness with the sun, but in an opposite direction; and this is the reason why the sun and Hermes and Lucifer [Venus] overtake and are overtaken by each other."[34]

---

[33] Plato, *Timaeus*.
[34] Plato, *Timaeus*.

According to the Timaeus, the planets were "living creatures having bodies" whose task was to measure time. The planets, especially the sun, were composed of fire. The fixed stars "were created, to be divine and eternal animals, ever-abiding and revolving after the same manner and on the same spot…" The indestructible soul of the person "who lived well during his appointed time was to return and dwell in his native star, and there he would have a blessed and congenial existence."

For Plato, God was not a deity with personality, such as the Greek gods. He merely saw it as an embodiment of the Idea of the Good and he also calls it the Demiurge, the principle that patterned objects and entities in the world on the prototypes of the eternal ideas or forms.[35]

Aristotle did away with the teachings of his master, Plato, that there existed eternal prototypes of everything in a celestial realm. For him, every object had its own form or qualities, and these could change as time went on. An acorn, for instance, had the potential to become an oak tree.[36]

Aristotle's ideas on cosmology can be summarized thus:

> "We must explain what we mean by 'heaven' and in how many senses we use the word, in order to make clearer the object of our inquiry. In one sense, then, we call 'heaven' the substance of the extreme circumference of the whole, or that natural body whose place is at the extreme circumference. We recognize habitually a special right to the name 'heaven' in the extremity or upper region, which we take to be the seat of all that is divine. In another sense, we use this name for the body continuous with the extreme circumference which

[35] Barnes, "Plato".

[36] Kenny, "Aristotle".

> contains the moon, the sun, and some of the stars; these we say are 'in the heaven'. In yet another sense we give the name to all body included within extreme circumference, since we habitually call the whole or totality 'the heaven'. The word, then, is used in three senses."[37]

It is clear that Aristotle's conception of the heavens more or less coincided with that of the Judeans and other ancient peoples. He also taught that the heavenly bodies are not composed of the four terrestrial elements but are made up of a superior and indestructible fifth element, the so-called "quintessence." In addition, the heavenly bodies have souls, or supernatural intellects, which guide them in their travels through the heavens.[38]

Philo of Alexandria

Philo of Alexandria (10 BC – AD 50), a Hellenized Jewish theologian and philosopher and contemporary of Jesus, wrote the following regarding the cosmos in his book On the Giants:

> "Those beings, whom other philosophers call demons, Moses usually calls angels; and they are souls hovering in the air. And let no one suppose, that what is here stated is a fable, for it is necessarily true that the universe must be filled with living things in all its parts, since every one of its primary and elementary portions contains its appropriate animals and such as are consistent with its nature; – the earth containing terrestrial animals, the sea and the rivers containing aquatic animals, and the fire such as are born in the fire (but it is said, that such as these last are found chiefly

[37] Aristotle, *On the Heavens*, Liber 1: 9.

[38] Kenny, "Aristotle".

> in Macedonia), and the heaven containing the stars: for these also are entire souls pervading the universe, being unadulterated and divine, inasmuch as they move in a circle, which is the kind of motion most akin to the mind, for every one of them is the parent mind. It is therefore necessary that the air also should be full of living beings. And these beings are invisible to us, inasmuch as the air itself is not visible to mortal sight. But it does not follow, because our sight is incapable of perceiving the forms of souls, that for that reason there are no souls in the air; but it follows of necessity that they must be comprehended by the mind, in order that like may be contemplated by like."[39]

The illustration (below) shows how generations of people, including Christians, after the time of Aristotle visualized the cosmos.
Philo was clearly influenced by the Old Testament as well as the prevalent Hellenistic intellectual climate of his day. It will be shown that the authors of the various writings in the New Testament were children of their time and that they held similar views.

The early Christian biblical authors could not escape the influence of Mesopotamian astrology and Greek philosophy. They were, of course, also influenced by the Hebrew Scriptures, their only Bible in the time before the letters of Paul and the Gospels were recognized as inspired Scripture.

The early Christians lived in this world. How pervasive the influence of astrology was, is demonstrated by the fact that Paul sailed from Malta to Italy in a ship called the "Twin Gods" or the "Twin Brothers" (Acts 28: 11). In Greek the name was Διόσκουροι (*Dioskouroi*), the name of the constellation known to us as Gemini with Castor and Pollux as the principal stars.

---

[39] Philo, *On the Giants,* 6–9.

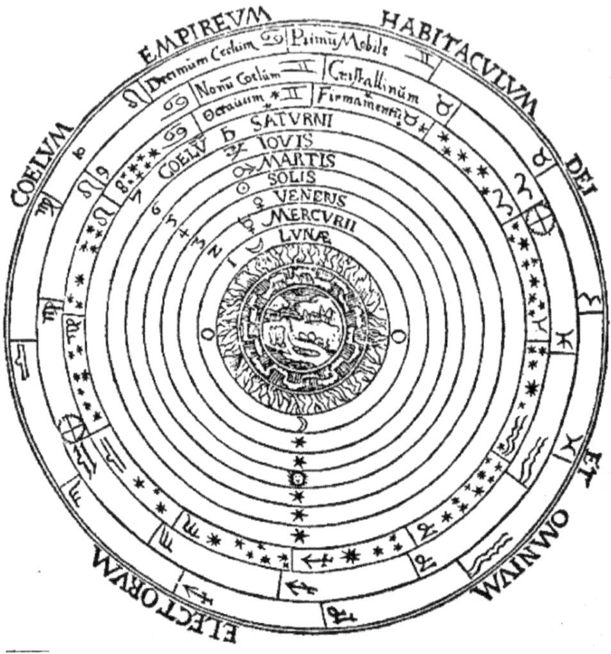

The Aristotelian worldview, as adapted by Christian theologians. Earth forms the stationary center and is surrounded by the clouds, the orbits of the planets and the firmament upon which the fixed stars with the Zodiac were located. The description given on the outer rim of the cosmic vault reads: COELUM EMPIRIUM (sic) HABITACULUM DEI ET OMNIUM ELECTORUM (the empire of heaven, the dwelling of God and all of the elect).

The Early Christian View of Heaven and Earth

The word used for *heaven* in the New Testament is οὐρανός (*ouranos*). This Greek word has a wide range of meanings: "the vaulted expanse of the sky with all things visible in it, the universe, the world, the aerial heavens or sky, the region where the clouds and the tempests gather and where thunder and lightning are produced, the starry heavens, the region above the starry heavens, the seat of order of things eternal and where God and the angels dwell." This is more or less the range of meanings as used by Aristotle.

The name Ouranos is also known in its Latin transcription, namely Uranus. This was the name of the ancient Greek god of the heaven or the sky. He ruled over the whole expanse above the earth and that means that the single word "ouranos" was applicable to all the spaces above the earth. This name was, incidentally, given to a planet discovered in 1781 with the aid of a telescope.[40]

The early Christians regarded heaven in a very concrete way as the vault surrounding the earth, the whole space occupied by the winds and clouds, the stars and the home of God and the angels – just as in the Old Testament – and for them the one word for *heaven* encompassed all its various aspects. The influence of Plato, Aristotle, and Philo may also be detected. Heaven is, therefore, always described as being "up there" or "above" (Mark 1: 10; John 3: 13; John 6: 38; Acts 7: 55; Acts 10: 11; Eph 4: 10; Col 3: 1–2). Paul wrote that he received visions and revelations when he was "caught up into the third heaven" and was "caught up into Paradise" (2 Cor 12: 2, 4). For him, the third heaven would have consisted of the dwelling of God himself; the second heaven being the heaven of the stars and the first heaven being the sky filled with clouds – just as the Hebrews and Aristotle regarded the heavens.

We read of various persons who saw the heavens opened and had a vision of God, Jesus or the angels. The following examples come to mind:

- Jesus, directly after his baptism (Mark 1: 10–12);
- Stephen, who was stoned to death (Acts 7: 55–56);
- Paul, on the road to Damascus (Acts 9: 3–7);
- Peter, who had a vision of a cloth lowered from the sky (Acts 10: 11–13); and
- John of Patmos (the whole book of Revelation).

---

[40] Enc Brit, "Uranus".

Revelation 4: 1 mentions "a door opened in heaven", through which John of Patmos could see the throne of God. That implies that the starry heaven was conceptualized as a huge dome and that God's residence was on the outer side of this dome.

John included many hymns sung by the heavenly choirs in his book. That implies that he simply must have assumed that sound could travel in the space between the stars and in God's heaven. We know, of course, that sound needs air to be transmitted and that the atmosphere of the earth extends only a few kilometers above the surface of the earth. John and his contemporaries could not have known that, of course.

According to Luke 24: 51 and Acts 1: 9, when Jesus ascended bodily into heaven after his resurrection from the grave he levitated visibly skywards and it was an event that could be observed by his disciples, until he disappeared behind a cloud. Luke, who wrote these reports, must have likewise assumed that Jesus could still breathe when he reached the highest heaven.

Bruce Malina and Adelbert Scholtz have convincingly demonstrated that the visions which John of Patmos had of God and Jesus on the heavenly throne, as well as various angels and other heavenly beings, as described in the book of Revelation, were merely descriptions of the starry skies – planets, stars and constellations. Therefore: God and the risen Christ, together with all the other heavenly creatures, dwelled between and beyond the stars, according to John. The stars were grouped into constellations, which were seen as living entities, just as the ancient Babylonians did.[41]

That the authors of the New Testament Scriptures were influenced by the prevailing astrology appears from various texts. Paul wrote (Eph 1: 20) that Jesus was raised by God from the dead

---

[41] Malina, *On the Genre and Message of Revelation*; Scholtz, *The Prophecies of Revelation.*

and that he ascended to God's "right hand in the heavenly places". The word for "heavenly places" does not only point to God's domicile above the stars, but also the starry and cloudy heavens. According to the ancient astrology, many a mythological hero, such as Perseus, Hercules, Cepheus, and Andromeda, was elevated to the starry skies after his or her death and became constellations.

The Jewish historian, Flavius Josephus, thought that fallen heroes became stars and constellations in the sky. He declared in his book The Wars of the Jews (ca AD 78) "that those souls which are severed from their fleshly bodies in battles by the sword are received by the ether, that purest of elements[42], and joined to that company which are placed among the stars; that they become good demons, and propitious heroes, and show themselves as such to their posterity afterwards".[43]

Paul seems to think that something similar happened to Jesus Christ when he was taken up into heaven. In Phil 2: 9–10, Paul writes that Christ was exalted and that "at the name of Jesus every knee would bow, of those in heaven, those on earth, and those under the earth". Paul clearly included the stars and other heavenly beings under "those in heaven".

It seems likely that there is a reference to astrological constellations in Luke 10: 19 – "Behold, I give you authority to tread on serpents and scorpions, and over all the power of the enemy." Jesus uttered these words directly after his disciples had reported that they were able to drive out demons from people and Jesus had mentioned that he saw Satan fall from heaven like a bolt of lightning. The words quoted from Jesus may, therefore, refer to the

---

[42] A reference to Aristotle's "quintessence" – the fifth element of which the stars were supposed to be composed.

[43] Josephus, *Wars,* Liber VI (1/5).

constellations of Serpens and Scorpius, which he must have regarded as embodiments of Satan and all that is evil.

Jesus clearly thought that events on earth and in the heavens were connected and therefore he could tell his disciples that he would provide them with the keys of the kingdom of heaven and that would mean that "whatever you will bind on earth will be bound in heaven; and whatever you will loose on earth will be loosed in heaven" (Matt 16: 19; see also Matt 18: 18).

The author of the letter of Jude regarded the planets – revered by his pagan contemporaries as gods – to be evil entities and, therefore, these "wandering stars" (ἀστέρες πλανῆται – *asteres planetai*) were fated to be banished to "the blackness of darkness" (Jud 1: 13).

The second letter of Peter contains a somewhat eccentric explanation of the creation myth of the first chapter of Genesis in which the four basic elements – fire, air, water, and earth – figure. The readers of this letter are reminded "that there were heavens from of old, and an earth formed out of water and amid water, by the word of God; by which means the world that then was, being overflowed with water, perished. But the heavens that now are, and the earth, by the same word have been stored up for fire, being reserved against the day of judgment and destruction of ungodly men" (2 Pet 3: 5–7). It is noteworthy that this text mentions "the heavens" in the plural (οἱ οὐρανοι – *hoi ouranoi*) – in other words: the heaven of the atmosphere, the heaven of stars, and the heaven as God's dwelling. These heavens, together with the earth, were formed by God's creative word out of water and they are destined to be destroyed by fire. Three of the four Greek elements, namely fire, water, and earth, are mentioned explicitly, while air is implied in the plurality of heavens.

That these four elements are meant, is clear from verse 10 in the same chapter: "But the day of the Lord will come as a thief in the night; in which the heavens [plural!] will pass away with a great noise, and the elements will be dissolved with fervent heat, and the earth and the works that are in it will be burned up." Verse 12 also mentions "the coming of the day of God, by reason of which the heavens [plural!] being on fire will be dissolved, and the elements will melt with fervent heat". The Greek word used for "element" is στοιχεῖον (*stoicheion*); this word was usually used for the four elements of the cosmos – fire, air, water, and earth.

A similar end for the world was foreseen by Jesus, according to Matthew: "But immediately after the oppression of those days, the sun will be darkened, the moon will not give her light, the stars will fall from the sky, and the powers of the heavens will be shaken" (Matt 24: 29).

Paul seems to have been critical of the prevailing philosophy of his time:

- "So we also, when we were children, were held in bondage under the elements of the world" (Gal 4: 3).
- "But now that you have come to know God, or rather to be known by God, why do you turn back again to the weak and miserable elements, to which you desire to be in bondage all over again?" (Gal 4: 9).
- "Be careful that you don`t let anyone rob you through his philosophy and vain deceit, after the tradition of men, after the elements of the world, and not after Christ" (Col 2: 8).
- "If you died with Christ from the elements of the world, why, as though living in the world, do you subject yourselves to ordinances" (Col 2: 20).

It is not quite clear what Paul regarded as "elements". It may be the notion that Christians ought not to be obsessed with worldly things composed of the four elements, but that they rather had to attach value to heavenly things that are indestructible. After all, he also wrote: "Set your mind on the things that are above, not on the things that are on the earth" (Col 3: 2).

There can be no doubt that the writings of the New Testament contain various pagan Greek views regarding the composition of the cosmos.

The Early Christian View of the Underworld and Hell

The New Testament employed more than one Greek word to name the underworld, the realm of the dead:

- Hades (Greek: ᾅδης) – *Hades* was the Greek god of the underworld and was also known as Pluto.[44] This name was also used for the grave, death, or hell. In the Greek translation of the Old Testament this word was used as the equivalent of Sheol, the abode of the dead. This word was used in the New Testament in Matt 16: 18, Luke 10: 15; Luke 16: 23; Acts 2: 31, Rev 1: 18, and Rev 20: 13–14. In all these texts it may mean hell or simply the underworld where the deceased are being kept.
- The abyss (Greek: ἄβυσσος – *abyssos*) – a pit of immeasurable deepness, the destination of the dead and especially the abode of demons. In Greek mythology, it was used as a synonym for "chaos" – the condition of the world before it was ordered.[45] This word appears in the following texts: Luke 8: 30–31, Rom 10: 7, Rev 1: 18, Rev 11: 7, Rev 17: 8, and Rev 20: 1–3, 13 and it was always used of the netherworld.

---

[44] Enc Brit, "Hades".

[45] Enc Brit, "Chaos".

- Tartarus (Greek: ταρταρος - *Tartaros*) – the name of the doleful and dark subterranean region, the deepest part of the underworld and regarded by the ancient Greeks as the abode of the most wicked dead, where they suffered punishment for their evil deeds.[46] This name is only found in 2 Pet 2: 4.
- The underworld (Greek: καταχθόνιος – *katachthonios*) – this word means "subterranean" and it is used in Phil 2: 10 for "those who dwell in the world below, the departed souls."
- Darkness (Greek: ζόφος – *Zofos*) – the darkness or blackness of the netherworld and hell. It is used in Jud 1: 6, 13 and 2 Pet 2: 4.
- Gehenna (Greek: γέεννα – *Geenna*). This is actually a Hebrew word that means Hell. It is the place of the future punishment call Gehenna or Gehenna of fire. This was originally the valley of Hinnom, south of Jerusalem, where the filth and dead animals of the city were cast out and burned; a fit symbol of the wicked and their future destruction. It is used in Matt 10: 28, Matt 18: 8–9, and Mark 9: 43.

It must be gathered that the authors of the Christian Scriptures thought that the netherworld was located somewhere below the surface of the (flat) earth.

The New Testament also contains the concept of *hell* where the godless sinners were to be punished for their evil deeds, which they committed while still alive on earth. In the following texts this place is pictured as a huge fire or a "pool of fire and sulfur": Matt 5: 22, Matt 13: 42, 50, Matt 18: 8, Matt 25: 41, Heb 10: 27, Jud 1: 7, Rev 19: 20, Rev 20: 10, 15, and Rev 21: 8.

Hell is, though, also described as "the outer darkness; there is where the weeping and grinding of teeth will be" (Matt 8: 12; Matt

---

[46] Enc Brit, "Tartarus".

22: 13; Matt 25: 30).

That Paul thought of the cosmos as consisting of three layers has already been shown. In Phil 2: 9–10 he quoted a hymn about Christ where this cosmology also appears: "Therefore God also highly exalted him, and gave to him the name which is above every name; that at the name of Jesus every knee would bow, of those in heaven, those on earth, and those under the earth…" John of Patmos likewise wrote that "no one in heaven, or on the earth, or under the earth" was able to open the book in the hand of God (Rev 5: 3).

In contrast with this, there are also texts that suggest that the faithful and repentant sinners would enter heaven immediately after death and that evil people were to enter eternal punishment directly after having died (Luk 16: 19–31; Luk 23: 43; Acts 7: 59).

Lucifer, King of Hell, by Paul Gustave Doré.

The New Testament concepts regarding the fate of the dead do seem to be rather confusing since hell and the netherworld, the realm of the dead, were seen as one and the same place; after all, the same words were used to name or describe both. We must remember, though, that the first Christians lived in a prescientific age and it did not matter very much to them that they sometimes held irrational, conflicting, and confusing beliefs.

It is clear from the preceding that the authors of the New Testament were profoundly influenced by Greek mythology in their conception of the fate of the dead. That meant that the dead were thought to be kept in the underworld, somewhere below the surface of the earth, awaiting Judgment Day, after which the faithful would be allowed into heavenly bliss and the ungodly would suffer eternal pain in hell.

The influence of Egyptian concepts regarding the fate of the dead cannot be ruled out, either. It is well known that the ancient Egyptians embalmed the bodies of their deceased kings and other important people to prepare them for the afterlife in a heavenly realm, among the stars. The dead were supplied with copies of the "Book of the Dead", a manual to guide them through all the dangers they could expect on their travels to the afterlife, including the "weighing of the heart", a trial in which their earthly lives were judged. The big difference was that the Egyptians believed that only royalty and the elite would reach the afterlife; the souls of rest of the population would cease to exist if their bodies were not embalmed.[47] In contrast, Christians believed that all believers would inherit everlasting life after death.

The Early Christian View of God

The New Testament authors followed the Old Testament by often linking God to fire and light. Hebr 12: 29, for instance, states outright: "Our God is a consuming fire."

---

[47] Oakes and Gahlin, *Egypt,* 390–95.

The Holy Spirit often appears in fire or flames:

- "John answered them all, 'I indeed baptize you with water, but he comes who is mightier than I, the latchet of whose sandals I am not worthy to loosen. He will baptize you in the Holy Spirit and fire'" (Luk 3: 16).
- "Tongues like fire appeared and were distributed to them, and it sat on each one of them. They were all filled with the Holy Spirit…" (Acts 2: 3–4).
- "Out of the throne proceed lightnings, sounds, and thunders. There were seven lamps of fire burning before the throne, which are the seven Spirits of God" (Rev 4: 5).

We are also informed:

- "This is the message which we have heard from him and announce to you, that God is light, and in him is no darkness at all" (1 John 1: 5).
- "The city [the New Jerusalem] has no need for the sun, neither of the moon, to shine, for the very glory of God illuminated it, and its lamp is the Lamb" (Rev 21: 23).

The second coming of Christ will also be a fiery event:

> "… when the Lord Jesus is revealed from heaven with his mighty angels in flaming fire…" (2 Thess 1: 7).

The exalted Christ was described as follows:

- "His head and his hair were white as white wool, like snow. His eyes were like a flame of fire" (Rev 1: 14).
- 1 Tim 6: 16 proclaims that the exalted and immortal Jesus Christ is "dwelling in unapproachable light".

In addition, we are assured:

> "God is a Spirit" (John 4: 24).

It has to be reminded that Plato taught that the celestial bodies were composed of fire. It may also be argued that the authors of the New Testament books were influenced by the Greek philosophers who taught that the cosmos was composed of the four elements, fire, air, water, and earth. Of these, fire was the least tangible and that may be the reason why God, Christ, and the Holy Spirit were associated with fire and light.

It must be concluded that the Biblical views of God, heaven, the netherworld, and hell were influenced to such an extent by pagan notions that it is impossible to divorce the biblical ideas from certain aspects of ancient paganism.

The Early Christian View of Angels

The New Testament mentions many instances where angels appeared to humans and they are portrayed as the servants and messengers of God. After all, the Greek word for angel, ἀγγέλος (*angelos*), literally means "messenger".

That John of Patmos thought that the stars in the sky were actually angels is clear from Rev 1: 16, 20:

> "He had seven stars in his right hand. (. . .) The seven stars are the angels of the seven assemblies.

The author of Hebr 1: 7 quotes Ps 104: 4 – "Of the angels he says, 'Who makes his angels winds, and his servants a flame of fire.'"

This author seems to have held the belief that these celestial beings are composed of the two less solid elements, namely air or wind and fire. Something similar is encountered in Matt 28: 2 where we read of the angel who opened Jesus' grave: "His appearance was like lightning."

The Early Christian View of Spirits

There are numerous references to *spirits* in the New Testament. The word utilized is πνεῦμα (*pneuma*). It has many meanings: "a movement of air, the wind; breath; the spirit, i.e. the vital principal by which the body is animated, the rational spirit, the power by which the human being feels, thinks, decides; the soul; a spirit higher than man but lower than God, i.e. an angel; the Spirit of God; also used of demons, or evil spirits, who were conceived as inhabiting the bodies of men".

Since this single word has such a rich variety of meanings it might be argued that all the meanings are really synonyms. That means that the early Christians – just as their Greek contemporaries, as well as the Judeans before them – regarded the wind, a person's breath, and his spirit to be the same thing. Their prescientific and concrete way of thinking leaves us no other conclusion, as will be shown in the analysis that follows.

The *spirit* often represents the whole person or his mind:

- "When Jesus had said this, he was troubled in the spirit, and testified, 'Most assuredly I tell you that one of you will betray me'" (John 13: 21).
- "Now while Paul waited for them at Athens, his spirit was provoked within him as he saw the city full of idols" (Acts: 17: 16).
- "God is my witness, whom I serve in my spirit" (Rom 1: 9).

The *spirit* is often seen as the life-giving force, the (invisible) breath, of a person. The following texts illustrate this idea:

- "Her [the girl who was resurrected by Jesus] spirit [or breath] returned, and she rose up immediately. He [Jesus] commanded that something be given to her to eat" (Luk 8: 55).

- "Jesus, crying with a loud voice, said, 'Father, into your hands I commit my spirit!' Having said this, he breathed his last" (Luk 23: 46). [This verse may just as well be translated: "Jesus, crying with a loud voice, said, 'Father, into your hands I commit my breath!' Having said this, he breathed his last." Another way of translating it would be: "Jesus, crying with a loud voice, said, 'Father, into your hands I commit my spirit!' Having said this, he gave up the spirit".]
- When Jesus met his disciples after his resurrection he said to them: "See my hands and my feet, that it is I myself. Touch me and see, for a spirit doesn`t have flesh and bones, as you see that I have" (Luk 24: 39).
- "They stoned Stephen, as he called on the Lord, saying, 'Lord Jesus, receive my spirit!'" (Acts 7: 59).
- "Then will the lawless one be revealed, whom the Lord will kill with the breath of his mouth, and bring to nothing by the brightness of his coming" (2 Thess 2: 8) [The expression "breath of his mouth" may equally be translated as "spirit of his mouth"].
- "For as the body apart from the spirit [breath?] is dead, even so faith apart from works is dead" (James 2: 26).
- "After the three and a half days, the breath of life from God entered into them, and they stood on their feet" (Rev 11: 11) [An alternative translation would be: "After the three and a half days, the *spirit* of life from God entered into them, and they stood on their feet" – which proves that the words "breath" and "spirit" were regarded as synonyms.]

These texts also contain the idea that at death a separation between spirit and body takes place – although the spirit was thought of as a rather refined type of matter, like air, wind, or the last breath of a dying person. The *spirit* was also often seen as identical with the *soul*. That means that the dualism between body and spirit or soul and the immortality of the spirit or soul, as taught by Plato, probably had an influence on the authors of the New Testament. In this, they differed from the Old Testament where a dualism between body and spirit was not to be found – except in the late book of Ecclesiastes.

The New Testament often equates the *Spirit* of God with the wind. In John 3: 8 this word is used in this double sense: "The wind blows where it wants to, and you hear its sound, but don`t know where it comes from and where it is going. So is everyone who is born of the Spirit." When the Holy Spirit was poured out on Pentecost Day, "there came from the sky a sound like the rushing of a mighty wind" (Acts 2: 2). In other words: God's Spirit is associated with the wind and may even be regarded as God's breath.

There is often a contrast between *spirit* and *flesh* in the New Testament (Rom 8: 1, 4; Gal 5: 17). By *flesh* the physical body is meant, but also the sinful nature of man. *Spirit* in this sense has a connection with man's conscience and his relationship with God. Therefore, Jesus could say: "The spirit indeed is willing, but the flesh is weak" (Matt 26: 41). The influence of neo-platonic philosophers may perhaps be detected here since they taught that matter was evil and spirit was noble and that the spirit had to be rescued from the vile body at death.[48]

Paul taught in 1 Cor 15 that the faithful will be resurrected on Judgment Day with a "spiritual body" or a "celestial body" – just as Jesus Christ. He describes this body as being incorruptible and he explains the difference between this spiritual body and an earthly body by stating that celestial bodies, such as the sun, moon, and

---

[48] Enc Brit, "Platonism".

stars, differ in glory and power from terrestrial bodies. In the same way, the resurrected spiritual body is totally different from the earthly human body. It seems likely that Paul was – directly or indirectly – influenced by the teaching of Aristotle that heavenly bodies were not composed of one or more of the four usual elements, but of a different indestructible fifth element, the so-called quintessence or aether, and that he applies that notion to the resurrected incorruptible bodies of the faithful with which they will be ready to enter heaven.

Paul teaches something similar in Rom 8: 21, 2 Cor 5: 1 and Phil 3: 20–21 where he states that the decaying creation and our humiliating bodies will be transformed into a state of eternal glory at the second coming of Christ, a state that cannot be compared to anything on earth.

Although Paul doesn't state it *expressis verbis*, it does seem as if he thought that the "spiritual body" or the "celestial body" with which the faithful would be resurrected on Judgment Day, could be equated with the stars shining in heaven – an idea he would have found in the book of Daniel (12: 2–3). After all, Paul thought of the heaven, comprised of the sky filled with clouds, stars, and spirits, to be parts of the same system. According to him, the sun, moon, and stars have "bodies" and he uses the same word for the "body" of a star, the "body" of a living human being, and the "spiritual body" of resurrected believers, namely σῶμα (*soma*) – more or less as Philo and Josephus also taught.

Heb 1: 14 declares that *angels* are "ministering spirits, sent forth to do service for the sake of those who will inherit salvation".

The Early Christians' View of the Soul

The concept of *soul* plays an important role in the New Testament. The Greek word is ψυχή (*psyche*). It has the following meanings:

breath, the vital force which animates the body and shows itself in breathing; the soul, the seat of the feelings, desires, affections, aversions; the soul regarded as a moral being designed for everlasting life; the soul as an essence that differs from the body and is not dissolved by death.

The word *soul* is often used for the whole person:

- "Take my yoke on you, and learn from me, for I am humble and lowly in heart; and you will find rest for your souls" (Matt 11: 29).
- "I will tell my soul, 'Soul, you have many goods laid up for many years. Take your ease, eat, drink, be merry'" (Luke 12: 19).
- "Then those who gladly received his word were baptized. There were added that day about three thousand souls" (Acts 2: 41).
- "It will be, that every soul that will not listen to that prophet will be utterly destroyed from among the people" (Acts 3: 23).

The word *soul* is also used as a synonym for *life:*

> For what will it profit a man, if he will gain the whole world, and forfeit his life [soul]? Or what will a man give in exchange for his life [soul]?

Man is composed of body, soul, and spirit (Matt 22: 37; 1 Thess 5: 23; Heb 4: 12). The *soul* is the part or aspect of the person that is saved through faith in Jesus Christ (Luke 12: 20; Luke 21: 19; Heb 10: 39; Heb 13: 17; Jas 1: 21; Jas 5: 20; 1 Pet 1: 9). The *soul* is also the part of man that survives death and receives life everlasting in heaven (Rev 6: 9; Rev 20: 4). It seems likely that the dualism between body and *soul*, as taught by Plato, must have influenced the early Christian authors.

There are, however, also texts that signify that more than just the *soul* will survive death. Jesus said: “Don`t be afraid of those who kill the body, but are not able to kill the soul. Rather, fear him who is able to destroy both soul and body in Gehenna [hell]” (Matt 10: 28). Jesus also thought that the dead still possessed material bodies when in hell. In Matt 18: 8–9 he taught:

> “If your hand or your foot causes you to stumble, cut it off, and cast it from you. It is better for you to enter into life maimed or crippled, rather than having two hands or two feet to be cast into the eternal fire. If your eye causes you to stumble, pluck it out, and cast it from you. It is better for you to enter into life with one eye, rather than having two eyes to be cast into the Gehenna of fire.”

It may be concluded that the teaching of the New Testament regarding the *soul* is sometimes rather confusing. There are texts that contradict each other. It is clear, though, that the soul was conceptualized in a concrete manner where it was seen as representing the whole (visible) person or where it was seen as the breath and life force of a person. The soul was the part of the person that was saved by Christ and that survived physical death.

These prescientific ideas held by the Jews and the early Christians are at odds with what believers believe today. And, yet, believers still believe what they read in the sacred Scriptures. It will be necessary to illuminate how it came about that contemporary believers do not accept these prescientific notions anymore.

Summary

The following conclusions about the cosmology of the New Testament may be made:

- The influence of ancient Greek philosophy and Mesopotamian astrology on the authors of the New Testament Scriptures cannot be denied.
- Earth was thought to be the center of the universe with all the celestial bodies circling around it.
- Heaven, as the abode of God, was deemed to be above and beyond the stars.
- Angels, heavenly spiritual beings, acted as God's servants and messengers.
- Spirits or souls were composed of wind and breath. The human spirit or soul survived after death and was transported, either to heaven, or to the underworld.

THE QUR'AN

The holy book of Islam, the Qur'an, was purportedly dictated to the prophet Muhammad by the archangel Gabriel. He memorized the words and taught them to his followers after which they were written down. In some cases, he dictated a certain passage directly to a scribe.[49]

Muhammad was active during the first part of the seventh century AD on the Arabian peninsula. He had contact with Jews and Christians and he was evidently deeply influenced by their religious ideas. The Qur'an, therefore, contains numerous allusions to biblical stories and figures, including Adam, Abraham, Moses, and Jesus.[50]

It may be safely said the Qur'an contains a simplified Old Testament theology. It is also not a very voluminous book, containing only 114 surahs or chapters of unequal length.

---

[49] Rodwell and Jones, *The Koran*, xix.

[50] Armstrong, *Islam,* 2–30.

The main characteristic of the Qur'an is its insistence on monotheism (Surah 2: 255) and an antagonistic attitude towards polytheism and the Christian doctrine of the divine Trinity.

Since Mohammed lived in a cultural backwater, the Arabian peninsula, during the so-called dark ages in Europe, it is to be expected that the teachings of the Qur'an regarding the cosmos would be less detailed and sophisticated and more naïve than those of the Hebrew Scriptures and the Christian New Testament. There are some similarities, however.

The Qur'an describes heaven as a physical place above the clouds and that is where God's throne is situated (Surah 2: 210, 255; 8: 8; 11: 12;). God's throne is also described as a couch on earth with the clouds as a canopy (Surah 2: 22). It is also situated over the waters (Surah 11: 7) – presumably the source of rain water in the sky. Angels are hovering around the throne (Surah 39: 75), while they also carry the throne (Surah 69: 17). The heavens are kept in place by invisible pillars (Surah 13: 2).

God also created seven heavens or firmaments above the earth, which are layered one above the other (Surah 2: 29; 17: 44; 23: 86; 65: 12; 67: 3; 71: 16-17). It is possible that these seven heavens can be equated with the orbits of the seven planets, although the Qur'an nowhere mentions any planets, apart from the sun and the moon. These seven heavens are, however, also characterized as "seven pathways" (Surah 23: 17), which may be interpreted as the orbits of the planets.

God created angels from fire (Surah 7: 13) and Adam, the first human being, was formed from clay (Surah 15: 27–28).

After death, resurrected true believers will be transported by angels to heaven (Surah 6: 61), which is described as a beautiful garden that is irrigated by a river (Surah 3: 15, 31; 7: 42). This garden is "as wide as the heavens and the earth" (Surah 3: 133).

Heaven has gates or doors, which will be opened on Judgment Day by the angels for the faithful to enter (Surah 7: 40).

God is seen as the eternal, all-knowing, and all-powerful creator of the world and he is composed of light (Surah 13: 2; 24: 35; 39: 69). He created the heavens and the earth in six days (11: 7) and created all living creatures from water (Surah 24: 45). He placed the sun, the moon, and the constellations in the sky to act as light-bearers and time keepers (Surah 13: 2; 25: 61).

Hell, the destination of the godless unbelievers after death and Judgment Day, is somewhere below the earth and is also called the "Abyss" (Surah 4: 121–122; 7: 41; 8: 11; 101: 9). The resurrected unbelievers are transported thither by the angels of hell after they have died and after Judgement Day (Surah 8: 50; 10: 109; 37: 20). Satan, who refused to bow before Adam (Surah 2: 34), was banished to Hell, although he still exerts power over the earth by tempting people (Surah 2: 36, 268). Hell is described as a never-ending fire (Surah 2: 167; 3: 131; 8: 14) and it is clear that the Qur'an describes it in physical terms.

On Judgment Day, believers and sinners will be resurrected: "And on the Day of Resurrection, they [the unbelievers] will be assigned to the most severe torment. God is not unaware of what you do" (Surah 2: 85; see also 2: 113 and 3: 55).

When the Qur'an mentions the word "soul" it is usually meant to denote the whole human being. On occasion, it also describes the condition of a person after death. In Surah 3: 161 we read for instance: "Whoever acts dishonestly will bring his dishonesty on the Day of Resurrection. Then every soul will be paid in full for what it has earned, and they will not be wronged."

The concept of "spirit" is used exclusively for God, who is often called the "Holy Spirit" (Surah 2: 87; 5: 110;16: 102).

BELIEVERS OF OUR TIME

It is common knowledge that a limited number of educated people of our time who regard themselves as believing Jews, Christians, or Muslims, and who see the world, themselves, and the cosmos in the same way as the authors of the ancient Scriptures. They are jokingly called "flat-earthers".

There is, for instance, a body calling itself the Flat Earth Society, with headquarters in London. They have their own website on which they publish articles to motivate their stance that the earth is not a globe, but a flat disk. They rely mainly on texts found in the Bible, the Qur'an, and the literature of other religions to bolster their point of view.[51]

Most believers have discarded a belief in a flat earth, which is the center of the universe. They do not believe that heaven, the home of God, is situated directly beyond the stars. They reject the idea that the stars are angels. They cannot accept that there are hollow spaces below the earth's surface where the souls of deceased people are gathered.

Educated believers of our time have been profoundly influenced by the progress of science. This progress must be briefly described in the next chapter.

---

[51] The website of the Flat Earth Society is to be found at – https://theflatearthsociety.org/home/index.php

Chapter 4
THE PROGRESS OF SCIENCE

DEFINITION OF SCIENCE

It is perfectly understandable that the authors of the ancient Scriptures held views about the cosmos that differ widely from those harbored by educated people of our time. After all, they didn't have the tools to conduct scientific investigations, observations, and experiments, such as telescopes, X-ray machines, fMRI scanners, microscopes, accurate scales, computers to do complicated calculations, cameras, or advanced mathematics. Since these scientific tools became available, our knowledge of the world, ourselves, and the universe has increased exponentially.

The word "science" is derived from the Latin *scientia.* This word means basically "knowledge" – that is, knowledge about the world and natural processes. The late eminent South African Christian philosopher, Herman Stoker (1899–1993), explained that scientific knowledge is not simply a description of phenomena. It is systemized knowledge that endeavors to understand, to explain, and to evaluate. It seeks relationships in order to combine knowledge into a system or a finished whole.[52] Heyns and Jonker, two theologians, agreed: "Science is systemized knowledge and verified knowledge of reality."[53]

It is necessary to provide a brief description of the level of scientific theories, insights, and knowledge available to educated people today. It will become clear that this knowledge differs

---

[52] Stoker, *Beginseks en Metodes in die Wetenskap,* 135–36.

[53] Heyns and Jonker, *Op Weg met die Teologie,* 28 (own translation).

substantially and fundamentally from the ideas found in the Scriptures. It also must be pointed out that a civilized and comfortable life in the 21st century would not have been possible without all the technological marvels and developments we nowadays take for granted. These marvels depend upon the application of various scientific theories that have proven their validity in practice.

PHYSICS AND ASTRONOMY

Galileo Galilei

Galileo Galilei (1564–1642) started the scientific revolution of the 16th century. Galileo probably contributed more to the establishment of modern natural science than anyone else with his observations and experiments.

Various clashes between science and theology have occurred during the last few centuries. The best known is that between the Italian mathematicians, physicists, and astronomers Giordano Bruno (1548–1600) and Galileo on the one hand and the Inquisition or ecclesiastical court of the Roman Catholic Church on the other hand during the sixteenth and seventeenth centuries.

Bruno declared that the universe was infinite and composed of an infinite number of worlds. He could not provide empirical evidence for his theories but his speculations make sense when modern insights are considered and he influenced scientific investigations in the centuries after his time. His ideas provoked the ire of the Inquisition because they contradicted the teachings of the Bible and of Aristotle. When he refused to retract his theories, he was burnt alive on the stake on 8 February 1600.[54]

Galileo was the first to use the newly invented telescope to

[54] Aquilecchia, "Bruno, Giordano".

study the stars. He discovered the mountains on the moon, the phases of Venus, the moons of Jupiter, the unusual shape of Saturn (due to its rings), the fact that the Milky Way contains many more stars than those visible to the naked eye, and sunspots. He wrote Istoria e Dimostrazioni Intorno Alle Macchie Solari e Loro Accidenti ("History and Demonstrations Concerning Sunspots and Their Properties," or "Letters on Sunspots"), which appeared in 1613 and this led to a warning from the Inquisition that he should not continue defending the viewpoint of Nicolaus Copernicus (1473–1543), who argued that the earth revolved around the sun and not the other way.

Frontispiece to Galileo's Dialogo Sopra di Due Massimi Sistemi del Mondo, Tolemaico e Copernicano (1632; Dialogue Concerning the Two Chief World Systems, Ptolemaic & Copernican). From left to right are Aristotle, Ptolemy, and Copernicus (their names are written on the hems of their robes). Ptolemy holds an astrolabe and Copernicus clasps a model of a planet orbiting the sun.

His most famous book, Dialogo Sopra di Due Massimi Sistemi del Mondo, Tolemaico e Copernicano ("Dialogue Concern-ing the Two Chief World Systems, Ptolemaic & Copernican"), was finished in 1630, and he dedicated it to the Pope, who was a friend. Since he presented the book as a mere hypothesis he initially got the approval of the ecclesiastical censors. However, the Inquisition, the Vatican's doctrinal police, subjected Galileo to a hearing in 1633 and he was forbidden to teach his views any longer and he was put under house arrest. Galileo was rehabilitated only in 1979 when Pope John Paul II conceded that the church treated him unjustly.[55]

On 31 October 1992 the Pope addressed the Pontifical Academy of Sciences in Rome and confessed that the Inquisition was wrong in condemning Galileo. This was one of the rare occasions where the Pope admitted an error of the church.[56]

Galileo also performed experiments with falling objects and noted that the increase in speed when a metal ball fell a long way, could be calculated mathematically. With this, he paved the way for scientific experiments of later times.

Isaac Newton

Isaac Newton(1642–1727) was undoubtedly the greatest scientist before Einstein and his pioneering work regarding the methodology of experimental science is still guiding scientists today.

Newton studied at Cambridge and he was appointed professor of mathematics and physics there (1669–1699). He was later master of the Royal Mint in London until his death. He was knighted in 1705, partly due to his struggle to keep Cambridge Protestant.

His two most famous works are Principia Mathematica

---

[55] Van Helden, "Galileo"; Galileo, *Dialogue Concerning the two Chief World Systems.*

[56] The New York Times, 01.11.1992.

(1687) and Opticks (1704). In the first he sets out the mathematical laws of mechanics, gravity, the movement of heavenly bodies, and the movement of liquids. In the second book he described the mathematics behind light refraction. He is also the inventor of the reflector telescope.[57]

Albert Einstein

Albert Einstein (1879–1955) was described by the American magazine Time as "the man of the century" at the end of the 20th century.

Einstein grew up in Munich, Germany, the son of Jewish parents. The family later moved to Italy and he completed his school career in Switzerland. After failing the entrance exam for a course in engineering, he qualified as a teacher in mathematics. He could not find a permanent teaching position and from 1902 worked as a clerk in the patent office in Bern.

During his stay in Bern, he published one of his most important writings in 1905. It deals with the special theory of relativity and it is based on the principle that the speed of light remains constant, regardless of the speed with which the observer moves, and that time passes more slowly the faster the observer moves. In 1907 he showed that matter and energy are reducible to each other. He expresses this with the famous formula $E=mc^2$ (E: energy; m: mass; c: speed of light).

---

[57] Scholtz, "Newton, Isaac."

He published his general theory of relativity in 1915. He showed that the force of gravity is really a distortion of space caused by massive bodies.

After obtaining his doctorate in 1905, from 1908 he was successively a lecturer in theoretical physics in Bern, Zurich, Prague, and Berlin. Einstein was visiting the USA when Hitler came to power in Germany in 1933, and he decided to remain in the USA. He was appointed as a professor in Princeton.

A consequence of Einstein's theories is that the universe must have had a beginning – am idea that he initially did not want to accept. Later he admitted this as his biggest mistake. Einstein received the Nobel Prize in Physics in 1921 for his work on the photoelectric effect.[58]

The Contemporary View of the Cosmos

Ever since the time of Copernicus and Galileo, our view of the cosmos has undergone various radical changes. We now know that the stars are bodies like our sun, only at far greater distances. Nowadays, it is universally accepted within educated circles that the earth is a tiny speck of dust in a vast expanse of space in which billions of galaxies are spread out.

The universe is about 13,7 billion years old and it is accepted that it started with a gigantic explosion, dubbed the Big Bang, during which all matter, space, and time were created. With our strongest optical and radio telescopes and other instruments we are able to observe most of this still expanding universe.

The observable universe is about 26 billion light years in diameter, although the universe must be bigger than that since we can only see the furthest galaxies as they were billions of years ago. Since that time, the universe must have continued to grow in size.

---

[58] Scholtz, "Einstein, Albert"; Zee, *Einstein's Universe.*

We will, however, never be able to detect the non-observable sections of the universe because the combined speed with which the earth and those parts of the universe are receding from each other is greater than the speed of light. No light or other radiation from those parts of the universe can ever catch up with us.

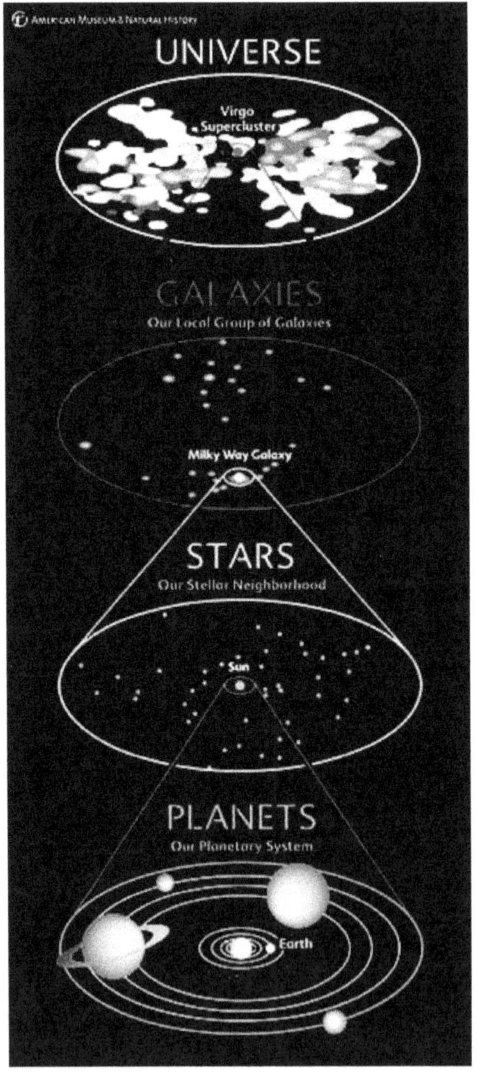

How our Solar System fits into the bigger picture of the Universe

The accompanying illustration (previous page) provides a simplified view of how we regard the cosmos today. In this cosmos, there is no place for a heaven as the dwelling place of God. Believers argue, though, that God as the creator cannot be part of his creation, that he is transcendent (that means, outside the universe, perhaps in another dimension), and that he must be a spiritual, non-material, all-powerful, all-knowing, and omnipresent intelligence.[59]

The age of the earth and the solar system is calculated to be around 4,6 billion years.[60]

BIOLOGY

Charles Darwin

Before Charles Robert Darwin (1809–1882) published his ground-breaking book, On the Origin of Species in 1859, there were many botanists and zoologists who did sterling work in describing and classifying all forms of plant and animal life. It was taken for granted that all the different species were created by God in their present forms, although selective breeding could change the appearance of species over time.

Darwin initially studied medicine, but then enrolled in theology and natural studies at the University of Cambridge. At 22, he joined the Beagle, a research ship, as an unpaid naturalist on a research cruise around the world. During the five-year trip, he collected material for his work. Darwin's theory that all life forms developed through a slow process of natural selection is considered the basis of the modern theory of evolution.

---

[59] Clark, *The Universe;* Hawking, *The Grand Design;* Joubert, *Die Groot Gedagte;* Steinhardt and Turok, *Endless Universe : Beyond the Big Bang.*
[60] Clark, *The Universe,* 29.

In The Descent of Man (1871) he discussed human evolution and gender selection as an alternative mode of change. In The Expression of The Emotions in Man and Animals (1872) he contributed to comparative psychology, with his own observations of his children's early development as background.

Darwin, also a renowned botanist, still exerts a great influence on the natural sciences, social sciences, and economics. His theories, though, caused severe controversy, especially in churches where his ideas were seen as contradicting the biblical creation narrative. Despite this, his important role in the development of the sciences is recognized worldwide. [61]

Gregor Mendel

Gregor Mendel (1822–1884) was an Austrian monk and teacher. He experimented since 1854 with peas in the monastery's garden by creating hybrids of peas with opposing qualities or characters, for instance: long plants versus short plants, or green pods versus yellow pods.

He continued breeding with the hybrids and found that certain traits were more often inherited than others. He termed then dominant and the others recessive traits. Since he experimented with a large plant population, he found that dominant traits appeared three times more often in the second generation of hybrids than the

[61] Van Lill, "Darwin, Charles Robert."

recessive characters. As a trained mathematician, he could prove this ratio of 3:1 mathematically.

He delivered a paper in 1865 at a local conference of natural scientists with the title Experiments on Plant Hybrids and his paper was published the next year. Few biologists took note of this paper and its importance was only realized after the start of the twentieth century.[62]

Today, it is generally recognized that Darwin and Mendel, whose work complement each other, must be regarded as the founding pioneer of the discipline of genetics, the science that investigates biological heredity.

The Science of Genetics

An important development regarding the discipline of genetics was achieved by molecular biologists Francis Crick (1916–2004) and James Watson (1928 –) who discovered the double helix structure of DNA (deoxyribonucleic acid), the molecule in each living cell that carries the genetic code for that particular organism. They received the Nobel Prize for Physiology in 1962 for this achievement.

The Human Genome Project, under the leadership of Francis Collins, managed to unravel the human genetic code to determine which part of the genetic material in die DNA molecule was responsible for which development in the growth and development of a human being since conception.[63]

The theory of evolution, as first formulated by Darwin, is the dominant and almost universally-accepted paradigm in biology today. Proponents of this theory state that the development of all forms of life on earth came about as the result of a process of

---

[62] Collins, *The Language of God,* 100–102; Olby, "Mendel, Gregor".

[63] Collins, *The Language of God.*

evolution or development, during which certain traits of organisms deviated from the norm due to chance and that these deviations made them more competitive in a changing environment, with the result that they produced more offspring than other members of the same species who were less adapted to changing conditions.[64]

FUNDAMENTALISM AND ANTI-EVOLUTIONISM

Origins

It is necessary to devote some attention to a movement within Christianity known as fundamentalism. This movement takes the Protestant position regarding the infallibility of the Bible to absurd extremes. Christian fundamentalism had its origins towards the end of the nineteenth century in America as a reaction towards Charles Darwin's theory of evolution – which seemed to clash with a literal reading of the creation story in Genesis 1. This movement is of the view that the Bible has to be taken literally in all respects because it is God's Word. For them, "science" and "evolution" are dirty words.

"Scientific Creationism" and "Intelligent Design"

In an effort to counter the theory of evolution, a rival philosophy based on a literal interpretation of the creation myth in Genesis 1 was devised, called "scientific creationism", later renamed "intelligent design" (ID).

Theologians who support this movement declare that God created the earth and all extinct and existing species of plants and animals separately about six thousand years ago. They derived this number from the genealogical lists in the Bible, stretching back to the first human being, Adam. They argue that no form of life can de-

---

[64] Dawkins, *The Greatest Show on Earth;* Fortey, *Life:L an Unauthorised Biography;* Rousseau, *Die Groot Avomtuur.*

velop into something else over time.[65]

Their alternatives to the theory of evolution, namely "scientific creationism" or "intelligent design" cannot be proven scientifically or experimentally and are flatly rejected by most biologists and other scientists.[66]

According to Carl Zimmer, there is "very little real science" in ID. The claims of ID, that God miraculously created each life form or species independently and separately, cannot be tested empirically and no scientific investigation has ever been able to pinpoint God's supposed intervention in the natural world.[67]

David Mills argues that ID is nothing but religious propaganda; it cannot claim to be a scientific theory since it fails to show through empirical observations or experiments exactly how God intervened to bring the present state of affairs in the universe and on earth about. Supporters of ID simply claim that God was responsible for phenomena for which scientists at present do not yet have a clear explanation, such as the origin of life on earth. They utterly fail to provide empirical proof for their assertion that God was responsible for the phenomena in question.[68]

Greg Graffin points out that creationists and supporters of ID have, up to date, contributed nothing to further scientific knowledge. All they do is to postulate that the only explanation for gaps in our knowledge of the world is that a particular gap is an indication of God's creative interference in the universe. All they do is to criticize

---

[65] Clark, *The Universe, 28;* Sandeen, "Fundamentalism"; Glick, "Intelligent Design".

[66] Ayala, "Evolution"; Glick, "Intelligent Design"; Graffin and Ohlson, *Anarchy Evolution*, 60–61; Cunningham, *Decoding the Language of God*, 233–45.

[67] Zimmer, *Evolution,* 403–04.

[68] Mills, *Atheist Universe,* 76.

the findings of scientists in an endeavor to "prove" that God must have designed and created the universe, including life on earth. They don't ever perform independent scientific investigations by conducting laboratory work or going on field expeditions.[69]

Creationists are convinced that God created everything, including man, within the span of a single week, called "creation week" – the seven days of creation of Genesis 1. They read Genesis 1 as if it is a scientific explanation of the origin of the world, while disregarding the very evident poetical flavor of this part of the Bible. This interpretation implies that Adam and Eve must be exactly one day younger than the dinosaurs and that they were actually contemporaries, just as tigers and trilobites are supposed to have been living at the same time. The geological record shows that this was never the case; no human fossils were ever found together with dinosaur fossils in the same geological strata. Dinosaurs became extinct millions of years before the appearance of man.[70]

David Mills hammered the final nail into the coffin of so-called "creation science" and ID by asking: will any practitioner of these philosophies ever be nominated for a Nobel Prize in science? The answer is, of course, "No".[71]

Christians who Accept the Theory of Evolution

That the theory of evolution and the Christian message do not necessarily have to clash has been eloquently argued by eminent Christian scientists, such as Denis Alexander, Francis Collins (the former head of the human genome project), and Leon Rousseau[72],

---

[69] Graffin and Olson, *Anarchy Evolution,* 60–61.

[70] Mills, *Atheist Universe,* 118.

[71] Mills, *Atheist Universe,* 253–54.

[72] Alexander, *Creation or Evolution*; Collins, *The Language of God*; Rousseau, *Die Groot Gedagte*.

as well as eminent reformed theologians, such as Adrio König.[73]

Professor Joseph Ratzinger, who later became Pope Benedict XVI, wrote:

> "Der Schöpfungsglaube fragt nach dem Daβ des Seins als solchen; sein Problem ist, warum überhaupt etwas ist und nicht nichts. Der Entwicklungsgedanke hingegegen fragt, warum gerade diese Dinge sind und nicht andere, woher sie ihre Bestimmtheit erlangt haben ..."[74]

This means that the belief in creation and the theory of evolution deal with different aspects of reality and, therefore, need not clash with each other.

The present leader of the Roman Catholic Church, Pope Francis, has a diploma in chemistry, a master's degree in philosophy, as well as a doctorate in theology, and he openly declared that he finds that the big bang theory as an acceptable explanation of the origin of the universe and that the theory of evolution is compatible with his Christian faith and his belief in a divine creator.[75]

Christians who find the theory of evolution acceptable, usually point out that the supporters of so-called scientific creationism or ID make the mistake of reading the first chapter of Genesis as if it were a scientific report, while ignoring its clear poetical qualities and its cultural background. The text of this chap-

---

[73] König, *Die Groot Geloofswoordeboek*.

[74] Ratzinger, *Schöpfungsglaube und Evolutionstheorie*, 234. ("The belief in creation asks about the 'that' of being as such; its problem is: why is there something and not rather nothing? The idea of development, on the other hand, asks why things are as they are and not something different and how they have received their qualities...")

[75] Biography.com Editors, "Pope Francis Biography".

ter makes it clear that a literal explanation is impossible. It is stated, for instance, that the sun only appeared on Day 4 of the six days of creation and that leads to the question: how were the first three days measured? They could not have been periods of 24 hours each as creationists insist because there was no sun to define a day. The six days may, rather, be seen as astronomical and geological ages.

MEDICAL SCIENCE

It is common knowledge that the discipline of medical science, together with all its permutations in the field of health care, is of great benefit to mankind.

The International Classification of Diseases (tenth edition – also known as the ICD-10), of the World Health Organization, contains a description and the diagnostic criteria of all diseases, disorders, and disabilities known to the medical world. The causes of all these ailments and afflictions are known – bacteria and other micro-organisms, viruses, injuries, genetic deviations, toxic substances, and so forth. Supernatural causes, such as demonic possession, are not recognized and are ruled out.[76]

There are various techniques available to diagnose a certain health condition or complaint: a physical examination, X-rays, electronic scans, blood tests, biopsies, a description of symptoms by the patient, and many more.

Treatments for most of these conditions are available, consisting in many cases of medication, surgery, radiation therapy, transplants, physiotherapy, psychotherapy, *etcetera.*

Although most health practitioners won't discourage pastoral care and counseling for their patients, including readings from the Scripture and prayers by spiritual advisors, they rely

---

[76] Wiseman. *Paranormaility : What we See Isn't There,* 303–308.

exclusively on tested and tried medical methods for the treatment of all sorts of diseases, distempers, and disorders.[77]

PSYCHOLOGY

Sigmund Freud

Sigmund Freud (1856–1939) stands out in the history of the disciplines of psychology and psychiatry as perhaps the most influential figure.

He grew up mainly in Vienna, Austria, and spent practically his entire adult life there. After his studies in medicine, he specialized in neurology. He used hypnosis to cure hysterical patients and this led to the formulation of his psychological theory, namely psychoanalysis. This approach relies largely on free association. The patient is allowed to talk about anything that comes to his/her mind, thereby (it is hoped) bringing to consciousness his unconscious and repressed fears, urges, and desires. Much attention is also paid to the interpretation of dreams. Insight into his/her problems and their causes was supposed to help the patient to overcome these problems.

Psychotherapy usually consists of daily or weekly sessions for months and even years. In the process, the psychiatrist strives to reconstruct the patient's personality. According to Freud, the human personality has three components: the Ego (the conscious part), the Superego, or conscience, which is largely determined by the person's education and includes his value system, and the Id, the unconscious seat of urges and desires, especially the sex drive. Clashes between the Superego and the Id would, according to Freud, give rise to neuroses. He argued that the presence of a religious belief is a sign of neuroticism and that this can be overcome with

---

[77] Scholtz, *Pastoral Care,* 129–143.

psychoanalysis.

The approach of psychoanalysis was the dominant paradigm of psychotherapy for decades. Nowadays, most psychotherapists regard most of Freud's ideas and theories as outdated and they employ other techniques in dealing with psychological and emotional problems.

A lasting contribution made by Freud was to point out the importance of unconscious and subconscious feelings, urges, memories, and drives, and their influence on human behavior.[78]

Neuropsychology

The field of neuropsychology has gained the position of the cutting-edge discipline in the field of psychology. Knowledge about the human brain and central nervous system has increased dramatically during the recent past. It became possible to find a neurological mechanism at the root of almost all psychological or emotional problems in man. These problems can be explained in terms of defects or lesions in the architecture of the brain, defective chemical processes in the nervous system, and abnormal or defective electrical currents and networks in the brain.[79]

Neuroscientists have not been able to precisely locate or explain the brain centers and neurological processes connected to the phenomenon of consciousness, self-consciousness, and the "ego" of human beings. They are, nevertheless, convinced that these processes and functions are totally dependent upon a healthy and operational brain.[80]

At death, these functions cease and there is no empirical evi-

---

[78] Scholtz, "Freud, Sigmund".

[79] Carter, *Mapping the Mind;* Kolb and Wishaw, *Fundamentals;* Lezak et al., *Neuropsychological Assessment.*

[80] Papineau and Selina, *Introducing Consciousness.*

dence of a separate soul of spirit that may survive death. Human beings are "instinctive dualists" and believe that they are composed of two elements: a body and a soul (just as the Greek philosopher Plato taught). There is, however, no supporting scientific evidence for this belief.[81]

Neuroscientists have also found no evidence for any form of demonic possession in human beings. All forms of abnormal or pathological behavior or experiences can be explained in terms of medical, neurological, or psychological processes and mechanisms.

Professor Joseph Pierre of the School of Psychiatry at the University of California, San Franscisco, made a study of so-called cases of demonic possession. He found that such cases can be due to a psychotic condition, such as schizophrenia where the patient loses contact with reality on account of abnormal chemical processes in the brain, brain lesions, other abnormalities in brain architecture or functioning, epilepsy, or mass hysteria.[82]

The authoritative manual of the American Psychiatric Association, the Diagnostic and Statistical Manual of Mental Disorders (fifth edition of 2013 – popularly known as the DSM-5), which discusses all known psychological conditions, circumstances, and complaints, doesn't contain anything about demonic possession or an infestation of evil and unclean spirits. The same applies to the ICD-10 of the World Health Organization, as has already been pointed out.

A Final Word

It is regarded as an unspoken axiom by most scientists that it is possible to find natural explanations for all observed phenomena.

---

[81] Kolb and Wishaw, *Fundamentals,* 6–8; Zwaab, *Wijn zijn of Brein,* 192, 424.

[82] Pierre, "Demonic Possession",

Any possibility of supernatural occurrences or events is regarded with skepticism.

The question now arises: is it possible to avoid clashes and contradictions between the faith and descriptions found in the Scriptures and the findings of scientists?

Chapter 5
READING AND UNDERSTANDING THE SCRIPTURES

THE JEWISH AND CHRISTIAN SCRIPTURES

The Bible and Anecdotal Evidence

Professor Flip Buys, a conservative reformed theologian who investigated demonic possession in an African context, is of the opinion that we can only rely on the teachings of the Bible, as the Word of God, for knowledge about the spirit world, including angels, the devil, and demons.

He refers to various authors on the subject of demonology who based their findings on anecdotal evidence – interviews with missionaries who encountered purported cases of demonic possession, people who claim to have been victims of this affliction, personal revelations received from the Holy Spirit, and even interviews with demons purportedly found in people who were thought to be possessed. He dismissed these anecdotal descriptions since they undermine the authority of Scripture as God's revelation about the spirit world.[83]

One must agree with Buys that this type of anecdotal evidence cannot be relied upon. The random collection and subjective interpretation of any number of anecdotes and unverifiable stories is not recognized as a valid research tool in the social sciences.[84]

---

[83] Buys, "A Reformed Perspective".

[84] Bless, *Fundamentals of Social Research.*

Certain Christian Beliefs in Retreat

It has been shown in the previous chapter that eminent Christians confessed that the opposition of their churches against certain scientific insights was wrong. Two popes admitted that Galileo was treated unjustly. With that, they agreed that the biblical cosmology, which he contradicted, cannot be accepted anymore and that modern astronomy can be trusted to provide valid knowledge about the cosmos.

The opposition of some Christian groups against the theory of evolution has largely evaporated. There are still certain Christians who oppose the idea that mankind descended from monkeys and apes, as they often put it, but overall, educated Christians find that the theory of evolution can be reconciled with their faith that God is the creator of the universe.

It must be granted that Christians had to relinquish certain traditional beliefs. It also seems as if a belief in the devil is not so pervasive as in the past when the Inquisition held certain parts of the world in a grip of terror in its campaigns against Satan.

A recent Gallup poll in America found that –

- 74% of Americans believe in God;
- 69% believe in angels;
- 67% believe in heaven;
- 59% believe in hell; and
- 58% believe in the devil.

This means that 42% of Americans do not believe in the devil or are unsure about him and that 26% reject a belief in God, or are not sure about his existence. The most believers were found to be elder people, less affluent people, and people without college education.[85]

This opinion poll was conducted only in America, but similar trends will certainly be found in most other western societies.

The question inevitably arises: how must believing Christians approach the Bible? How far can the Bible still be trusted? Can they believe the reports about the devil and demons in the Scriptures? After all, Christians usually base their faith on the teachings of the Bible, a collection of documents that can be regarded as the foundational documentation of Christianity.

It must be pointed out, though, that many Americans do not accept the infallibility of the Bible anymore. Gallup recently found:

> "A record-low 20% of Americans now say the Bible is the literal word of God, down from 24% the last time the question was asked in 2017, and half of what it was at its high points in 1980 and 1984. Meanwhile, a new high of 29% say the Bible is a collection of 'fables, legends, history and moral precepts recorded by man.' This marks the first time significantly more Americans have viewed the Bible as not divinely inspired than as the literal word of God."[86]

When reading and trying to understand the Bible, there are some important considerations and facts that cannot be ignored:

The Biblical Authors Lived Many Centuries Ago

The last book in the Bible, Revelation, is also the youngest. It was written during AD 96–97, more than two thousand years ago at a

---

[85] Gallup, "Belief in Five Spiritual Entities".

[86] Gallup, "Fewer in U.S. Now See Bible as Literal Word of God".

time when the Roman Empire was at its height.[87]

The oldest parts of the Old Testament seem to date from the time of the Israelite kingdom, many centuries before Christ.[88]

This all means that the authors of the various parts of the Bible lived in ancient times, when people held primitive and pre-scientific views regarding the world. It has already been shown how the authors of the Old Testament and the New Testament saw the world, themselves, the cosmos, and God. Believers of the 21st century find it hard to accept some of those beliefs.

Although conventional Christians believe that the authors of the Scriptures were inspired by the Spirit of God, which led them to provide their readers with a faithful rendering of who God is and what He expects from mankind, they also understand that it was inevitable and acceptable that the Scriptures contain primitive and pre-scientific notions. If the Scriptures were written in such a manner that the modern cosmology and the theory of evolution were incurporated, the original readers would not have understood what they were reading. The authors, as children of their times, automatically made use of the ideas, beliefs, and convictions of their readers to provide them with knowledge about God and his will for man.

That means that it will be a grave mistake to think that the authors of the Scriptures had the same mental pictures as people of our time regarding concepts such as heaven, hell, the world, angels, spirits, and souls. But that does not mean that their experiences with God were inaccurately reported. Educated Christians accept that they may adhere to current scientific insights, but that they are also convinced that they hear the voice of God in the Scriptures. They believe that the message(s) of the Bible can still be accepted and applied to our current circumstances.

---

[87] Scholtz, *The Prophecies of Revelation.*

[88] Boshoff, *Geskiedenis en Geskrifte,* 87–107.

Different Biblical Documents Were Written at Different Times
As has been pointed out, the oldest and the youngest parts of the Bible were produced centuries apart. There was, of course, a shift in certain beliefs during those years. In a previous chapter, the differences between the world-views of the Hebrew Scriptures and the New Testament were highlighted.

The authors of the Scriptures were influenced by the intellectual climates of the different civilizations that held sway during their times: Egypt, Babylonia, Persia, the heritage of Greece in the eastern Mediterranean, and the Roman Empire.

People who read the Scriptures today must keep these different influences in mind and that presupposes that they be informed about these cultures and how the biblical authors incorporated certain current ideas into their documents, or reacted against certain unacceptable notions of their pagan neighbors.

Certain books in the Bible were assembled by incorporating different parts that date from different times. The first five books of the Bible, which were traditionally regarded as the work of Moses, proved to be an amalgam of different sources from different epochs. These books, the so-called Pentateuch, only got their final form after the end of the Babylonian exile and during the Hellenistic Period, which started in 333 BC.[89]

The book of Isaiah contains the work of three authors from different periods.[90] The Gospels of Matthew and Luke contain three components each: extracts from the so-called Q Document, consisting of a collection of sayings of Jesus, excerpts from the earlier Gospel of Mark, and material unique to each of these Gospels.[91] The Gospel of John was assembled from two main

---

[89] Boshoff, *Geskiedenis en Geskrifte,* 217.

[90] Boshoff, *Geskiedenis en Geskrifte,* 215.

[91] Pretorius, *The Gospels,* 283–535.

components: a sober narrative part with reports about Jesus' ministry and crucifixion, together with sermons and dialogues, which were attributed to Jesus long afterwards.[92]

It is necessary to take note of the probable dates of composition of all these elements of these biblical books, because that may have a bearing on how they are to be understood.

The Scriptures Contain Various Genres

It is important to note that the Scriptures contain various literary genres and that certain passages can only be understood if the particular genre is recognized.

The Bible contains historical reports, reminiscences, poetry, prophecies, fictitious stories and parables, collections of wisdom sayings, and personal correspondence. Each of these genres calls for a different approach when being interpreted and understood. When they employ figures of speech, parables, or idiomatic expressions, knowledge of the background of those is required.

The Scriptures Wanted to Convince People

One may regard the various parts of the Bible as religious propaganda. The authors wished to convince their readers of their views and their faith. They wanted to preserve certain memories to serve as reminders for future generations of their experiences with God or with Jesus, with the hope that their readers would accept their points of view.

In this regard, John 20: 30–31 may be quoted:

> "Therefore Jesus did many other signs in the presence of his disciples, which are not written in this book; but these are written, that you may *believe* that Jesus is the Christ, the Son

[92] Pretorius, *The Gospels,* 176–253.

of God, and that *believing* you may have life in his name" (*emphasis added*).

No Translation is Perfect

Very few educated people of our time can read the Bible in its original languages – Hebrew, Aramaic, and Greek. The result is that they have to rely on translations. In English, there is a wide choice of translations.

However, no translation is ever perfect – especially if it is from a language that hasn't been used for many centuries. Modern Hebrew and modern Greek differ substantially from the ancient versions. Translators often struggle to find an equivalent for certain expressions in a modern language and it is not always easy to convey certain nuances in the original text. It is, therefore, perhaps a good idea if Bible students could consult more than one translation.

Another reason why translations are not always correct is the fact that there is uncertainty about the exact wording of the original documents. We only have copies of copies of copies of the originals. In the process of manual copying, many errors crept in. The discipline of textual criticism has been able to reconstruct most of the original text, but uncertainty about certain texts remain. In every edition of the Hebrew and Greek Scriptures, possible alternative wordings for certain texts are provided in the footnotes.

Finding the Core Message

That the Bible contains errors cannot be denied.

Descriptions of certain historical events differ from extra-biblical sources about those same events. Some contradictions occur where the same event is described in different biblical books. The books of Chronicles sometimes differ from the books of Samuel and Kings. There are differences between the four gospels about what

Jesus said and did. The descriptions of events in the life of the apostle Paul in Acts do not always agree with his own letters.

Another problem is that authors of documents in the New Testament often referred to events and ideas mentioned in the Old Testament, but got their facts wrong. Because of this, one must ask: which version is true or false? Two conflicting statements cannot both be true.

The geography of Palestine and the Mediterranean world as described in the gospels and Acts is not always accurate.

These differences and discrepancies are attributable to the fact that the biblical authors were fallible people with less reliable memories or who had to rely on the skewed memories of others.

It has also been pointed out that the biblical cosmology is outdated and cannot be accepted by informed people of our time.

Despite all this, Christians are convinced that they hear the voice of God in the Scriptures. They believe that the core message of the Bible is not affected by these problems. Despite these inaccuracies and mistakes, the Spirit of God is believed to have guided the authors to provide a faithful rendering of the core beliefs of their faith.[93]

Demythologization

The German theologian, Rudolf Bultmann (1884–1976), became famous for his program to "demythologize" the New Testament. By that, he proposed that Christians ought to reinterpret the mythological framework of the biblical authors and understand the message of the Bible in terms of our modern knowledge of the world and the existentialism of the philosopher Martin Heidegger.[94]

---

[93] König, *Groot Geloofswoordeboek,* 79–81.

[94] Perrin, "Bultmann, Rudolf (Karl)"; Van Aarde, "A Commemoration of the Legacy of Rudolf Bultmann".

This method of "demythologizing" the Bible is an integral part of biblical hermeneutics today. The ancient world view is reinterpreted or discarded, and the message of the Bible is presented in a manner consistent with contemporary scientific views.

The following question, though, must be asked: where does the demythologizing of the Bible end? How far must Christians of our time go to reinterpret and even remove the mythical aspects of the Bible? Do we restrict that merely to the biblical cosmology, as outlined above, or do we regard all references to God, Jesus as a divine figure, angels, Judgment Day, and the afterlife as myths that may be reinterpreted or even removed from the Christian faith?

And the most important questions in terms of the quest of this book, are as follows:

- Must Christians regard the references in the Bible to Satan, demons, and evil spirits as a part of an ancient mythology?
- How can Christians reconcile our present established scientific knowledge with a belief in a powerful devil who can destabilize God's creation and act as his adversary?

THE SCRIPTURES OF ISLAM

Muhammad

The founder of the religion of Islam, the prophet Muhammad (AD 570–632), left an indelible mark on the world's history because his followers, the Muslims, form the second largest religious group in the world, second only to Christianity.

He was a religious man who initially adhered to the traditional pagan religion of the Arabs. He often retreated to the desert to pray and meditate. When he was 40 he had his first vision of the Archangel Gabriel who appeared to him and commanded him to "recite". Muhammad was initially reluctant to recite anything, but then the first verses of the Qur'an started to flow from his lips.

A bewildered Muhammad told his wife about this incident and she called upon a cousin, a Christian, to guide her husband through this spiritual experience. He regarded this episode as his calling to become Gods messenger. For the next 23 years Muhammad received many more revelations and visions when the archangel appeared to him or when God spoke directly to him.

He recited these revelations to his family members and friends who learnt them by heart because none of them could read or write. These revelations were later written down and became the Qur'an. More and more people followed him and accepted him as a prophet.

Muhammad often had contact with Jews and Christians during his travels as a merchant, whom he described as the "People of the Book" (the Bible). There were Jewish and Christian communities in Arabia and Syria from whom Muhammad heard stories from the Bible, which convinced him that there is only one God, called Allah in Arabian.

Some researchers assert that Muhammad's visions and revelations were the result of temporal lobe epilepsy. Whether this was indeed the case cannot be determined with any degree of certainty today. However, he does seem to have displayed the typical symptoms of the so-called Geschwind Syndrome, a variety of a temporal lobe epilepsy, including hyper-religiosity, hallucinations or visions while having a fit, a quick temper, an active sex life (he was married to several women), and verbosity.[95]

---

[95] Aziz, "Did Prophet Muhammad (PBUH) have epilepsy?"; Freemon, "A Differential Diagnosis of the Inspirational Spells of Muhammad"; Veronelli *et al.*, "Geschwind Syndrome".

The Apostle Paul also seemed to have suffered from this condition.[96]

The Qur'an

The revelations of Muhammad were collected after his death into a single book, called the Qur'an. It is the holy book of Islam and it is regarded as the Word of God, dictated by the archangel Gabriel or God himself to Muhammad and, therefore, perfect and without any flaw or mistake.

The Qur'an only got its final form several decades after the death of Muhammad. There were several versions, which were suppressed in favor of the final one we have today. It is much shorter than the New Testament and contains 114 chapters or surahs of unequal length. They are arranged haphazardly with no rational order or sequence.[97]

It is only possible to understand the Qur'an adequately with a knowledge of the Bible since this sacred text repeatedly mentions characters and episodes from the Bible. One encounters, for instance, people such as Adam, Abraham, Jacob, Moses, Aaron, David, Solomon, Mary, Jesus – but also Satan.

Muhammad certainly did not always understand the stories from the Bible told to him correctly and he made mistakes in this regard. For instance, he mistook Jesus' mother Mary for Miriam, the sister of Aaron and Moses, although they lived centuries apart (Surah 3: 35–36; 19: 28).

Satan is mentioned 88 times in the Qur'an, while evil spirits – called "jinn" – are encountered 48 times.

Since the surahs are arranged haphazardly, no clear or syste-

---

[96] Pretorius, *Jesus of Nazareth,* 132–37.

[97] Rodwell and Jones. *The Koran;* Schimmel. "Islam".

matic presentation of Satan is to be found in the Qur'an. For that reason, the most important verses dealing with this figure will be presented and discussed systematically in a later chapter.

Chapter 6
SATAN IN THE HEBREW SCRIPTURES

This chapter deals with the way in which Satan or the devil, as well as demons or evil spirits, are introduced in the Old Testament and other Jewish literature before the time of the New Testament.

Relevant passages from the Scriptures will be quoted and that will be followed by comments and explanations. These passages will be presented in the order in which they were written during the centuries.

THE FIGURE OF SATAN

The Temptation of Eve

Genesis 3: 1 -6

1.	Now the serpent was more subtle than any animal of the field which YHWH God had made. He said to the woman, "Yes, has God said, `You shall not eat of any tree of the garden?`"
2.	The woman said to the serpent, "Of the fruit of the trees of the garden we may eat,
3.	but of the fruit of the tree which is in the midst of the garden, God has said, `You shall not eat of it, neither shall you touch it, lest you die.`"
4.	The serpent said to the woman, "You won`t surely die,
5.	for God knows that in the day you eat it, your eyes will be opened, and you will be as God, knowing good and evil."

6.	When the woman saw that the tree was good for food, and that it was a delight to the eyes, and that the tree was to be desired to make one wise, she took of the fruit of it, and ate; and she gave some to her husband with her, and he ate.

Albrecht Dürer: Adam and Eve

The talking snake in the Garden of Eden is usually interpreted as an appearance of Satan who coaxed Eve to eat fruit from the forbidden tree. She then seduced Adam to do the same.

In Rev 12: 9 and 20: 2, Satan is called "the old serpent". When John the Baptist addressed some Pharisees and Sadducees, he called them "you offspring of vipers" (Matt 3: 7). With these words, he hinted that they were children of the devil.

Shawna Dolansky, however, argued: "Introduced as 'the most clever of all of the beasts of the field that YHWH God had made,' the serpent in the Garden of Eden is portrayed as just that: a serpent. Satan does not make an appearance in Genesis 2–3, for the simple reason that when the story was written, the concept of the devil had not yet been invented."[98]

It will be shown later in this chapter that the concept of Satan or the devil, as the adversary or opponent of God, only appeared in the Hebrew Scriptures during the time when Judea was a province of the Persian Empire – centuries after Genesis 3 was written.

---

[98] Dolansky, "How the Serpent Became Satan", 4.

The Fate of the King of Babylon

Isaiah 14: 10–15

10.	All they shall answer and tell you, Are you also become weak as we? are you become like us?
11.	Your pomp is brought down to Sheol, [and] the noise of your viols: the worm is spread under you, and worms cover you.
12.	How you are fallen from heaven, day-star, son of the morning! How you are cut down to the ground, who laid the nations low!
13.	You said in your heart, I will ascend into heaven, I will exalt my throne above the stars of God; and I will sit on the mountain of congregation, in the uttermost parts of the north;
14.	I will ascend above the heights of the clouds; I will make myself like the Most High.
15.	Yet you shall be brought down to Sheol, to the uttermost parts of the pit.

It is tempting to interpret this passage as a prophecy describing the fall of Satan and banishment from heaven. The person addressed in this prophecy is, after all, addressed as the "day-star, son of the morning" – which seems to point to Lucifer. That is how this passage was often interpreted.

The context makes it clear, though, that the king of Babylon was meant – and not the devil. He is accused of regarding himself as a deity and who wanted to occupy God's throne in heaven between the stars in the north. He would, however, die as any other human being, become a rotting and worm-infested corpse, and descend into Sheol.

This prophecy was spoken and written during the time of the kingdom of Judah, during 740–700 BC, long before the Babylonians ransacked Jerusalem and deported the Judean elite to Babylon during 586 BC.[99] At that time, Satan has not yet been invented or copied from the Persian mythology.

Satan is Allowed to Test Job

Job 1: 6 – 2: 7

1:6	Now it happened on the day when the sons of God came to present themselves before YHWH, that Satan also came among them.
1:7	YHWH said to Satan, "Where have you come from?" Then Satan answered YHWH, and said, "From going back and forth in the earth, and from walking up and down in it."
1:8	YHWH said to Satan, "Have you considered my servant, Job? For there is none like him in the earth, a blameless and an upright man, one who fears God, and turns away from evil."
1:9	Then Satan answered YHWH, and said, "Does fear God for nothing?
1:10	Haven`t you made a hedge around him, and around his house, and around all that he has, on every side? You have blessed the work of his hands, and his substance is increased in the land.
1:11	But put forth your hand now, and touch all that he has, and he will renounce you to your face."

[99] Boshoff, *Geskiedenis,* 133, 135.

1:12	YHWH said to Satan, "Behold, all that he has is in your power. Only on himself don`t put forth your hand." So Satan went forth from the presence of YHWH.
1:13	It fell on a day when his sons and his daughters were eating and drinking wine in their eldest brother`s house,
1:14	that there came a messenger to Job, and said, "The oxen were plowing, and the donkeys feeding beside them,
1:15	and the Sabeans attacked, and took them away. Yes, they have killed the servants with the edge of the sword, and I alone have escaped to tell you."
1:16	While he was still speaking, there also came another, and said, "The fire of God has fallen from the sky, and has burned up the sheep and the servants, and consumed them, and I alone have escaped to tell you."
1:17	While he was still speaking, there came also another, and said, "The Chaldeans made three bands, and swept down on the camels, and have taken them away, yes, and killed the servants with the edge of the sword; and I alone have escaped to tell you."
1:18	While he was still speaking, there came also another, and said, "Your sons and your daughters were eating and drinking wine in their eldest brother`s house,
1:19	and, behold, there came a great wind from the wilderness, and struck the four corners of the house, and it fell on the young men, and they are dead. I alone have escaped to tell you."
1:20	Then Job arose, and tore his robe, and shaved his head, and fell down on the ground, and worshipped.

1:21	He said, "Naked I came out of my mother`s womb, and naked shall I return there. YHWH gave, and YHWH has taken away. Blessed be the name of YHWH."
1:22	In all this, did not sin, nor charge God with wrongdoing.
2:1	Again it happened on the day when the sons of God came to present themselves before YHWH, that Satan came also among them to present himself before YHWH.
2:2	YHWH said to Satan, "Where have you come from?" Satan answered YHWH, and said, "From going back and forth in the earth, and from walking up and down in it."
2:3	YHWH said to Satan, "Have you considered my servant Job? For there is none like him in the earth, a blameless and an upright man, one who fears God, and turns away from evil. He still maintains his integrity, although you incited me against him, to ruin him without cause."
2:4	Satan answered YHWH, and said, "Skin for skin. Yes, all that a man has will he give for his life.
2:5	But put forth your hand now, and touch his bone and his flesh, and he will renounce you to your face."
2:6	YHWH said to Satan, "Behold, he is in your hand. Only spare his life."
2:7	So Satan went forth from the presence of YHWH, and struck with painful sores from the sole of his foot to his head.

Rylaarsdam *et al.* remarked: "The Book of Job is not only the finest expression of the Hebrew poetic genius; it must also be accorded a place among the greatest masterpieces of world literature."[100] It has

[100] Rylaarsdam, "Biblical Literature".

been alleged that this book shows some similarities with the ancient Greek tragedies by three great Greek dramatists – Aeschylus (525–456 BC), Sophocles (c. 496–406 BC), and Euripides (c. 480–406 BC).[101]

Just as a Greek tragedy, the book starts with a prologue in prose, followed by a long part in poetic language during which various characters – Job, his friends Eliphaz, Bildad, Zophar, and Elihu – argue with each other. The climax is reached when God answers Job and his friends. The book ends off with a short epilogue.

Albrecht Dürer: Job and Satan

It is no surprise that more than one film version of this drama has been produced, some of which are available on the internet.

The book was most probably written during the period when Judea was a province of the Persian Empire after the end of the Babylonian exile, during the period 539–333 BC. This late date may explain the possible influence of the Greek tragedies of those times. It was mostly a peaceful time and some Jews – like the fictitious character of Job – became quite wealthy.

This is the first occasion in the Old Testament where Satan is depicted as a person, even as an angel who appeared at God's celestial court as one of the "sons of God".[102]

---

[101] Rylaarsdam, "Biblical Literature"; Conversi, "Tragedy".

[102] Boshoff, *Geskiedenis,* 203–07.

The meaning of the Hebrew word שָׂטָן (*satan*) is "adversary (in general – personal or national) or a superhuman adversary, namely Satan (as a personal name)." The word "satan" occurred earlier in the Old Testament, but then it always simply meant an "adversary" in general terms (1 Sam 19: 4; 2 Sam 19: 23;1 Kgs 5: 18; 11: 14, 23, 25; Ps 109: 6). In Num 22 we read of an occasion where an angel was called a satan or an adversary:

> "Then YHWH opened the eyes of Balaam, and he saw the angel of YHWH standing in the way, with his sword drawn in his hand; and he bowed his head, and fell on his face. The angel of YHWH said to him, Why have you struck your donkey these three times? behold, I am come forth for an adversary [satan], because your way is perverse before me" (Num 22: 31–32).

In the story of Job, Satan was a member of God's court – not God's enemy or opponent as described in the New Testament. He fulfilled the function of a prosecutor, and he accused Job of being pious only because he was rich. God allowed Satan to strike Job with calamities and cataclysms and catastrophes, including a health issue. Satan was not allowed to do anything without God's permission.[103]

The anonymous author of Job could, of course, not have known what happened in heaven when God allowed Satan to test Job's piety by transforming him from a rich and happy man to a pauper with painful health problems. Similarly, the author could not have known what God told Job and his friends. It must be surmised that he simply utilized the ideas and views of his contemporaries regarding God and Satan to compose this dramatic tragedy.

Job correctly called out that his misfortunes were the work

[103] Boshoff, *Geskiedenis,* 203–207.

of YHWH and that he, therefore, had to accept his fate with patience (Job 1: 21 and 2: 10). That means that Satan was not regarded as an independent agent, but that his actions were, at the deepest level, also God's management of events. In the last few chapters (Job 38–41), God accepted responsibility for Job's misfortunes.

Satan, the Adversary of the High Priest

Zechariah 3: 1-2

1.	He showed me Joshua the high priest standing before the angel of YHWH, and Satan standing at his right hand to be his adversary.
2.	YHWH said to Satan, YHWH rebuke you, Satan; yes, YHWH that has chosen Jerusalem rebuke you: is not this a brand plucked out of the fire?

Satan makes a brief appearance in a vision of the prophet Zachariah, which was written during the Persian period of Israel's history. He is presented as the accuser, prosecutor, or adversary of Joshua, the high priest. Satan was, though, silenced by God. He was, therefore, totally under the control of God and could not act independently. He is also not presented as God's enemy.

Satan Coaxes David into a Census

I Chronicles 21: 1–2

1.	Satan stood up against Israel, and moved David to number Israel.
2.	David said to Joab and to the princes of the people, Go, number Israel from Beersheba even to Dan; and bring me word, that I may know the sum of them.

This is the only occasion in the Old Testament where Satan acted on his own, without God's permission, when he manipulated David to organize a census. This census was wrong since David wanted to use the results to boast about his glory as the king of Israel.

This passage must, though, be compared with 2 Sam 24: 1–2, which was the source for the passage in 1 Chronicles:

> "Again the anger of YHWH was kindled against Israel, and he moved David against them, saying, 'Go, number Israel and Judah. Go now back and forth through all the tribes of Israel, from Dan even to Beersheba, and number you the people, that I may know the sum of the people.'"

One must conclude that the author of Chronicles could and would not accept the idea that it was YHWH who enticed David to do something wrong, as stated in Samuel. He, therefore, exchanged the name of YHWH with that of Satan.

The books of Chronicles were written during the Hellenistic period of Israel's history, after Alexander the Great had absorbed Palestine, Egypt, and the Persian Empire into his Greek empire. At that time, Jewish thought was already deeply influenced by the Persian religion of Zoroastrianism. This religion knew of a spiritual figure called Ahriman, akin to an evil and independent devil.[104]

Ahriman was clearly the prototype for the later Jewish Satan. He was the source of all evil, darkness, suffering, disasters, and misfortune in the world. He did his work with the aid of a gang of evil spirits. Their fate was sealed, though, because the continuing struggle between good and evil was due to be won by the chief Persian deity, Ahura Mazda, the source of light and all that is good.[105]

---

[104] Boshoff, *Geskiedenis,* 38, 223–226; Duchesne-Guillemin, "Zoroastrianism"; Jacobs and Blau, "Satan".

[105] Enc.com. "Ahriman."

The idea that Satan was the seducer and instigator of all the sin, wrongdoing, and crime in the world does not agree with earlier parts of the Old Testament. The following passages declare that it was God who brought misfortune, sickness, poverty, and accidents, as well as good fortune, good health, wealth, and prosperity:

- "Then the Lord your God will make your punishment, and the punishment of your seed, a thing to be wondered at; great punishments and cruel diseases stretching on through long years" (Deut 28: 59).
- "Joshua said, 'Hereby you shall know that the living God is among you, and that he will without fail drive out from before you the Canaanite, and the Hittite, and the Hivite, and the Perizzite, and the Girgashite, and the Amorite, and the Jebusite'" (Josh 3: 10).
- "The Lord is the giver of death and life: sending men down to the underworld and lifting them up. The Lord gives wealth and takes a man's goods from him: crushing men down and again lifting them up" (1 Sam 2: 6–7).
- "Shall we receive good at the hand of God, and shall we not receive evil?" (Job 2: 10).
- "Doesn`t evil and good come out of the mouth of the Most High?" (Lam 3: 38).
- "I am the giver of light and the maker of the dark; causing blessing, and sending troubles; I am the Lord, who does all these things" (Isa 45: 7).
- "Shall evil befall a city, and the Lord has not done it?" (Amos 3: 6).

In other words: the oldest parts of the Old Testament, from which these texts were quoted, did not use the concept of a devil to explain bad things. God, as the creator of the world, was the originator of everything, including disasters, pain, and evil.

EVIL SPIRITS

One reads of evil spirits in the Hebrew Scriptures. They were regarded as agents of God who lured people into committing wrong and bad actions. The following passages must be quoted and explained:

An Evil Spirit between Abimelech and the Men of Shechem

Judges 9: 23–24

23.	God sent an evil spirit between Abimelech and the men of Shechem; and the men of Shechem dealt treacherously with Abimelech:
24.	that the violence done to the seventy sons of Jerubbaal might come, and that their blood might be laid on Abimelech their brother, who killed them, and on the men of Shechem, who strengthened his hands to kill his brothers.

The book of Judges was written during the Babylonian Exile of the Judean elite after the fall of Jerusalem in 586 BC.[106] This passage tells of an episode from some centuries previously, of which some records seemed to have been preserved.

The animosity between Abimelech and the men of Shechem was blamed on an evil spirit sent by God. It must be noted that this sordid and sleazy spirit was in God's service and he could not be blamed for being mischievous or malicious. He can only be called evil because the results of his actions were bad.

---

[106] Boshoff, *Geskiedenis,* 170.

Saul Plagued by an Evil Spirit

1 Sam 16: 14–23

14.	Now the Spirit of YHWH departed from Saul, and an evil spirit from YHWH troubled him.
15.	Saul`s servants said to him, "See now, an evil spirit from God troubles you.
16.	"Let our lord now command your servants who are before you, to seek out a man who is a skillful player on the harp: and it shall happen, when the evil spirit from God is on you, that he shall play with his hand, and you shall be well."
17.	Saul said to his servants, "Provide me now a man who can play well, and bring him to me."
18.	Then answered one of the young men, and said, "Behold, I have seen a son of Jesse the Bethlehemite, who is skillful in playing, and a mighty man of valor, and a man of war, and prudent in speech, and a comely person; and YHWH is with him."
19.	Therefore Saul sent messengers to Jesse, and said, "Send me David your son, who is with the sheep."
20.	Jesse took a donkey [laden] with bread, and a bottle of wine, and a kid, and sent them by David his son to Saul.
21.	David came to Saul, and stood before him: and he loved him greatly; and he became his armor bearer.
22.	Saul sent to Jesse, saying, "Please let David stand before me; for he has found favor in my sight."
23.	It happened, when the [evil] spirit from God was on Saul, that David took the harp, and played with his hand: so Saul

	was refreshed, and was well, and the evil spirit departed from him.

1 Sam 18: 10 –12

10.	It happened on the next day, that an evil spirit from God came mightily on Saul, and he prophesied in the midst of the house: and David played with his hand, as he did day by day. Saul had his spear in his hand;
11.	and Saul cast the spear; for he said, I will strike David even to the wall. David avoided out of his presence twice.
12.	Saul was afraid of David, because YHWH was with him, and was departed from Saul.

1 Sam 19: 9–10

9.	An evil spirit from YHWH was on Saul, as he sat in his house with his spear in his hand; and David was playing with his hand.
10.	Saul sought to strike David even to the wall with the spear; but he slipped away out of Saul`s presence, and he struck the spear into the wall: and David fled, and escaped that night.

1 Sam 19: 23-24

23.	And he went on from there to Naioth in Ramah: and the spirit of God came on him, and he went on, acting like a prophet, till he came to Naioth in Ramah.
24.	And he took off his clothing, acting like a prophet before Samuel, and falling down he was stretched out, without his

> clothing, all that day and all that night. This is the reason for the saying, Is even Saul among the prophets?

King Saul seemed to have suffered from a serious psychiatric disorder, such as a bout of severe depression with psychotic features or even paranoidal schizophrenia. David was called upon to provide some music therapy, which did seem to help. In a fit of anger and a paranoid hallucination, Saul tried to kill David with his spear.

The episode where Saul "prophesied" – perhaps babbling incoherently – and lay naked for all to see, is a sign of a serious mental problem.[107]

With the complete lack of knowledge of psychiatric and psychological problems at that time, Saul's bizarre behavior was blamed on an evil spirit sent by God. Since the concept of Satan or the devil with his demonic helpers had not yet entered the religious thoughts of Israel, no other cause or explanation for Saul's condition seemed possible.

That Saul had some or other mental disorder may also have contributed to his suicide at a later stage (1 Sam 31).

Ben Reichert – just as other fundamentalist Christians – had a problem with the idea that these bad spirits were sent by God and not by Satan. He tried to circumvent this dilemma by declaring: "The passage implies that God can *still* command the demons when he wants them to serve his purposes. (…) It appears that, as in Job, God permitted them to do this to Saul to fulfill his greater purpose in raising David as king"[108] (*emphasis added*).This implies that Reichert supposed that the evil spirits were, in reality, the helpers of Satan – which cannot be deduced from the text. There cannot be the slightest doubt that these spirits were God's servants and his alone.

---

[107] APA, *DSM-5*, 99–106; 160 – 168.
[108] Reichert, "Demonology".

A Spirit of Perverseness for Egypt

Isa 19: 11–14

11.	The chiefs of Zoan are completely foolish; the wisest guides of Pharaoh have become like beasts: how do you say to Pharaoh, I am the son of the wise, the offspring of early kings?
12.	Where, then, are your wise men? let them make clear to you, let them give you knowledge of the purpose of the Lord of armies for Egypt.
13.	The princes of Zoan are become fools, the princes of Memphis are deceived; they have caused Egypt to go astray, who are the corner-stone of her tribes.
14.	YHWH has mingled a spirit of perverseness in the midst of her; and they have caused Egypt to go astray in every work of it, as a drunken man staggers in his vomit

This passage is part of a prophecy directed against the foolish rulers of Egypt. Their failures were due to a "spirit of perverseness", sent by YHWH.

The expression used for this spirit is רוּחַ עִוְעִים (*ruach av-im*) – meaning a spirit of distortion, warping, or chaos.

A Lying Spirit Sent by God

1 Kgs 22:16–23

16.	The king said to him [Micaiah], "How many times shall I adjure you that you speak to me nothing but the truth in the name of YHWH?"

17.	He said, "I saw all Israel scattered on the mountains, as sheep that have no shepherd: and YHWH said, 'These have no master; let them return every man to his house in peace.'"
18.	The king of Israel said to Jehoshaphat, "Didn`t I tell you that he would not prophesy good concerning me, but evil?"
19.	[Micaiah] said, "Therefore hear you the word of YHWH: I saw YHWH sitting on his throne, and all the host of heaven standing by him on his right hand and on his left.
20.	"YHWH said, 'Who shall entice Ahab, that he may go up and fall at Ramoth-Gilead?' One said on this manner; and another said on that manner.
21.	"There came forth a spirit, and stood before YHWH, and said, 'I will entice him.'
22.	"YHWH said to him, 'How?' He said, 'I will go forth, and will be a lying spirit in the mouth of all his prophets.' He said, 'You shall entice him, and shall prevail also: go forth, and do so.'
23.	"Now therefore, behold, YHWH has put a lying spirit in the mouth of all these your prophets; and YHWH has spoken evil concerning you."

Micaiah, the prophet, told the kings of Israel and Judah about a strange vision he had had. He saw God on his throne in heaven with a host of spirits or angels on both sides of Him. They functioned as his courtiers and councilors and He asked their advice on how to destroy King Ahab of Israel. One of these spirits proposed that he would act as an evil or lying spirit by persuading the Israelite prophets to give false prophecies, which would give Ahab false confidence in war, with a disastrous outcome.

God approved of the plan and gave the spirit the order to carry on. This passage makes it clear that evil spirits were seen as God's advisors and helpers and they took orders from Him – and certainly not from Satan.

The Leviathan

The Leviathan (Hebrew: לִוְיָתָן – *livyathan*) is a sea monster that is mentioned six times in the Old Testament, namely in Job 3: 8, Job 40: 25, 41: 26, Ps 74: 14, Ps 104: 26 and twice in Isa 27:1.

This monster is identified in Rev 13: 1 as the Antichrist, the chief lieutenant of the dragon, Satan. There were those who thought that the Leviathan of the Old Testament must be another name for Satan himself, but that cannot be justified from the six places where this monster is mentioned. He is specifically described as a sea monster that will be slain by God at the end of time (Isa 27: 1).

This sea monster must be regarded as a personification of all chaotic forces[109] – not as Satan.

THE BOOK OF ENOCH

Date and Authorship

The idea that Satan was an angel who rebelled against God and was driven from heaven, together with his followers and co-conspirators, does not occur in the Old Testament, as has been shown earlier in this chapter.[110] This view was found for the first time in the extrabiblical book of Enoch.

This book purportedly contains the description of the visions and revelations received by the ancient patriarch Enoch, According

---

[109] Van der Toorn et al., *Dictionary of Deities and Demons in the Bible*, 512–14.

[110] Denova, "The Origin of Satan".

to Gottheil and Littmann, this book was written to preserve legends and "Jewish folk-lore in the last pre-Christian centuries" about the patriarch Enoch, as well as ideas about the flood in Noah's time, angels, heaven, the netherworld, and hell.[111]

This book was regarded by some early Christians to be part of Scripture. The biblical letter of Jude states the following:

> "To these also Enoch, the seventh from Adam, prophesied, saying, 'Behold, the Lord came with ten thousands of his holy ones, to execute judgment on all, and to convict all the ungodly of all their works of ungodliness which they have done in'" (Jud 1: 14–15).

This is a quotation from Enoch 1: 9. Jude clearly thought that the book was written by the very ancient Enoch himself – and not by anonymous authors many centuries later.

John of Patmos, the author of Revelation, quoted repeatedly or referred to visions found in Enoch, without naming his source.[112]

No other documents in the New Testament seem to have quoted from Enoch directly, although more than one document made use of ideas found in Enoch. Around AD 300 the church fathers openly and finally rejected Enoch as part of Scripture.[113]

The only groups at present that regard Enoch as holy Scripture are Ethiopian sects. The only surviving complete text is in Ethiopic, which was translated from Greek, which was, in turn, translated from the original Aramaic.[114] Our knowledge about Enoch, therefore, depends upon a translation of a translation of a translation. This process of repeated translations could have caused

---

[111] Gottheil and Littmann, "Enoch".

[112] Scholtz, *Revelation,* 27, 33, 47, 64, 67, 190, 281, 295.

[113] Gottheil and Littmann, "Enoch".

[114] Enc Brit, "Enoch".

the English translations to be less than accurate or uncertain in certain spots.

This Ethiopic text was translated into English by George Schodde and Robert Charles respectively. The translation by Charles will be used in this chapter and the explanatory notes of Schodde will be consulted.

Some Aramaic fragments of Enoch were found in the caves at Qumran containing the Dead Sea Scrolls.[115] The former chief editor of the Dead Sea Scrolls editorial team, John Strugnell, has reportedly saw a complete Aramaic manuscript of Enoch, which was in the possession of a collector of antiquities, but who was unwilling to part with it or have it published.[116]

We read the following about the patriarch Enoch in Genesis:

> "Enoch lived sixty-five years, and became the father of Methuselah. Enoch walked with God after he became the father of Methuselah three hundred years, and became the father of sons and daughters. all the days of Enoch were three hundred sixty-five years. Enoch walked with God, and he was not, for God took him" (Gen 5: 21–22).

Since Enoch was such a pious man who walked with God, the anonymous author(s) of the book of Enoch argued that he must have been walking in heaven with God and the angels. This book is a description of these purported visions and experiences of Enoch, told in the first-person singular at times, but also written about Enoch in the third person singular.

The book consists of five distinct parts:

---

[115] Rylaarsdam, "Biblical Literature"; Wikipedia, "List of the Dead Sea Scrolls".

[116] Shanks, "An Interview with John Strugnell".

- The Book of the Watchers (ch 1–36);
- The Book of Parables (ch 37–71);
- The Book of the Heavenly Luminaries (ch 72–82);
- Two visions of Enoch regarding the Flood and the history of the world (ch 83–90); and
- A speech by Enoch (ch 91–107).[117]

The Book of the Watchers, which deals with the fallen angels, can be dated to between 250 and 200 BC, during the Hellenistic period in Israel's history, after various Persian influences from earlier centuries had been absorbed.[118]

The Book of the Watchers grapples with the question: where do evil, sin, iniquity, arrogance, pride, and violence come from? To answer this question, the author took as his starting point an enigmatic passage in Genesis 6:

> "It happened, when men began to multiply on the surface of the ground, and daughters were born to them, that God`s sons saw that men`s daughters were beautiful, and they took for themselves wives of all that they chose. YHWH said, 'My spirit will not strive with man forever, because he also is flesh; yet will his days be one hundred twenty years.' The Nephilim were in the earth in those days, and also after that, when God`s sons came to men`s daughters. They bore children to them: the same were the mighty men who were of old, men of renown" (Gen 6: 1–4).

The Hebrew word for *the Nephilim* (הַנְּפִילִים) is usually translated as "the giants".

---

[117] Rylaarsdam, "Biblical Literature".
[118] Denova, "The Origin of Satan".

It is theorized that Enoch had its origin amongst the sect of the Essenes of Qumran or its predecessors. After all, the only extant scraps of the original Aramaic text were found among the Dead Sea Scrolls, the hidden and forgotten library of the Essenes. The stance of Enoch regarding celibacy, the coming Messiah, and the fate of the soul after death seems to correspond with the known convictions of the Essenes.[119]

Another connection between the Essenes – or as they were later known, the Ebionites – and the Book of Enoch, is the fact that only two documents in the New Testament associated with this sect, quoted from it as if it were Scripture, namely the Epistle of Jude[120] and Revelation.[121] On occasion, other documents in the New Testament made indirectly use of ideas found in Enoch, without quoting directly from it.

The second part of Enoch, the Book of Parables, contains the name "Satan" or "satans" on four occasions. Ben-Daniel reported regarding the date of origin of this document that "at the Enoch Seminar held at Camaldoli, Italy, in 2005, a consensus crystallized among the majority of scholars, for a date towards the end of the reign of King Herod the Great, which is to say around the end of the first century BCE. A minority argue for a later date, in the second half of the first century CE."[122]

The Essenes of Qumran seem to have been unfamiliar with this part of Enoch because no fragments of this document were found among the Dead Sea Scrolls.[123]

---

[119] Rylaarsdam, "Biblical Literature".

[120] Pretorius, *Jesus of Nazareth,* 103–115.

[121] Scholtz, *Revelation*, 16.

[122] Ben-Daniel, "Enoch", 10.

[123] [123] Ben-Daniel, "Enoch", 1.

If this document does, indeed, date from the last part of the first century BC, then it is at most a few decades older than the first documents in the New Testament, written during the forties or fifties AD.[124] It will be shown in due course how these references to Satan may have influenced the authors of the New Testament books.

The following passages from Enoch must be analyzed:

The Seven Archangels

Enoch 20: 1–8

> And these are the names of the holy angels who watch. Uriel, one of the holy angels, who is over the world and over Tartarus. Raphael, one of the holy angels, who is over the spirits of men. Raguel, one of the holy angels who takes vengeance on the world of the luminaries. Michael, one of the holy angels, to wit, he that is set over the best part of mankind and over chaos. Saraqael, one of the holy angels, who is set over the spirits, who sin in the spirit. Gabriel, one of the holy angels, who is over Paradise and the serpents and the Cherubim. Remiel, one of the holy angels, whom God set over those who rise.

The author(s) of Enoch was/were rather obsessed with angels. Although they mentioned the names of the seven archangels only in chapter 20 of this book, it may be important to mention them right here.

The archangels Michael and Gabriel both appear in the New Testament. Their names were probably taken from the Book of Enoch – unless their names were part of popular folklore.

It has already been shown that the Hebrew Scriptures equated the angels with the stars and the celestial constellations. The

[124] Pretorius, *The Gospels,* 89.

seven archangels may perhaps be connected to the seven planets known in Antiquity.

Introduction to Enoch

Enoch 1: 1—9

The words of the blessing of Enoch, wherewith he blessed the elect and righteous, who will be living in the day of tribulation, when all the wicked and godless are to be removed. And he took up his parable and said – Enoch a righteous man, whose eyes were opened by God, saw the vision of the Holy One in the heavens, which the angels showed me, and from them I heard everything, and from them I understood as I saw, but not for this generation, but for a remote one which is for to come. Concerning the elect I said, and took up my parable concerning them: The Holy Great One will come forth from His dwelling, and the eternal God will tread upon the earth, (even) on Mount Sinai, [And appear from His camp] And appear in the strength of His might from the heaven of heavens. And all shall be smitten with fear and the Watchers shall quake, and great fear and trembling shall seize them unto the ends of the earth. And the high mountains shall be shaken, and the high hills shall be made low, and shall melt like wax before the flame. And the earth shall be wholly rent in sunder, And all that is upon the earth shall perish, and there shall be a judgement upon all (men). But with the righteous He will make peace. And will protect the elect, And mercy shall be upon them. And they shall all belong to God, and they shall be prospered, and they shall all be blessed. And He will help them all, and light shall appear unto them, and He will make peace with them'. And behold! He cometh with ten thousands of His holy ones to execute judgement upon all, and to destroy all the ungodly: And to convict all flesh of all the works of their ungodliness which they have ungodly committed, and of all the hard things which ungodly sinners have spoken against Him.

This first chapter is the introduction to the rest of the Book of the Watchers and it explains why the patriarch Enoch purportedly had his visions and heavenly experiences. This introduction contains a warning about the coming judgment of God to eradicate the ungodly Watchers. These watchers (Aramaic: עִירִין, *iyrin*) were the angels dispatched to watch over the humans on earth. Because they became ungodly, God planned to punish them by ravaging the earth. It will later transpire that this would happen during the flood in Noah's time.

The "elect" who would be saved, were the upright and God-fearing people – probably the predecessors of the Essenes.

A few key passages from the Book of the Watchers will be quoted to describe how it came about that certain angels were banished from heaven.

The Angels who Took Human Women

Enoch 5: 1–9

And it came to pass when the children of men had multiplied that in those days were born unto them beautiful and comely daughters. And the angels, the children of the heaven, saw and lusted after them, and said to one another: 'Come, let us choose us wives from among the children of men and beget us children.' And Semjaza, who was their leader, said unto them: 'I fear ye will not indeed agree to do this deed, and I alone shall have to pay the penalty of a great sin.' And they all answered him and said: 'Let us all swear an oath, and all bind ourselves by mutual imprecations not to abandon this plan but to do this thing.' Then sware they all together and bound themselves by mutual imprecations upon it. And they were in all two hundred; who descended in the days of Jared on the summit of Mount Hermon, and they called it Mount Hermon, because they had sworn and bound themselves by mutual imprecations upon it. And these are the names of their leaders: Samlazaz, their leader, Araklba, Rameel, Kokablel, Tamlel, Ramlel, Danel, Ezeqeel, Baraqijal, Asael, Armaros, Batarel, Ananel, Zaqiel, Samsapeel, Satarel, Turel, Jomjael, Sariel. These are their chiefs of tens.

Enoch 7:1–5

And all the others together with them took unto themselves wives, and each chose for himself one, and they began to go in unto them and to defile themselves with them, and they taught them charms and enchantments, and the cutting of roots, andmade them acquainted with plants. And they became pregnant, and they bare great giants, whose height was three thousand ells: Who consumed all the acquisitions of men. And when men could no longer sustain them, …

Some of the angels or watchers saw the beautiful daughters of men on earth and lusted after them. They formed a secret clique to which they were bound by an oath. This was the start of the rebellion against God because these angels preferred to live on earth and leave heaven. These sex-obsessed angels mated with mortal females and their offspring were giants. These giants demanded so much food that humans could not keep up to feed them and they suffered famine themselves.

These passages were obviously inspired by Gen 6: 1–4.

The group of watchers had twenty leaders and each one of them was over ten members. That means that 200 angels took part in this thrust and incursion to earth. Samlaza was the top leader.

Men were Taught Secret Knowledge

Enoch 8:1–4:

> And Azâzêl taught men to make swords, and knives, and shields, and breastplates, and made known to them the metals of the earth and the art of working them, and bracelets, and ornaments, and the use of antimony, and the beautifying of the eyelids, and all kinds of costly stones, and all colouring tinctures. And there arose much godlessness, and they committed fornication, and they were led astray, and became corrupt in all their ways. Semjâzâ taught enchantments, and root-cuttings, Armârôs the resolving of enchantments, Barâqijâl, taught astrology, Kôkabêl the constellations, Ezêqêêl the knowledge of the clouds, Araqiêl the signs of the earth, Shamsiêl the signs of the sun, and Sariêl the course of the moon. …

Enoch 9:6–9:

> Thou seest what Azâzêl hath done, who hath taught all unrighteousness on earth and revealed the eternal secrets which were preserved in heaven, which men were striving to learn: And Semjâzâ, to whom Thou hast given authority to bear rule over his associates. And they have gone to the daughters of men upon the earth, and have slept with the women, and have defiled themselves, and revealed to them all kinds of sins. …

Azazel, one of the chief watchers, taught men secret knowledge: how to produce instruments of war, cosmetics to make women more sexually attractive and to be able to seduce men more easily, and knowledge about sorcery and astrology. This all resulted in hatred, fighting, and fornication on earth.

Noah Warned of the Flood

Enoch 10: 1–4

> Then said the Most High, the Holy and Great One spake, and sent Uriel to the son of Lamech, 2 and said to him: 'Go to Noah and tell him in my name "Hide thyself!" and reveal to him the end that is approaching: that the whole earth will be destroyed, and a deluge is about to come upon the whole earth, and will destroy all that is on it. And now instruct him that he may escape and his seed may be preserved for all the generations of the world.'

God decided to cleanse the world of all the sinners and the gross and gluttonous giants. The only way to do that was to drown the lot of them in a great flood. However, Noah and his family had to be spared and he was to be warned to be ready when the deluge came.

Gabriel Complains to God

Enoch 10: 9

> And to Gabriel said the Lord: 'Proceed against the bastards and the reprobates, and against the children of fornication: and destroy the children of fornication and the children of the Watchers from amongst men: and cause them to go forth: send them one against the other that they may destroy each other in battle: for length of days shall they not have.

Gabriel, whose job was to watch over "Paradise and the serpents and the Cherubim", complained to God about the deterioration of mankind due to the secret knowledge they had obtained, their violence, their immoral lifestyles, and the destruction brought about by the giants.

The Evil Angels to be Arrested and Condemned

Enoch 10: 11

> And the Lord said unto Michael: 'Go, bind Semjâzâ and his associates who have united themselves with women so as to have defiled themselves with them in all their uncleanness.

After Gabriel's complaint, Michael was ordered to arrest Semjaza, the chief watcher of the group of 200 fallen angels. Together with his followers, Michael had the task "set over the best part of mankind and over chaos" – including the chaos created on earth by the watchers and their gigantic children.

Enoch 10: 12–15

> And, when their sons have slain one another, and they have seen the destruction of their beloved ones, bind them fast for seventy generations in the valleys of the earth, till the day of their judgement and of their consummation, till the judgement that is for ever and ever is consummated. In those days they shall be led off to the abyss of fire: and to the torment and the prison in which they shall be confined for ever. And whosoever shall be condemned and destroyed will from thenceforth be bound together with them to the end of all generations. …

Mankind was to be given the opportunity of destroying themselves by killing each other after having been given secret knowledge by Azazel. God ordered Michael to cast the rebellious angels and watchers into the abyss, the space beneath the earth. They were to be held there till Judgment Day.

Enoch 15: 2–4

> And go, say to the watchers of heaven, who have sent thee to intercede for them: "You should intercede for men, and not men for you: Wherefore have ye left the high, holy, and eternal heaven, and

> lain with women, and defiled yourselves with the daughters of men and taken to yourselves wives, and done like the children of earth, and begotten giants as your sons. And though ye were holy, spiritual, living the eternal life, you have defiled yourselves with the blood of women, and have begotten children with the blood of flesh, and, as the children of men, have lusted after flesh and blood as those also do who die and perish.

Michael was ordered by God to explain to the evil watchers that their lust for human women, their immorality, and the violence of their giant offspring led to their downfall and the judgment from God.

Enoch 16: 3

> "You have been in heaven, but all the mysteries had not yet been revealed to you, and you knew worthless ones, and these in the hardness of your hearts you have made known to the women, and through these mysteries women and men work much evil on earth."

The evil fallen angels had to be reminded that they, who previously lived in heaven and were driven out, had taught the human women some less important knowledge. The real knowledge about God and his plans for the world has not been disclosed to them.

Enoch 19: 1

> And Uriel said to me: 'Here shall stand the angels who have connected themselves with women, and their spirits, assuming many different forms, are defiling mankind, and shall lead them astray into sacrificing to demons as gods, here shall they stand, till the day of the great judgement in which they shall be judged till they are made an end of.

Uriel was the archangel who guided Enoch through his heavenly wanderings and visions. He explained that the fallen angels led mankind astray to worship demons and false gods. They would eventually have to face Judgment Day to receive their final punishment.

Gustave Doré: The Fallen Angel (engraving — 1866)

The Prison of the Fallen Angels

Enoch 21: 1–10

And I proceeded to where things were chaotic. And I saw there something horrible: I saw neither a heaven above nor a firmly founded earth, but a place chaotic and horrible. And there I saw seven stars of the heaven bound together in it, like great mountains and burning with fire. (…) And from thence I went to another place, which was still more horrible than the former, and I saw a horrible thing: a great fire there which burnt and blazed, and the place was cleft as far as the abyss, being full of great descending columns of fire: neither its extent or magnitude could I see, nor could I conjecture. Then I said: 'How fearful is the place and how terrible to look upon!' Then Uriel answered me, one of the holy angels who was with me, and said unto me: 'Enoch, why hast thou such fear and affright?' And I answered: 'Because of this fearful place, and because of the spectacle of the pain.' And he told me: 'This place is the prison of the angels, and here they will be imprisoned for ever.'

Uriel gave Enoch a vision of the abyss where the wicked angels were to be locked up until Judgment Day. He also saw the fires of hell where the evil angels would be tortured into eternity.

The rest of the Book of the Watchers is devoted to descriptions of Judgment Day and heaven where the souls of the blessed would rest in a beautiful garden.

Satans Forbidden in Heaven

Enoch 40: 1–2; 7–8

1. And after that I saw thousands of thousands and ten thousand times ten thousand, I saw a multitude
2. beyond number and reckoning, who stood before the Lord of Spirits. And on the four sides of the Lord of Spirits I saw four presences…
7. And I heard the fourth voice fending off the Satans and forbidding them to come before the Lord
8. of Spirits to accuse them who dwell on the earth..

This passage is part of the second section of Enoch, the Book of Parables. Enoch saw a vision of the host of angels, as well as four archangels. One of them told him that he would not allow the satans, the fallen angels who were evicted from heaven, to act as accusers of the people on earth.

These satans differed from the Satan encountered in the book of Job who was part of God's heavenly court and was allowed to accuse Job of false piety.

Enoch 55: 3–6

For I saw all the angels of punishment abiding (there) and preparing all the instruments of Satan.
And I asked the angel of peace who went with me: 'For whom are they preparing these Instruments?'
And he said unto me: ' They prepare these for the kings and the mighty of this earth, that they may thereby be destroyed.
And after this the Righteous and Elect One shall cause the house of his congregation to appear: henceforth they shall be no more hindered in the name of the Lord of Spirits.

Satan appears in this passage as a person who had to help prepare instruments of torture for the punishment of ungodly kings and mighty people in the afterlife. It seems strange that Satan's instruments were to be used to punish the ungodly and this idea may be the result of a faulty translation process. It is more probable that these torture instruments were also meant to punish Satan.

Enoch Warned of the Coming Flod

Enoch 54: 1–10

And I looked and turned to another part of the earth, and saw there a deep valley with burning fire. And they brought the kings and the mighty, and began to cast them into this deep valley.

> And there mine eyes saw how they made these their instruments, iron chains of immeasurable weight.
> And I asked the angel of peace who went with me, saying: "For whom are these chains being prepared ?"
> And he said unto me: "These are being prepared for the hosts of Azazel, so that they may take them and cast them into the abyss of complete condemnation, and they shall cover their jaws with rough stones as the Lord of Spirits commanded.
> And Michael, and Gabriel, and Raphael, and Phanuel shall take hold of them on that great day, and cast them on that day into the burning furnace, that the Lord of Spirits may take vengeance on them for their unrighteousness in becoming subject to Satan and leading astray those who dwell on the earth.'
> And in those days shall punishment come from the Lord of Spirits, and he will open all the chambers of waters which are above the heavens, and of the fountains which are beneath the earth.
> And all the waters shall be joined with the waters: that which is above the heavens is the masculine, and the water which is beneath the earth is the feminine. And they shall destroy all who dwell on the earth and those who dwell under the ends of the heaven. And when they have recognized their unrighteousness which they have wrought on the earth, then by these shall they perish.

Four archangels told Enoch that Azazel or Satan would be condemned to an everlasting fire. The people on earth who were seduced by Satan would be eradicated from the earth by a ferrocious flood in which all the waters in the heavens and under the earth would wash them away.

People who Produce Idols of Metal

Enoch 65: 6-9

> And a command has gone forth from the presence of the Lord concerning those who dwell on the earth that their ruin is accomplished because they have learnt all the secrets of the angels, and all the violence of the satans, and all their powers – the most secret ones – and all the power of those who practice sorcery, and the power of witchcraft, and the power of those who make molten images for the whole earth: And how silver is produced from the dust of the earth, and how soft metal originates in the earth. For lead and tin are not produced from the earth like the first: it is a fountainthat produces them, and an angel stands therein, and that angel is pre-eminent.

God wanted to get rid of the human race after the fallen angels, here called the violent satans, taught men the secret knowledge of sorcery and metallurgy. Their skills in working metals, such as silver, lead, and tin, enabled them to produce idols.

Summary

The Book of the Watchers is an effort to provide some background and make sense of the description of mankind's early history in Genesis – the sons of God or angels who took human wives and beget giants, as well as the flood in the time of Noah. The pious man, Enoch, who walked with God, was used as the vehicle to give the explanations.

An answer was given to the question as to why there is so much sin, immorality, violence, and godlessness on earth. A concept was borrowed from the Persian religion, namely an evil spirit and adversary of the chief god, Ahuramazda. It was unthinkable for the author of the book of Enoch to blame God for all the calamities, disasters, and iniquities on earth and a gang of fallen and malevolent angels were blamed for all that – exonerating the good God in the process.

There can be no doubt that the concept of a devil, as found in the New Testament, was influenced by the book of Enoch. The name Satan does not occur in the Book of the Watchers and the leader of the evil angels had the name of Semjâzâ. As leader of the evil angels he is the prototype of the devil, Satan.

In the Book of Parables, the fallen angel Azazel was identified as Satan.

THE BOOK OF JUBILEES

Date and Authorship

The Book of Jubilees is another extra-biblical book, probably dating from the second or first century BC. It is impossible to determine who wrote it.[125]

The only extant complete manuscripts are in Ethiopic and an English translation has been made from those by R.H. Charles in 1895. It seems that the Ethiopic version is a translation from Greek. Some fragments of this book in the original Hebrew were found among the Dead Sea Scrolls.[126] Other documents of this Essene library contain various quotations from the Book of Jubilees, which indicates that this Jewish sect regarded the Book of Jubilees as authoritative.[127]

There is no indication that early Christians regarded it as part of Scripture and no known quotations from it are contained in the New Testament, although some of its ideas resonated in the New

---

[125] Boshoff, *Geskiedenis,* 253; Rylaarsdam, "Biblical Literature."

[126] Wikipedia, "List of the Dead Sea Scrolls".

[127] Enc Brit, "Jubilees, Book of"; Rylaarsdam, "Biblical Literature".

Testament. It is regarded as Scripture only in Ethiopia.[128]

This book contains a summary and commentary on parts of Genesis and Exodus. There is a great interest in angels and demons.[129] Toy and Kohler observed that the author of this book "transfers to Satan and his hosts those acts of God which seem unworthy of Him – such as the tempting of Abraham, the attempt on Moses' life, the hardening of the heart of Pharaoh, and the slaying of the first-born."[130] This tendency to blame Satan for all evil, bad, wrong things to exonerate God often occurs in the New Testament.

Some Angels Take Human Women

Jubilees 5: 1–7

1. And it came to pass when the children of men began to multiply on the face of the earth and daughters were born unto them, that the angels of God saw them on a certain year of this jubilee, that they were beautiful to look upon; and they took themselves wives of all whom they chose, and they bare unto them sons and they were giants.
2. And lawlessness increased on the earth and all flesh corrupted its way, alike men and cattle and beasts and birds and everything that walks on the earth -all of them corrupted their ways and their orders, and they began to devour each other, and lawlessness increased on the earth and every imagination of the thoughts of all men (was) thus evil continually.

[128] Boshoff, *Geskiedenis,* 253; Toy and Kohler, "The Book of Jubilees".

[129] Toy and Kohler, "The Book of Jubilees."

[130] Toy and Kohler, "The Book of Jubilees."

3. And God looked upon the earth, and behold it was corrupt, and all flesh had corrupted its orders, and all that were upon the earth had wrought all manner of evil before His eyes.
4. And He said that He would destroy man and all flesh upon the face of the earth which He had created.
5. But Noah found grace before the eyes of the Lord.
6. And against the angels whom He had sent upon the earth, He was exceedingly wroth, and He gave commandment to root them out of all their dominion, and He bade us to bind them
7. in the depths of the earth, and behold they are bound in the midst of them, and are (kept) separate.
8. And against their sons went forth a command from before His face that they should be smitten with the sword, and be removed from under heaven.

This passage from Jubilees 5 tells how certain angels lusted after human women, who bore them giants as offspring.

These giants were violent and cruel and God decided to destroy them. According to the following verses (not quoted) they fought each other and all of them were wiped out. The evil angels, their fathers, were rounded up and locked up in an abyss to await Judgement Day.

God also sent a deluge upon earth to drown all the evil humans, but decided to spare Noah and his family.

This tale is essentially the same as that told in Enoch and one may speculate that they had a common source, which was part of the Jewish legends and mythology of those times.

Evil Spirits of the Dead Giants

Jubilees 10: 1–14

1. And in the third week of this jubilee the unclean demons began to lead astray the children of the sons of Noah, and to make to err and destroy them.
2. And the sons of Noah came to Noah their father, and they told him concerning the demons which were leading astray and blinding and slaying his sons' sons.
3. And he prayed before the Lord his God, and said: 'God of the spirits of all flesh, who hast shown mercy unto me. And hast saved me and my sons from the waters of the flood, And hast not caused me to perish as Thou didst the sons of perdition; For Thy grace has been great towards me, and great has been Thy mercy to my soul; let Thy grace be lift up upon my sons, and let not wicked spirits rule over them Lest they should destroy them from the earth.
4. But do Thou bless me and my sons, that we may increase and Multiply and replenish the earth.
5. And Thou knowest how Thy Watchers, the fathers of these spirits, acted in my day: and as for these spirits which are living, imprison them and hold them fast in the place of condemnation, and let them not bring destruction on the sons of thy servant, my God; for these are malignant, and created in order to destroy. And let them not rule over the spirits of the living; for Thou alone canst exercise dominion over them. And let them not have power over the sons of the righteous from henceforth and for evermore.'
6. And the Lord our God bade us [the archangels] to bind all.
7. And the chief of the spirits, Mastêmâ, came and said: 'Lord, Creator, let some of them remain before me, and let them harken to my voice, and do all that I shall say unto them; for if some of them are not left to me, I shall not be able to execute the power of my will on the sons of men; for these

are for corruption and leading astray before my judgment, for great is the wickedness of the sons of men.'

8. And He said: Let the tenth part of them remain before him, and let nine parts descend into the place of condemnation.' And one of us [the archangels] He commanded that we should teach Noah all their medicines; for He knew that they would not walk in uprightness, nor strive in righteousness.

9. And we did according to all His words: all the malignant evil ones we bound in the place of condemnation and a tenth part of them we left that they might be subject before Satan on the earth.

10. And we explained to Noah all the medicines of their diseases, together with their seductions, how he might heal them with herbs of the earth.

11. And Noah wrote down all things in a book as we instructed him concerning every kind of medicine. Thus the evil spirits were precluded from (hurting) the sons of Noah.

12. And he gave all that he had written to Shem, his eldest son; for he loved him exceedingly above all his sons.

The reader is told that the unclean demons or wicked spirits of the deceased giant sons of the watchers or fallen angels, led the sons of Noah astray.

Noah prayed to God to punish these sordid spirits. The leader of these spirits, Mastema or Satan, begged God not to imprison all the evil spirits, but to allow him to keep one tenth of them. These spirits were needed to keep wicked men in check and cause them to become sick. The archangels were sent to teach Noah and his sons the use of medicines to heal the sick and to resist these evil spirits.

According to the book of Jubilees, the evil spirits were the spirits of the dead giants or Nephilim of Gen 6: 1–4. They brought diseases upon humankind and their leader was Mastema. His other name of Satan seems to have functioned as a title.

FINAL RUNDOWN

This chapter has shown that the books of the Old Testament did not know the devil. The figure of Satan is mentioned a few times, but he was not the enemy of God. He was merely the accuser of Job and the accuser of the high priest. In the late books of Chronicles, Satan influenced King David to organize a census so that he could boast about his own greatness.

Evil spirits are encountered more than once. They were, without exception, God's servants and they did not operate independently or under the authority or leadership of the devil.

The concept of evil spirits or demons, the spirits of dead giants, only appear in the Book of Jubilees. Enoch explained how these giants were born; they were the offspring of the 200 rebellious angels who were kicked out of heaven.

Gustave Dore: Satan at the Gates of Hell

Satan also appeared under more than one name. He was caught by Michael, thrown into the abyss, where he must stay until Judgment Day.

Enoch and the Book of Jubilees are not part of Scripture, but they contain indications of how the Jews thought about Satan and evil spirits in the two centuries before the time of Jesus. These ideas were incorporated into the New Testament and they were evidently borrowed from these books.

For instance, in Jud 1: 6 we are informed:

> "Angels who didn`t keep their first domain, but deserted their own dwelling place, he has kept in everlasting bonds under darkness for the judgment of the great day."

2 Peter 2: 4 tells us:

> "For if God didn`t spare angels when they sinned, but cast them down to Tartarus, and committed them to pits of darkness, to be reserved to judgment."

These two excerpts from the New Testament clearly show the influence of the books of Enoch and Jubilees. Although the book of Daniel briefly mentioned Judgment Day, this concept was made an integral part of the teachings of Jesus, Paul, and the rest of New Testament after it became part of Jewish and early Christian thinking on account of the influence of Enoch and Jubilees.

In other words: It is impossible to understand the New Testament without keeping the books of Enoch and Jubilees in mind. The topic of the next chapter is an exploration of how the authors of the New Testament expanded upon the ideas popularized by Enoch and the Book of Jubilees – without quoting directly from them.

It is important to point out that there are similarities between the presentation of the giants in Enoch and Jubilees on the one hand and the Greek mythological figures of the Titans on the other hand.

There were twelve Titans, gigantic deities, the offspring of the god of Heaven and the goddess of the earth. They rebelled against their father, who locked them up in Tartarus, the netherworld. They escaped, but after a battle of ten years, Zeus defeated them and incarcerated them in an abyss beneath Tartarus.[131]

---

[131] Enc Brit. "Titan".

Azazel, one of the fallen angels who taught men the technology of metallurgy, seems to be modelled on the Greek god Hephaestus, the god of fire and the divine smith. He was thrown out of Olympus after a quarrel with Zeus.[132]

Since Enoch and the book of Jubilees were written during the Hellenistic period in Israel's history, it may not be too farfetched to assume that the stories of the giants in these two books were partly copied from Greek mythology. The use of the name "Tartarus" in 2 Peter suggests some connection to the Greek mythology, via the books of Enoch and Jubilees.

[132] Enc Brit. "Hephaestus".

Chapter 7

SATAN IN THE CHRISTIAN SCRIPTURES

The oldest parts of the New Testament are most probably the letters of James and Jude[133], as well as the so-called Q Document, which was later incorporated into the Gospels of Matthew and Luke. The epistles of the Apostle Paul, who wrote them during the fifties and early sixties of the first century AD – a little more than twenty years after the crucifixion of Jesus – are also fairly early documents.

The four gospels, Matthew, Mark, Luke, and John, only got their final forms after the end of the Jewish War against the Romans (AD 66–70). They were – except for Mark – partly based on earlier material. The Q Document, which contains some saying of Jesus, was probably written during the forties or fifties AD in Galilee and it was later absorbed int Matthew and Luke, who also copied large parts of Mark. Matthew and Luke also contain some material unique to them, gathered from various other sources.[134]

John contains mainly two elements: a narrative part, which seems to have been written before the Jewish War, and a part containing discourses, debates, and dialogues of Jesus, which were merged with the earlier part during the nineties of the first century.[135]

The last book in the New Testament, Revelation, can be accurately dated to AD 96–97.[136] The other documents in the New Testament may also be of a rather later date – the last decade of the

---

[133] Pretorius, *The Gospels,* 254.

[134] Pretorius, *The Gospels,* 84–89; 263–73; 387–90; 449–56.

[135] Pretorius, *The Gospels,*536–37.

[136] Scholtz, *The Prophecies of Revelation.*

first century AD, or even later.

These documents will be discussed in more or less chronological order to trace any developments in thought about the devil and demons, if any.

THE Q DOCUMENT

It has already been mentioned that the Gospels of Matthew and Luke assimilated this earlier source, the so-called Q Document, containing a collection of sayings of John the Baptist and Jesus, into their gospels – together with parts of Mark and other material. This document was reconstructed by removing the material taken from Mark and the unique material of Matthew and Luke from their texts. It was named Q after the German word “Quelle”, which means “source”. It seems to have originated during the forties or fifties of the first century AD – a decade or more after Jesus’ execution.[137]

This document often refers to the devil and to unclean spirits and those parts must be discussed and dissected.

It is important to remember that Jesus was a member of the sect of the Essenes or Nazoreans (Matt 2: 23; 26:71; Luke 18: 37, John 18: 5, 7; 19: 19; Acts 2: 22; 3: 6; 4: 10; 6: 14; 22: 8; and 26: 9). It is not possible to understand Jesus’ teachings and actions adequately if this fact is not kept in mind.[138]

The text of Q, as reconstructed by Robert J. Miller, appears below. Headings were added at appropriate places.[139]

The Sons of the Devil

Luke 3: 7–9 (Matt 3: 7–9)

---

[137] Pretorius, *The Gospels,* 84–90.

[138] Pretorius, *Jesus of Nazareth,* 31–37; Pretorius, *The Gospels,* 31–43.

[139] Miller, *The Complete Gospels*, 249–300.

7.	John said to the crowds that came out to be baptized by him, "You brood of vipers! Who warned you to flee from the wrath to come?
8.	Bear fruits worthy of repentance. Do not begin to say to yourselves, `We have Abraham as our ancestor'; for I tell you, God is able from these stones to raise up children to Abraham.
9.	Even now the ax is lying at the root of the trees; every tree therefore that does not bear good fruit is cut down and thrown into the fire".

These words of John the Baptist were certainly aimed at the haughty and corrupt Sadducees, the rich and liberal priestly class in Jerusalem who cooperated with the pagan Roman authorities and regarded this wild prophet with suspicion. He warned them that their ancestry from Abraham would not guarantee their survival and that Judgment Day was awaiting them.

By calling his opponents a "brood of vipers", he accused them of being the spiritual offspring of the devil, the serpent of Genesis 3 – and not of Abraham.

The Temptation of Jesus

Luke 4: 1–13 (Matt 4: 1–4, 9–12, 5–7, 13)

1.	Jesus, full of the Holy Spirit, returned from the Jordan and was led by the Spirit in the wilderness,
2.	where for forty days he was tempted by the devil. He ate nothing at all during those days, and when they were over, he was famished.
3.	The devil said to him, "If you are the Son of God, command this stone to become a loaf of bread."
4.	Jesus answered him, "It is written, `One does not live by bread alone.'"

5.	Then the devil led him up and showed him in an instant all the kingdoms of the world.
6.	And the devil said to him, "To you I will give their glory and all this authority; for it has been given over to me, and I give it to anyone I please.
7.	If you, then, will worship me, it will all be yours."
8.	Jesus answered him, "It is written, `Worship the Lord your God, and serve only him.'"
9.	Then the devil took him to Jerusalem, and placed him on the pinnacle of the temple, saying to him, "If you are the Son of God, throw yourself down from here,
10.	for it is written, `He will command his angels concerning you, to protect you,'
11.	and `On their hands they will bear you up, so that you will not dash your foot against a stone.'"
12.	Jesus answered him, "It is said, `Do not put the Lord your God to the test.'"
13.	When the devil had finished every test, he departed from him until an opportune time.

The details of the story of Jesus' temptation could only have come from Jesus himself, since there were no other witnesses of these events. Jesus certainly related his experiences later to his followers, who passed their knowledge on to the compiler(s) of Q. Jesus must have been dehydrated and starving after fasting for a protracted period, which could easily have led to hallucinations.[140] These experiences, though, were so real to him that he regarded them as part of God's calling to become *the* Messiah of Israel.

The devil could have been a personification in Jesus' mind of the Sadducees and priests who opposed John the Baptist and him,

[140] Pretorius, *Jesus of Nazareth,* 53–54.

as well as of the pagan Roman oppressors.[141]

Belief in the devil and evil spirits was part and parcel of the ancient world view, shared by the Jews and early Christians. The compiler(s) of Q, therefore, did not deem it necessary to explain who and what the devil was.

The Greek word for "devil" is διάβολος (*diabolos*), which means "a devil, false accuser, slanderer".

The quotations from the Old Testament were taken from Deut 8: 3; Deut 6: 13 and 16; and Deut 10: 20.

Jesus and Beelzebul

Luke 11: 14–23 (Matt 12: 22–30)

1. Now he was casting out a demon that was mute; when the demon had gone out, the one who had been mute spoke, and the crowds were amazed.
2. But some of them said, "He casts out demons by Beelzebul, the ruler of the demons."
3. (…)
4. But he knew what they were thinking and said to them, "Every kingdom divided against itself becomes a desert, and house falls on house.
5. If Satan also is divided against himself, how will his kingdom stand? — for you say that I cast out the demons by Beelzebul.
6. Now if I cast out the demons by Beelzebul, by whom do your exorcists cast them out? Therefore they will be your judges.
7. But if it is by the finger of God that I cast out the demons, then the kingdom of God has come to you.

[141] Pretorius, *The Gospel,* 94.

8.	When a strong man, fully armed, guards his castle, his property is safe.
9.	But when one stronger than he attacks him and overpowers him, he takes away his armor in which he trusted and divides his plunder.
10.	Whoever is not with me is against me, and whoever does not gather with me scatters.

Jesus was maligned by his Jewish opponents, when he was accused of casting out demons with the power of Beelzebul (Greek: Βεελζεβούλ – *Beelzeboul*), the prince or ruler of the demons. Jesus easily pointed out the logical flaw in this ridiculous accusation by arguing that it is impossible that Satan (Beelzebul) would have been willing to get rid of his helpers, the lesser little devils. Jesus also compared himself with a strong man who overpowered another strong man (Satan) by looting his armor and his treasures.

The name Beelzebul is derived from the name of a Philistine deity (mentioned in 2 Kgs 1: 2–3, 6, and 16) where he is called Beelzebub (Baal or Lord of the Flies) (Hebrew: בְּבַעַל זְבוּב – *Baal–Zebub*). Those who accused Jesus of using the power of Beelzebul tried to discredit him as an imposter, somebody in an alliance with Satan or a pagan god. Jesus countered by declaring that the demons were driven out "by the finger of God" and that that was a sign that God's kingdom would be established soon. He added that those who did not gather (followers or helpers for his campaign) together with him, were against him and only scattering the people of God.

John the Baptist and Jesus Slandered

Luke 7: 31–35 (Matt 11: 16–19)

31.	"To what then will I compare the people of this generation, and what are they like?

32.	They are like children sitting in the marketplace and calling to one another, `We played the flute for you, and you did not dance; we wailed, and you did not weep.'
33.	For John the Baptist has come eating no bread and drinking no wine, and you say, `He has a demon';
34.	the Son of Man has come eating and drinking, and you say, 'Look, a glutton and a drunkard, a friend of tax collectors and sinners!'
35.	Nevertheless, wisdom is vindicated by all her children."

With these enigmatic sayings, Jesus defended John the Baptist and himself, despite being slandered by unwise people, such as the Jerusalem elite. Those who played the flute – John and Jesus – expected a positive response from their audience. Those who wept – John and Jesus – hoped that others would weep along with them about the sins of the Jews. Instead, John and Jesus were defamed and accused of being under the influence of an evil spirit or fraternizing with the dregs of society. John and Jesus were, however, children of the Lady Wisdom (Prov 7–9 and Enoch 42) and their messages were the result of their wisdom.

Demons Returning

Luke 11: 24–26 (Matt 12: 43–45)

11.	"When the unclean spirit has gone out of a person, it wanders through waterless regions looking for a resting place, but not finding any, it says, 'I will return to my house from which I came.'
12.	When it comes, it finds it swept and put in order.

13.	Then it goes and brings seven other spirits more evil than itself, and they enter and live there; and the last state of that person is worse than the first."

Jesus must have had the experience that expelling evil spirits – regarded in those days as the cause of diseases, disabilities, and disorders, on account of the Book of Jubilees – had no lasting effects and that a person, who was seemingly healed, only became worse afterwards. This is a tacit admission that Jesus' ministry of healing did not always help sick people in the long run.

THE EPISTLES OF JAMES AND JUDE

One of the shorter documents in the New Testament, the Epistle of James, may be one of the earliest parts of the New Testament, written probably during the forties or fifties of the first century AD.[142] It contains some references to the devil and demons.

The Epistle of Jude, written by a brother of James, is the second shortest document in the Bible. It is also a relatively early document and it has certainly been inspired by Enoch.[143]

The Demons Know God

James 2: 19

19.	You believe that God is one. You do well. The demons also believe, and shudder.

Demons, evil spirits, have knowledge of God. That knowledge gives them the shivers, because they know that they will have to face God on Judgment Day

[142] Pretorius, *The Gospels,* 254.

[143] Pretorius, *Jesus of Nazareth,* 118.

Hatred with a Demonic Origin

James 3: 13–16

13.	Who is wise and understanding among you? Let him show his deeds done in gentleness of wisdom by his good life.
14.	But if you have bitter jealousy and selfish ambition in your heart, don`t boast and don`t lie against the truth.
15.	This wisdom is not that which comes down from above, but is earthly, sensual, and demonic.
16.	For where jealousy and selfish ambition are, there is confusion and every evil deed.

The message of this passage is that spite, strife, and selfish ambitions have a demonic origin – as described in the Books of Jubilees and Enoch. People who are guilty of these sins have been captured by demons.

Resist the Devil

James 4: 6–8

6.	But he gives more grace. Therefore it says, "God resists the proud, but gives grace to the humble."
7.	Be subject therefore to God. But resist the devil, and he will flee from you.
8.	Draw near to God, and he will draw near to you. Cleanse your hands, you sinners; and purify your hearts, you double-minded.

James advised his readers to resist the devil so that he could flee from them. This resistance seems to entail a drawing nearer to God. That is to be accomplished by living with a pure heart, avoiding temptations, and sin. The devil is regarded as a nasty character.

Fallen Angels

Jude 1: 6

6.	Angels who didn`t keep their first domain, but deserted their own dwelling place, he has kept in everlasting bonds under darkness for the judgment of the great day.

This statement by Jude is a clear reference to the descriptions in Enoch and the Book of Jubilees of how some angels rebelled against God, were exiled from heaven, and are kept under lock and key in anticipation of Judgment Day.

Michael and the Devil Argued

Jude 1: 9

9.	But Michael, the archangel, when contending with the devil and arguing about the body of Moses, dared not bring against him an abusive condemnation, but said, "May the Lord rebuke you!"

This verse is a reference to Zech 3: 1–2:

> "He showed me Joshua the high priest standing before the angel of YHWH, and Satan standing at his right hand to be his adversary. YHWH said to Satan, YHWH rebuke you, Satan; yes, YHWH that has chosen Jerusalem rebuke you: is not this a brand plucked out of the fire?"

It is not known when and where the debate or dispute between Michael and Satan took place. In any case, the devil is depicted here as an intelligent being who can argue with an archangel.

According to Enoch 10: 11, Michael had to capture Semjaza, the chief of the watchers.

An Army of Angels

Jude 1: 14

14.	To these also Enoch, the seventh from Adam, prophesied, saying, "Behold, the Lord came with ten thousands of his holy ones."

Jude quoted a prophecy from Enoch 1: 9 that God would come with a huge army of angels on Judgment Day to finally destroy and demolish Satan and his band of demons.

THE LETTERS OF PAUL

The Apostle Paul was a prolific writer and some of his letters were collected after his death as a martyr in Rome during the sixties of the first century AD when Emperor Nero clamped down on the Christians. His letters form a substantial part of the New Testament.

These letters were probably written in the following order during the fifties and early sixties of the first century AD:

The apostle Paul (ceiling mosaic, Archiepiscopal Chapel of St. Andrew, Ravenna, Italy)

- 1 Thessalonians;
- 1 Corinthians;
- 2 Corinthians;
- Galatians;
- Philippians; and
- Romans.

The following letters are regarded as "Deutero-Pauline" – probably written by Paul's followers on his behalf, namely Ephesians, Colossians, and 2 Thessalonians. The so-called pastoral epistles, 1 and 2 Timothy and Titus, are "Trito-Pauline" and were probably also written by members of the Pauline school according to his directives, or a generation after his death.[144]

His hometown was a major Greek city in Asia Minor and a Roman colony, which automatically made him a Roman citizen. He grew up in a Jewish home and belonged to the tribe of Benjamin (Phil 3: 5). As a youngster, he must have been exposed to the intellectual and mythological heritage of Greece.

According to Acts 22: 3, he sat as a student "at the feet of Gamaliel", a leader and teacher of the party of the Pharisees in Jerusalem. His studies made him familiar with the contents of the Hebrew Scriptures and he often quoted from them in his letters.

During the late fifties Paul returned to Jerusalem with the money he had raised for the poor followers of Jesus in Jerusalem. There he was arrested and after a series of trials he was sent to Rome.

Paul's writings were already accepted as "Scriptures" and authoritative at an early date because 2 Pet 3: 15–16 informs us:

> "Regard the patience of our Lord as salvation; even as our beloved brother Paul also, according to the wisdom given to him, wrote to you; as also in all of his letters, speaking in them of these things. In those are some things hard to be understood, which the ignorant and unsettled twist, as they do also to the *other scriptures*, to their own destruction" (*emphasis added*).

In the passages that follow, Paul's views regarding Satan and demons will be examined and explained:

Satan Sabotaged Paul

1 Thess 2: 17–18

---

[144] Sanders, "Paul, the Apostle, Saint."

17.	But we, brothers, being bereaved of you for a short season, in presence, not in heart, tried even harder to see your face with great desire,
18.	because we wanted to come to you – indeed, I, Paul, once and again – but Satan hindered us.

Paul took it for granted that his readers would know who or what Satan was. The Greek name for Satan is ὁ Σατανᾶς (*ho Satanas*), which means "the adversary, enemy". It is a transliteration of the Hebrew name of Satan (הַשָּׂטָן).

Paul wanted to visit the Christians in Thessalonica again, but the enemy of God, Satan, somehow made that impossible. Satan had a personality in Paul's view and he had power to influence events.

Fallen Angels to be Judged

1 Cor 6: 2 –3

2.	Don`t you know that the saints will judge the world? And if the world is judged by you, are you unworthy to judge the smallest matters?
3.	Don`t you know that we will judge angels? How much more, things that pertain to this life?

According to Paul, the saints, the Christians, will take part in Judgment Day. The godless, wicked, and wayward people of the world will be judged, but also the fallen angels mentioned in Enoch and the Book of Jubilees.

Communion with Demons

1 Cor 10: 20–21

20.	But I say that the things which the Gentiles sacrifice, they sacrifice to demons, and not to God, and I don`t desire that you would have communion with demons.
21.	You can`t both drink the cup of the Lord and the cup of demons. You can`t both partake of the table of the Lord, and of the table of demons.

Paul was convinced that the pagan gods, to whom the Gentiles offered sacrifices, were actually demons or evil spirits. Christians had to avoid all contact with pagan ceremonies. Paul had knowledge of pagan rites, having grown up in a Greek city.

Evil Powers to be Condemned

1 Cor 15: 24–28

24.	Then the end comes, when he will deliver up the kingdom to God, even the Father; when he will have abolished all rule and all authority and power.
26.	For he must reign until he has put all his enemies under his feet.
26.	The last enemy that will be abolished is death.
27.	For, "He put all things in subjection under his feet." But when he says, "All things are put in subjection," it is evident that he is excepted who subjected all things to him.
28.	When all things have been subjected to him, then the Son will also himself be subjected to him who subjected all things to him, that God may be all in all.

This text states that Christ will eradicate "all rule and all authority and power", as well as "all his enemies" on Judgment Day. This is in accordance with Enoch and the Book of Jubilees that both envisaged the final removal to the flames of hell of Satan, all other angry angels, and all stubborn and savage spirits on Judgment Day.

The Plans of Satan

2 Cor 2: 10–11

10.	Now I also forgive whomever you forgive anything. For if indeed I have forgiven anything, I have forgiven that one for your sakes in the presence of Christ,
11.	that no advantage may be gained over us by Satan; for we are not ignorant of his schemes.

Paul did not elaborate about what the schemes of Satan were, but it may be supposed that he was of the view that Satan did his best to wreck Paul's efforts to bring the Gospel to a pagan world.

The God of this World

2 Cor 4: 3–4

3.	Even if our gospel is veiled, it is veiled in those who perish;
4.	in whom the god of this world has blinded the minds of the unbelieving, that the light of the gospel of the glory of Christ, who is the image of God, should not dawn on them.

Paul called the devil "the god of this world" because the godless world was under his influence and in his grip and he did his best to obstruct the preaching of the gospel.

Christ and Belial

2 Cor 6: 14–16

14.	Don`t be unequally yoked with unbelievers, for what fellowship have righteousness and iniquity? Or what communion has light with darkness?
15.	What agreement has Christ with Belial? Or what portion has a believer with an unbeliever?
16.	What agreement has a temple of God with idols? For you are a temple of the living God. Even as God said, "I will dwell in them, and walk in them; and I will be their God, and they will be my people."

Paul contrasted various entities with each other: believers and unbelievers, righteousness and iniquity, Christ and Belial, and the temple of God and idols. The Greek word for "Belial" is Βελιάρ (*Beliar*), which is the transcription of a Hebre בְּלִיַּעַל (*Belial*), meaning "worthless or wicked" (for instance, in 1 Kgs 21: 13). Paul, used this nickname to affirm that Satan was worthless and wicked – the exact opposite of Christ.

An Angel of Light

2 Cor 11: 3, 14–15

3.	But I am afraid that by any means, as the serpent deceived Eve in his craftiness, your minds might be corrupted from the simplicity that is toward Christ.
13.	For such men are false apostles, deceitful workers, masquerading as Christ`s apostles.
14.	No wonder, for even Satan masquerades as an angel of light.

Paul compared the false apostles, who brought a gospel that differed from his message, with Satan who "masquerades as an angel of light" – an oblique reference to Enoch and the Book of Jubilees where he was presented as a fallen angel. Paul, therefore, taught that Satan disguised himself by pretending to still be a good angel, although he was imprisoned in the abyss. Satan's other name, Lucifer (Bringer of Light), is partly derived from this verse.

A Messenger of Satan

2 Cor 12: 7–9

7.	By reason of the exceeding greatness of the revelations, that I should not be exalted excessively, there was given to me a thorn in the flesh, a messenger of Satan to buffet me, that I should not be exalted excessively.
8.	Concerning this thing, I begged the Lord three times that it might depart from me.
9.	He has said to me, "My grace is sufficient for you, for my power is made perfect in weakness." Most gladly therefore will I rather glory in my weaknesses, that the power of Christ may rest on me.

Paul did not supply any details about this "thorn in the flesh" he suffered from. It must have been something extremely painful and embarrassing, probably a serious health issue. The Greek word used for buffet, κολαφίζω (*kolafizo*), means literally to strike with the fist, as in a boxing match. That suggests that Paul may have been knocked out and unconscious at times, perhaps during an epileptic fit.[145] He attributes it to a messenger or angel of Satan. He prayed in

[145] Pretoris, *Jesus of Nazareth,* 126–39.

vain to God to get rid of this affliction, but God replied that He would not grant him his prayer to keep him humble.

Paul – just as other believers of his time – thought that maladies and painful conditions were caused by evil spirits, but that God was able to neutralize their evil actions – which, unfortunately, did not happen in this case.

Christ the Victor

Phil 2: 9–11

9. Therefore God also highly exalted him [Christ], and gave to him the name which is above every name;
10. that at the name of Jesus every knee would bow, of those in heaven, those on earth, and those under the earth,
11. and that every tongue would confess that Jesus Christ is Lord, to the glory of God, the Father.

With "those in heaven, those on earth, and those under the earth", Paul had all creatures in creation in mind who would acknowledge that Christ is the Lord on Judgment Day. These creatures clearly included the damned devil and all sullen and sulking spirits who were being held in the abyss, awaiting Judgment Day.

The Love of God Stronger

Rom 8: 38–39

38. For I am persuaded, that neither death, nor life, nor angels, nor principalities, nor things present, nor things to come, nor powers,

39. nor height, nor depth, nor any other creature, will be able to separate us from the love of God, which is in Christ Jesus our Lord.

Paul ensured his readers that nothing in creation would be able to separate them from God's love. He included evil spirits in his list of possible dangers, namely (fallen) angels, principalities, and powers in the heights of heaven or in the deep abyss under the earth.

Christ the Victor

Eph 1: 20–22

20.	… which he worked in Christ, when he raised him from the dead, and made him to sit at his right hand in the heavenly places,
21.	far above all rule, and authority, and power, and dominion, and every name that is named, not only in this world, but also in that which is to come.
22.	He put all things in subjection under his feet, and gave him to be head over all things to the assembly,
23.	which is his body, the fullness of him who fills all in all

Paul wrote that when Christ was raised from the dead, God exalted him to a position where all powers and authorities, of this world or of the spirit world, were subject to him. This idea differs somewhat from Enoch where it was written that Satan and his demons were arrested and bound by Michael. Here, Christ is the victor.

The Prince of the Demons

Eph 2: 1–3

1.	You were made alive when you were dead through your trespasses and sins,
2.	in which you once walked according to the course of this world, according to the prince of the powers of the air, of the spirit who now works in the sons of disobedience;
3.	among whom we also all once lived in the lust of our flesh, doing the desires of the flesh and of the mind, and were by nature children of wrath, even as the rest.

Paul used a strong expression to describe Satan, namely "the prince of the powers of the air, of the spirit who now works in the sons of disobedience". With the "powers in the air" he evidently thought of evil angels in the starry skies; in other words: demons. With the sons of disobedience, he has ungodly sinners in mind – people who are under the influence of this savage spiritual being, Satan.

No Place for the Devil

Eph 4: 26–27

26.	Don`t let the sun go down on your wrath,
27.	neither give place to the devil.

With the advice not to give a place to the devil, Paul evidently admonished his readers not to give in to sinful temptations.

Spiritual Warfare

Eph 6: 11–18

11.	Put on the whole armor of God, that you may be able to stand against the wiles of the devil.
12.	For our wrestling is not against flesh and blood, but against

	the principalities, against the powers, against the world`s rulers of the darkness of this age, and against the spiritual hosts of wickedness in the heavenly places.
13.	Therefore, put on the whole armor of God, that you may be able to withstand in the evil day, and, having done all, to stand.
14.	Stand therefore, having the utility belt of truth buckled around your waist, and having put on the breastplate of righteousness,
15.	and having fitted your feet with the preparation of the gospel of peace;
16.	above all, taking up the shield of faith, with which you will be able to quench all the fiery darts of the evil one.
17.	Take the helmet of salvation, and the sword of the Spirit, which is the word of God;
18.	with all prayer and requests, praying at all times in the Spirit, and being watchful to this end in all perseverance and requests for all the saints:

According to Paul, Christians were locked in a spiritual war against the evil spirits "in heavenly places" – including certain stars and starry constellations. He seems to have exhausted his vocabulary to describe these ferocious, foul, and filthy friends of Satan, the "evil one". Believers were being attacked by these wily and wicked worms by means of temptations to forsake Christ and to revert to paganism with its worship of inferior idols and dreadful demons.

The Evil One

2 Thes 3: 3

3.	But the Lord is faithful, who will establish you, and guard you from the evil one.

Paul was convinced that the believers would be protected against the devil, the evil one, by the faithful God.

The Devil's Snares

1 Tim 3: 6-7

6.	(The overseer therefore must be) not a novice, to avoid being puffed up and falling into the condemnation of the devil.
7.	Moreover he must have good testimony from those who are outside, to avoid falling into reproach and the snare of the devil.

The requirements for overseers in the church meant that they had to be ethical examples. That held in that they had to be wary of the temptation the devil may place in front of them. They ought not to be novices who could easily become filled with pride, which would lead to their condemnation, just as the devil was condemned for his arrogance – as pointed out in Enoch and the Book of Jubilees.

The Snares of the Devil

2 Tim 2: 24–26

24.	The Lord`s servant must not quarrel, but be gentle towards all, able to teach, patient,
25.	in gentleness correcting those who oppose him; if perhaps God may give them repentance to the knowledge of the truth,

26.	and they may recover themselves out of the devil`s snare, having been taken captive by him to his will.

It was a requirement for servants of the Lord to be peaceful and patient people who had to take care that they escaped from the traps of the devil. They were captives of the devil in the past, which meant that they did what the devil wanted.

Seducing Spirits

1 Tim 4: 1–3

1.	But the Spirit says expressly that in later times some will fall away from the faith, paying attention to seducing spirits and doctrines of demons,
2.	through the hypocrisy of men who speak lies, branded in their own conscience as with a hot iron;
3.	forbidding marriage and commanding to abstinence from foods which God created to be received with thanksgiving by those who believe and know the truth.

This warning against the doctrines of demons seems to have been directed against the Ebionites or Essenes, the ascetic Jewish followers of Jesus, who advocated celibacy and had strict dietary laws, including an avoidance of olive oil.[146] Paul (or his follower who wrote this letter on his behalf) regarded all those whose ideas differed from his to harbor some detestable doctrines of demons.

[146] Josephus, *The Jewish War, Book II,* VIII/II & III; Pretorius, *Jesus of Nazareth,* 31–35.

THE NARRATIVE PARTS OF JOHN'S GOSPEL

The earliest parts of the Gospel of John, the narrative parts – without the later-added discourses, lectures, sermons, and dialogues – was almost certainly written during the fifties or early sixties of the first century AD, probably by John, the disciple of Jesus, or somebody who heard the story from him.[147] This proto-gospel contains very little about Satan and demons.

The Devil and Judas

John 13: 2, 27

2.	After supper, the devil having already put into the heart of Judas Iscariot, Simon`s son, to betray him,
27,	After the morsel, then Satan entered into him. Jesus therefore said to him, "What you do, do quickly."

Satan appears only in one episode in the Proto-Gospel of John. The treason by Judas was due to the influence of Satan on him. Satan is, therefore, someone who could motivate men towards abhorrent actions.

The Powers of Demons

John 10: 19–21

19.	Therefore a division arose again among the Jews because of these words.
20.	Many of them said, "He has a demon, and is mad! Why do you listen to him?"
21.	Others said, "These are not the sayings of one possessed with a demon. Can a demon open the eyes of the blind?"

[147] Pretorius, *The Gospels,* 185.

This episode was the aftermath of an occasion where Jesus restored the eye-sight of a blind man on the Sabbath. Some Jews accused Jesus of being possessed of a demon, which enabled him to perform this miracle. The demon was also supposed to make him mad. Others thought that demons did not have those powers.

THE GOSPEL OF MARK

As has been mentioned, the Gospels of Matthew and Luke are composed of parts of the Q Document, parts of the Gospel of Mark, and material unique to each of these two gospels. These three gospels are called the "Synoptic Gospels", which means that they offer essentially the same view of Jesus. That is not a surprise since Matthew and Luke both copied parts of Q and parts of Mark.[148]

The most likely date for the composition of Mark is during the seventies AD, after the destruction of Jerusalem during the Jewish War in AD 70. The Gospels of Matthew and Luke followed later, probably during the eighties of the first century.[149]

In the explanation that follows, the Gospel of Mark will be dealt with first. Thereafter, the parts of Matthew and Luke not containing parts of Q and parts of Mark will be dissected.

The Temptation of Jesus

Mark 1: 13 (Matt 3: 14: 11; Luke 4: 1–13)

13.	He was there in the wilderness forty days tempted by Satan. He was with the wild animals. The angels ministered to him.

[148] Pretorius, *The Gospels,* 85–86.

[149] Pretorius, *The Gospels,* 389.

Mark mentioned the temptation of Jesus in a single sentence. Matthew and Luke added many more details, which they took from the Q Document.

It has been shown in the discussion of Q that this episode of Jesus' struggle with Satan was most likely a case of hallucination on account of severe dehydration and malnutrition after prolonged fasting in the desert. For Jesus, his encounter with Satan was real enough and he must have told his followers about it afterwards.

Jesus and Beelzebul

Mark 3: 20–30 (Matt 12: 22–32; Luke 11: 14 – 12:10)

20.	The multitude came together again, so that they could not so much as eat bread.
21.	When his friends heard it, they went out to lay hold on him: for they said, "He is insane."
22.	The scribes who came down from Jerusalem said, "He has Beelzebul," and, "By the prince of the demons he casts out the demons."
23.	He called them to him, and said to them in parables, "How can Satan cast out Satan?
24.	If a kingdom is divided against itself, that kingdom cannot stand.
25.	If a house is divided against itself, that house cannot stand.
26.	If Satan has risen up against himself, and is divided, he can`t stand, but has an end.
27.	But no one can enter into the house of the strong man to plunder, unless he first binds the strong man; and then he will plunder his house.

28.	Most assuredly I tell you, all their sins will be forgiven to the sons of men, and their blasphemies with which they may blaspheme;
29.	but whoever may blaspheme against the Holy Spirit never has forgiveness, but is guilty of an eternal sin"
30.	— because they said, "He has an unclean spirit."

A somewhat similar episode is narrated in Matt 12: 22–32 and Luke 11: 14 – 12:10, which is part of the Q Document. The differences between Mark and the other two Synoptic Gospels are big enough to warrant the conclusion that they come from different sources.

This is an example where Jesus was maligned, when he was accused of casting out demons with the power of Beelzebul (Greek: Βεελζεβούλ – *Beelzeboul*), the prince or ruler of the demons. Jesus easily ridiculed this accusation by pointing out that it is impossible that Satan (Beelzebul) would be willing to get rid of his assistants, the destructive demons.

Jesus also declared that it was an unforgivable sin, a sin against the Holy Spirit (the mind of God or God himself) to accuse Jesus, the Messiah and anointed of God, of making use of dark and evil powers.

For Jesus and his audience, Satan or Beelzebul was a reality.

The Parable of the Sower Explained

Mark 4: 13–15 (Matt 13: 18–20; Luke 8: 11–13)

13.	He said to them, "Don`t you understand this parable? How will you understand all of the parables?
14.	The farmer sows the word.

15.	These are they by the road, where the word is sown; and when they have heard, immediately Satan comes, and takes away the word which has been sown in them.

This is part of Jesus' explanation of the Parable of the Sower to his disciples. Jesus compared the seed sown onto the hard road surface, where the birds ate the seed, with the Pharisees and teachers of the Law who heard his message, but did not accept it. That was because Satan prevented that.

Matthew and Luke essentially repeated the passage in Mark unaltered.

Jesus Speaks about his Suffering and Death

Mark 8: 31–33; 9: 1 (Matt 16: 21–23; Luke 9: 22–24).

31.	He began to teach them that the Son of Man must suffer many things, and be rejected by the elders, the chief priests, and the scribes, and be killed, and after three days rise again.
32.	He spoke to them openly. Peter took him, and began to rebuke him.
33.	But he, turning around, and seeing his disciples, rebuked Peter, and said, "Get behind me, Satan! For you have in mind not the things of God, but the things of men."

Mark (as well as Matthew and Luke) included this story in his gospel to prepare his readers for the crucifixion at a later stage.

Jesus knew very well that his actions were being watched by the Jewish religious authorities and the Roman overlords. It happened regularly that the Romans crucified dangerous criminals and rebels. Jesus' movement had to be crushed because he presented himself as the rightful king of the Jews – and that was exactly the reason why he was crucified at a later stage (Mark 15: 2 and 26; Matt 27: 11 and 37; Luke 23: 3 and 38; John 19: 19). Therefore, he warned his disciples that such a fate may await him and them. Peter rebuked Jesus because he didn't want Jesu as the Messiah s to be executed. Jesus warned Peter that Satan was putting those thoughts into his mind, because the crucifixion was inevitable.

A Man with an Evil Spirit

Mark 1: 21–28 (Luke 4: 31–37)

21.	They went into Capernaum, and immediately on the Sabbath day he entered into the synagogue and taught.
22.	They were astonished at his teaching, for he taught them as having authority, and not as the scribes.
23.	Immediately there was in their synagogue a man with an unclean spirit, and he cried out,
24.	saying, "Ha! What do we have to do with you, Jesus, you Nazarene? Have you come to destroy us? I know you who you are: the Holy One of God."
25.	Jesus rebuked him, saying, "Be quiet, and come out of him!"
26.	The unclean spirit, convulsing him and crying with a loud voice, came out of him.
27.	They were all amazed, so that they questioned among themselves, saying, "What is this? A new teaching? For with authority he commands even the unclean spirits, and they obey him."

28.	The report of him went out immediately everywhere into all the region of Galilee and its surrounding area.

Jesus proved to be a capable preacher in the synagogue of Capernaum, speaking with more authority than the teachers of the Law the congregants usually heard. It must be concluded that Jesus had received a thorough training in the Scriptures, probably at the Essene center at Qumran. According to the Jewish philosopher, Philo of Alexandria, some Essenes were known as "Therapeutae" (Healers) in those days.[150]

A man with a psychiatric disorder disrupted a meeting and he quietened down after Jesus took care of him. With the lack of medical knowledge in those days, his disorder was seen as being caused by a dirty despicable demon.

Luke repeated this report without any additions.

Jesus Heals Many People

Mark 1: 29–34 (Matt 8: 14–17; Luke 4: 38–41)

29.	Immediately, when they had come out of the synagogue, they came into the house of Simon and Andrew, with James and John.
30.	Now Simon`s wife`s mother lay sick with a fever, and immediately they told him about her.
31.	He came and took her by the hand, and raised her up. The fever left her, and she served them.
33.	All the city was gathered together at the door.

[150] Enc Brit, "Therapeutae".

34.	He healed many who were sick with various diseases, and cast out many demons. He didn`t allow the demons to speak, because they knew him.

Jesus' reputation as a healer grew rapidly as he helped Simon's mother-in-law to get better and he healed some other people from the town. Some were supposedly possessed of detestable demons because the causes of their complaints were unknown, due to the lack of medical knowledge at that time.

Matthew and Luke copied this story essentially unchanged.

A Crowd by the Lake

Mark 3: 7–12 (Luke 6: 12–17)

7.	Jesus withdrew to the sea with his disciples, and a great multitude followed him from Galilee, from Judea,
8.	from Jerusalem, from Idumaea, beyond the Jordan, and those from around Tyre and Sidon. A great multitude, hearing what great things he did, came to him.
9.	He spoke to his disciples, that a little boat should stay near him because of the crowd, so that they wouldn`t press on him.
10.	For he had healed many, so that as many as had diseases pressed on him that they might touch him.
11.	The unclean spirits, whenever they saw him, fell down before him, and cried, "You are the Son of God!"
12.	He sternly warned them that they should not make him known.

Jesus drew crowds from the south, east, and north of Galilee to hear his message. He healed many people with diseases with the result that the evil spirits reportedly cried out that he must be the Son of God. What rather really happened was that the people who were healed cried out in amazement, but it was interpreted that the evil spirits that supposedly left them, used their voices.

This is another case where health complaints and conditions were seen as the work of disgusting demons.

Luke has essentially the same information, but he rearranged the wording.

Jesus Chooses the Twelve Apostles

Mark 3: 13–19 (Matt 10: 1–4; Luke 6: 12–16)

13.	He went up into the mountain, and called to himself whom he wanted, and they went to him.
14.	He appointed twelve, that they might be with him, and that he might send them out to preach,
15.	and to have authority to heal sicknesses and to cast out demons.

Jesus chose exactly twelve disciples or apostles (envoys or missionaries) to symbolize the new Israel that he wanted to create. The twelve had to represent the twelve patriarchs and the twelve tribes of Israel. He trained them to heal sicknesses and to cast demons out – an indication that these two activities were seen as identical.

Jesus Heals a Man with Evil Spirits

Mark 5:1–20 (Matt 8: 28–34; Luke 8: 26–39)

1.	They came to the other side of the sea, into the country of the Gadarenes.
2.	When he had come out of the boat, immediately there met him out of the tombs a man with an unclean spirit,
3.	who had his dwelling in the tombs. Nobody could bind him anymore, not even with chains,
4.	because he had been often bound with fetters and chains, and the chains had been torn apart by him, and the fetters broken in pieces. Nobody had the strength to tame him.
5.	Always, night and day, in the tombs and in the mountains, he was crying out, and cutting himself with stones.
6.	When he saw Jesus from afar, he ran and bowed down to him,
7.	and crying out with a loud voice, he said, "What have I to do with you, Jesus, you Son of the Most High God? I adjure you by God, don`t torment me."
8.	For he said to him, "Come out of the man, you unclean spirit!"
9.	He asked him, "What is your name?" He said to him, "My name is Legion, for we are many."
10.	He begged him much that he would not send them away out of the country.
11.	Now there was there on the mountainside a great herd of pigs feeding.
12.	All the demons begged him, saying, "Send us into the pigs, that we may enter into them."

13.	At once Jesus gave them permission. The unclean spirits came out, and got hold of the pigs. The herd of about two thousand rushed down the steep bank into the sea, and they were drowned in the sea.
14.	Those who fed them fled, and told it in the city, and in the country. The people came to see what it was that had happened.
15.	They came to Jesus, and saw him who was possessed by demons sitting, clothed and in his right mind, even him who had the legion; and they were afraid.
16.	Those who saw it declared to them how it happened to him who was possessed by demons, and about the pigs.
17.	They began to beg him to depart from their borders.
18.	As he was entering into the boat, he who had been possessed by demons begged him that he might be with him.
19.	He didn`t allow him, but said to him, "Go to your house, to your friends, and tell them how the Lord has done great things for you, and how he had mercy on you."
20.	He went his way, and began to proclaim in Decapolis how Jesus had done great things for him, and everyone marveled.

When Jesus and the disciples reached the eastern shore of the lake of Galilee a man with a serious psychiatric problem – probably a bipolar (manic-depressive) disorder with psychotic features[151] – confronted Jesus. It is doubtful that he addressed Jesus as the Son of

[151] APA, *DSM-5,* 123–27, 152.

God or king of Israel because Jesus was certainly not known in those parts. Mark or his source must have added this exclamation because he thought the demons would recognize Jesus for whom and what he was.

Jesus, somehow, calmed the man down. If he had a bipolar disorder with psychotic tendencies, he could have entered a more normal phase after having been in an extreme manic phase previously.[152]

A herd of pigs somehow got a fright and rushed into the water where they drowned. This event was linked to Jesus who was thought to have driven the demons from this poor distressed man's mind and that they invaded the suffering swine.

The people of that town became afraid of Jesus, taking him for a magician, and begged him to leave – too afraid of his powers to throw him out.

Matthew and Luke copied the story faithfully, although Matthew wrote that two men, instead of one man, were healed from their evil spirits. In Luke's account, the demons begged Jesus not to banish them to "the Abyss," the place of captivity where dangerous demons were being held, according to Enoch and the Book of Jubilees.

The Mission of the Twelve Disciples

Mark 6: 7–13 (Matt 10: 5–15; Luke 9: 1–6)

7.	He called to himself the twelve, and began to send them out two by two; and he gave them authority over the unclean spirits.
12.	They went out, and preached that people should repent.

[152] APA, *DSM-5,* 149–52.

13.	They cast out many demons, and anointed many with oil who were sick, and healed them.

Jesus sent his disciples out in pairs to spread his message and to heal the sick by driving out evil spirits. Many of these healings were certainly the effect of the placebo effect where the body reacts positively if the person believes that he will recover from his malady.

A Woman's Faith

Mark 7: 24–30 (Matt 15: 21–28)

24.	From there he arose, and went away into the borders of Tyre and Sidon. He entered into a house, and wanted no one to know it, but he couldn`t escape detection.
25.	For a woman, whose little daughter had an unclean spirit, having heard of him, came and fell down at his feet.
26.	Now the woman was a Greek, a Syrophoenician by race. She begged him that he would cast the demon out of her daughter.
27.	But Jesus said to her, "Let the children be filled first, for it is not appropriate to take the children`s bread and throw it to the dogs."
28.	But she answered him, "Yes, Lord. For even the dogs under the table eat the children`s crumbs."
29.	He said to her, "For this saying, go your way. The demon has gone out of your daughter."
30.	She went away to her house, and found the child laying on the bed, with the demon gone out.

Jesus took his disciples to Phoenicia to escape the crowds in Galilee. However, a local Greek-speaking woman recognized him and asked him to heal her daughter. Jesus initially insulted her by comparing the pagans with dogs, but relented when she refused to be insulted and he freed the child from the demon – whatever her medical condition was.

Matthew added a saying of Jesus, namely that he was only interested in helping "the lost sheep of the house of Israel."

Jesus Heals a Boy with an Evil Spirit

Mark 9: 14–29 (Matt 17: 14–21; Luke 9: 37–43a)

14. Coming to the disciples, he saw a great multitude around them, and scribes questioning them.
15. Immediately all the multitude, when they saw him, were greatly amazed, and running to him greeted him.
16. He asked the scribes, "What are you asking them?"
17. One of the multitude answered, "Teacher, I brought to you my son, who has a mute spirit;
18. and wherever it seizes him, it dashes him down, and he foams at the mouth, and grinds his teeth, and wastes away. I asked your disciples to cast it out, and they weren`t able."
19. He answered them, "Unbelieving generation, how long will I be with you? How long will I bear with you? Bring him to me."
20. They brought him to him, and when he saw him, immediately the spirit convulsed him, and he fell on the ground, wallowing and foaming at the mouth.

21.	He asked his father, "How long has it been since this has come to him?" He said, "From childhood.
22.	Often it has cast him both into the fire and into the water, to destroy him. But if you can do anything, have compassion on us, and help us."
23.	Jesus said to him, "If you can believe? All things are possible to him who believes."
24.	Immediately the father of the child cried out with tears, "I believe. Help my unbelief!"
25.	When Jesus saw that a multitude came running together, he rebuked the unclean spirit, saying to him, "You mute and deaf spirit, I command you, come out of him, and enter no more into him!"
26.	Having cried out, and convulsed him greatly, it came out. The boy became like one dead; so much that most of them said, "He is dead."
27.	But Jesus took him by the hand, and raised him up; and he arose.
28.	When he had come into the house, his disciples asked him privately, "Why couldn`t we cast it out?"
29.	He said to them, "This kind can come out by nothing, except by prayer and fasting."

The description of the disorder from which this boy was ailing, makes it clear that he suffered from severe epileptic fits. Whether Jesus effected a permanent cure is unclear.

Whoever is not Against Us is for Us

Mark 9: 38–40 (Luke 9: 49–50)

38.	John said to him, "Teacher, we saw someone who doesn`t follow us casting out demons in your name; and we forbade him, because he doesn`t follow us."
39.	But Jesus said, "Don`t forbid him, for there is no one who will do a mighty work in my name, and be able quickly to speak evil of me.
40.	For whoever is not against us is on our side.

The disciples were dismayed because other people copied Jesus by casting out demons – probably other Essenes who practiced their healing skills. However, Jesus regarded them as allies.

THE GOSPEL OF MATTHEW

The unique parts of Matthew, which do not also appear in Q and Mark, must be scrutinized next.

The Multitudes Seek Jesus

Matthew 4: 23–25

23.	Jesus went about in all Galilee, teaching in their synagogues, preaching the gospel of the kingdom, and healing every disease and every sickness among the people.
24.	The report about him went forth into all Syria. They brought to him all who were sick, afflicted with various diseases and torments, possessed with demons, epileptics, and paralytics; and he healed them.
25.	Great multitudes from Galilee, Decapolis, Jerusalem, Judea and from beyond the Jordan followed him.

This passage demonstrates that Jesus was a popular teacher and healer and that people flocked to see and hear him. He must have been a charismatic figure and people felt drawn to him. He somehow managed to heal people with psycho-somatic ailments, caused by the stress brought about by poverty and the repression by the Roman authorities, as well as cases of paralysis and epilepsy. All these conditions were seen as the work of stinking septic spirits.

Jesus Heals Peter's Mother-in-Law

Matt 8: 14–18

14.	When Jesus came into Peter`s house, he saw his wife`s mother lying sick of a fever.
15.	He touched her hand, and the fever left her. She got up and served him.
16.	When evening came, they brought to him many possessed with demons. He cast out the spirits with a word, and healed all who were sick;
17.	that it might be fulfilled which was spoken through Isaiah the prophet, saying: "He took our infirmities, and bore our diseases."

This passage records some healings performed by Jesus, including the mother-in-law of Peter. Matthew regarded this as the fulfillment of Isaiah 53: 4 where it is said of the suffering servant of God: "Surely he has borne our infirmities, and carried our sorrows; yet we esteemed him stricken, struck of God, and afflicted."

It is clear that being sick and being invaded by a destructive demon were regarded as synonyms.

A Mute Man

Matt 9: 32–34

32.	As they went forth, behold, there was brought to him a mute man who was demon possessed.
33.	When the demon was cast out, the mute man spoke. The multitudes marveled, saying, "Nothing like this has ever been seen in Israel!"
34.	But the Pharisees said, "By the prince of the demons, he casts out demons."

Jesus' fame as a healer spread far and wide. He healed a mute man by scaring away the evil spirit suspected of causing his condition. Some Pharisees accused him of expelling the demons by the power he had received from Satan, the prince of the demons.

The Judgment

Matt 25: 31–33. 41

31.	"But when the Son of Man comes in his glory, and all the holy angels with him, then will he sit on the throne of his glory.
32.	Before him all the nations will be gathered, and he will separate them one from another, as the shepherd separates the sheep from the goats.
33.	He will set the sheep on his right hand, but the goats on the left.
41.	Then will he say also to them on the left hand, `Depart from me, you cursed, into the eternal fire which is prepared for the devil and his angels…

This is an excerpt of Jesus' parable of the sheep and the goats. He made it clear that the godless people, who didn't practice any charity and hospitality, would be assigned on Judgment Day to the eternal fire that was prepared for the devil and his angels – as described in Enoch and the Book of Jubilees.

THE GOSPEL OF LUKE

Luke's Gospel contains some material that doesn't come from the Q Document or Mark. The following texts must be examined:

Jesus Teaches and Heals

Luke 6: 17–19

17.	He came down with them, and stood on a level place, with a crowd of his disciples, and a great number of the people from all Judea and Jerusalem, and the sea coast of Tyre and Sidon, who came to hear him, and to be healed of their diseases;
18.	also those who were troubled with unclean spirits, and they were being healed.
19.	All the multitude sought to touch him, for power came forth from him, and healed them all.

This passage merely relates that people came from far and wide, even from outside Palestine, to see and hear Jesus. He healed many who were infected by unclean spirits. He became a celebrity and a star.

Women who Accompanied Jesus

Luke 8: 1–3

1.	It happened soon afterwards, that he went about through cities and villages, preaching and bringing the good news of the kingdom of God, and with him the twelve,
2.	and certain women who had been healed of evil spirits and infirmities: Mary who was called Magdalene, from whom seven demons had gone out;
3.	and Joanna, the wife of Chuzas, Herod`s steward, Susanna; and many others; who ministered to them from their possessions.

Jesus had several companions who accompanied him during his campaign to recruit supporters while preaching his message about the coming kingdom of God. This group included his twelve disciples, as well as several women who shared their wealth with Jesus in accordance of the Essene tradition. Mary Magdalene, one of these women, was rescued from seven demons – an episode not described in any of the gospels and only briefly mentioned in Mark 16: 9.

Return of the Seventy-Two

Luke 10: 17–20

17.	The seventy returned with joy, saying, "Lord, even the demons are subject to us in your name."
18.	He said to them, "I saw Satan having fall like lightning from heaven.
19.	Behold, I give you authority to tread on serpents and scorpions, and over all the power of the enemy. Nothing will in any way hurt you.

20.	Nevertheless, don`t rejoice in this, that the spirits are subject to you, but rejoice that your names are written in heaven."

In a preceding passage, Luke 10: 1–12 (which is part of Q and corresponds with Matt 9: 37–38; 10: 7–16), Jesus sent out seventy–two of his supporters to spread his message regarding the coming kingdom of God.

Only Luke related how these messengers reported back, telling Jesus that they were able to help people contaminated by demons. Jesus replied that he had seen Satan fall like a thunderbolt from heaven. This may be an oblique reference to Enoch where it is described how the Archangel Michael threw the rebellious and sex-crazed angels out of heaven (Enoch 10: 12–15).

The disciples also got the promise that their names were written in heaven, somewhere between the stars. That guaranteed their immunity from attacks by the evil powers in the sky.

It is possible that the followers of Jesus who were able to drive evil spirits from ill people were either fellow-Essenes who received some training at Qumran in the healing arts, or were trained by Jesus himself in these skills.

Jesus Heals a Woman on the Sabbath

Luke 13: 10–17

10.	He was teaching in one of the synagogues on the Sabbath day.
11.	Behold, there was a woman who had a spirit of infirmity eighteen years, and she was bent over, and could in no way lift herself up.

12.	When Jesus saw her, he called her, and said to her, "Woman, you are freed from your infirmity."
13.	He laid his hands on her, and immediately she stood up straight, and glorified God.
14.	The ruler of the synagogue, being moved with indignation because Jesus had healed on the Sabbath, answered to the multitude, "There are six days in which men ought to work. Therefore come on those days and be healed, and not on the Sabbath day!"
15.	Therefore the Lord answered him, "You hypocrites! Doesn`t each one of you free his ox or his donkey from the stall on the Sabbath, and lead him away to water?
16.	Ought not this woman, being a daughter of Abraham, whom Satan had bound eighteen long years, to have been freed from this bondage on the Sabbath day?"
17.	As he said these things, all his adversaries were put to shame, and all the multitude rejoiced for all the glorious things that were done by him.

Jesus, as an Essene, thought that charity and compassion were more important than the observance of all sorts of ceremonial laws, like doing nothing at all on the Sabbath. His charitable deed was freeing a woman from bondage by Satan with her chronic condition.

Jesus Answers Herod

Luke 13: 31–33

31.	On that same day, some Pharisees came, saying to him, "Get out of here, and go away, for Herod wants to kill you."

32.	He said to them, "Go and tell that fox, 'Behold, I cast out demons and perform cures today and tomorrow, and the third day I complete my mission.
33.	Nevertheless I must go on my way today and tomorrow and the next day, for it can`t be that a prophet perish out of Jerusalem.'

There were some Pharisees who were well-disposed towards Jesus and they warned him against Herod Antipas, the superstitious ruler of Galilee, who regarded him as a resurrected John the Baptist and wanted to get rid of him.

Jesus sent a cheeky message back to Herod, calling him a sly fox and declaring that he still had work to do in Galilee, like casting out demons like Herod himself, before he had to go as a prophet to Jerusalem.

THE BOOK OF ACTS

The book of Acts contains a continuation of the story of the Gospel of Luke. Both were dedicated to a certain Theophilus by the unnamed author of both these books. Acts displays the same world-view as the Synoptic Gospels, as will become apparent when the following passages are analyzed:

Satan led Ananias to Tell a Lie

Acts 5: 1–4

1.	But a certain man named Ananias, with Sapphira, his wife, sold a possession,

2.	and kept back part of the price, his wife also being aware of it, and brought a certain part, and laid it at the apostles` feet.
3.	But Peter said, "Ananias, why has Satan filled your heart to lie to the Holy Spirit, and to keep back part of the price of the land?
4.	While you kept it, didn`t it remain your own? After it was sold, wasn`t it in your power? How is it that you have conceived this thing in your heart? You haven`t lied to men, but to God."

The first congregation of followers of Jesus in Jerusalem after his crucifixion, consisting mostly of Essenes, continued with the Essene tradition of sharing all their possessions. A couple, Ananias and Sapphira, sold a plot and claimed that they donated all the proceeds of the sale to the congregation, while secretly keeping a portion of it for themselves. Peter ascribed Ananias lie to the influence of Satan.

Jesus Healed those who were Oppressed by the Devil

Acts 10: 36–38

36.	The word which he sent to the children of Israel, preaching good news of peace by Jesus Christ (he is Lord of all):
37.	that spoken word you yourselves know, which was proclaimed throughout all Judea, beginning from Galilee, after the baptism which John preached;
38.	even Jesus of Nazareth, how God anointed him with the Holy Spirit and with power, who went about doing good,

	and healing all who were oppressed by the devil; for God was with him.

Peter, the leader of the apostles in Jerusalem, explained that Jesus healed those with diseases, caused by the devil.

Paul Calls a Sorcerer a Son of the Devil

Acts 13: 6–10

6.	When they had gone through the island to Paphos, they found a certain sorcerer, a false prophet, a Jew, whose name was Bar-Jesus,
7.	who was with the proconsul, Sergius Paulus, a man of understanding. The same called Barnabas and Saul to him, and sought to hear the word of God.
8.	But Elymas the sorcerer (for so is his name by interpretation) withstood them, seeking to turn aside the proconsul from the faith.
9.	But Saul, who is also called Paul, filled with the Holy Spirit, fastened his eyes on him,
10.	and said, "Full of all deceit and all cunning, you son of the devil, you enemy of all righteousness, will you not cease to pervert the right ways of the Lord?

This sorcerer, Bar Jesus or Elymas, tried to prevent Paul from proclaiming the gospel to the governor of the Island of Paphos. Paul accused him of being a son of the devil.

Paul was Called to the Pagans

Acts 26: 15–18

15.	I said, `Who are you, Lord?` He said, `I am Jesus, whom you persecute.
16.	But arise, and stand on your feet, for to this end have I appeared to you, to appoint you a servant and a witness both of the things which you have seen, and of the things which I will reveal to you;
17.	delivering you from the people, and from the Gentiles, to whom I send you,
18.	to open their eyes, that they may turn from darkness to light and from the power of Satan to God, that they may receive remission of sins and an inheritance among those who are sanctified by faith in me.`

Paul explained to King Herod Agrippa how it came that he was called by the exalted Jesus to open the eyes of the pagans so that they could escape from darkness to the light and from the clutches of Satan to God. In other words: Paul regarded pagan religions as the worship of Satan.

Paul Accused of Preaching Demons

Acts 17: 18

18.	Some of the Epicurean and Stoic philosophers also encountered him. Some said, "What does this babbler want to say?" Others said, "He seems to be advocating foreign demons," because he preached Jesus and the resurrection.

When Paul addressed the men of Athens, some philosophers accused him of advocating and promoting some foreign demons. If this account is accurate, it demonstrates that even learned Greek philosophers were convinced of the reality of demons.

Jewish Exorcists were Overpowered by a Man with Evil Spirits
Acts 19: 11–16

11.	God worked special miracles by the hands of Paul,
12.	insomuch that handkerchiefs or aprons were carried away from his body to the sick, and the evil spirits went out.
13.	But some of the itinerant Jews, exorcists, took on themselves to name over those who had the evil spirits the name of the Lord Jesus, saying, "We adjure you by Jesus whom Paul preaches."
14.	There were seven sons of one Sceva, a Jewish chief priest, who did this.
15.	The evil spirit answered, "Jesus I know, and Paul I know, but who are you?"
16.	The man in whom the evil spirit was leaped on them, and overpowered them, and prevailed against them, so that they fled out of that house naked and wounded.

While Paul was working in Ephesus, he managed to heal sick people and drive their evil spirits away. When Jewish exorcists, the sons of a certain high priest, tried the same, the man who had an evil spirit assaulted them and they fled, wounded and without their clothes.

This story tells us that there were Jewish exorcists active in the ancient world. The Greek word is ἐξορκιστης (*exorkistes*) and the English word is clearly derived from it. The ancient world knew of many such people who dismissed evil spirits from sick people by means of magic formulae and convoluted ceremonies.[153] These seven sons of Sceva tried to copy Paul's formula, with a disastrous outcome.

Acts 23: 8

8.	For the Sadducees say that there is no resurrection, neither angel, nor spirit; but the Pharisees confess all of these.

Paul was defending himself at a meeting of the Jewish Council. The parties of the Pharisees and the Sadducees reacted differently towards his testimony. We are informed that the Sadducees, the party to which most priests belonged, didn't believe in angels, spirits, and the resurrection of the dead. It is known that they argued that the Pentateuch, the five books attributed to Moses and containing the Israelite Law, nowhere mentions these notions and that such ideas, therefore, had no value or validity.[154]

HEBREWS

The so-called letter to the Hebrews is not really a letter, but rather an anonymous treatise or a sermon from the last part of the first century AD. The unknown author wanted to demonstrate that Jesus Christ is the final and perfect high priest and that Christianity is superior to Judaism, which was abolished with the destruction of the Jerusalem temple with its priesthood in AD 70.[155]

---

[153] Enc Brit, "Exorcism".

[154] Enc Brit, "Sadducees".

[155] Rylaarsdam, "Biblical Literature"; Enc Brit, "Hebrews".

Demons and evil spirits are nowhere mentioned in this book, although the reader often encounters angels. The devil is only mentioned once in the following passage:

The Devil's Power

Hebr 2: 14–16

14.	Since then the children have shared in flesh and blood, he [Christ] also himself in like manner partook of the same, that through death he might bring to nothing him who had the power of death, that is, the devil,
15.	and might deliver all of them who through fear of death were all their lifetime subject to bondage.
16,	For most assuredly, not to angels does he give help, but he gives help to the seed of Abraham.

The author of Hebrews thought that the devil had power of death. This expression is anything but clear but perhaps it was meant to convey the idea that the devil was king in the abyss, the abode of the fallen angels, demons, and godless people. He will be brought to "nothing" by Christ.

THE SERMNS AND DISCOURSES IN JOHN'S GOSPEL

Some followers and students of the Apostle John, who probably wrote the narrative parts of his gospel, completed the proto-gospel by adding dialogues, debates, and discourses purportedly spoken by Jesus. These parts actually contain the ideas and convictions of second- or third-generation Christians, towards the nineties of the first century AD – and not those of Jesus himself.[156]

The devil is mentioned twice in this part of the gospel:

Jesus Calls Judas a Devil

John 6: 68–71

68.	Simon Peter answered him, "Lord, to whom would we go? You have the words of eternal life.
69.	We have come to believe and know that you are the Christ, the Son of the living God."
70.	Jesus answered them, "Didn`t I choose you, the twelve, and one of you is a devil?"
71.	Now he spoke of Judas, the son of Simon Iscariot, for it was he who would betray him, being one of the twelve.

Jesus called Judas a devil when he betrayed him. The Greek word used for "devil", namely διάβολος *(diabolos)* means "(false) accuser or slanderer" – a good description of Judas.

The Jews are Children of the Devil

John 8: 44

44.	You are of your Father, the devil, and it is your desire to do the lusts of your father. He was a murderer from the beginning, and doesn`t stand in the truth, because there is no truth in him. When he speaks a lie, he speaks of his own; for he is a liar, and the father of it.

[156] Pretorius, *The Gospels,* 536–37.

According to Jesus, the Jews who opposed him were the children of the devil – not the children of Abraham. The devil is the father of the lie and the enemy of truth. He is, therefore, the source of all that is dishonest, untruthful, or without integrity.

The Jews Accuse Jesus of Having a Demon

John 7: 20

20.	The multitude answered, "You [Jesus] have a demon! Who seeks to kill you?"

John 8: 48–52

48.	Then the Jews answered him, "Don`t we say well that you are a Samaritan, and have a demon?"
49.	Jesus answered, "I don`t have a demon, but I honor my Father, and you dishonor me.
50.	But I don`t seek my own glory. There is one who seeks and judges.
51.	Most assuredly, I tell you, if a person keeps my word, he will never see death."
52.	Then the Jews said to him, "Now we know that you have a demon. Abraham died, and the prophets; and you say, `If a man keeps my word, he will never taste of death.`

There were Jews who opposed Jesus. They are reported as accusing Jesus of hallucinating or being over-suspicious. That was due to a demon that supposedly took hold of him. Jesus denied this, of course.

1, 2, AND 3 JOHN

Although the three short letters known as the letters of John, they must rather be regarded as the work of some of John's followers and students. The style and contents of these documents show some similarities with the discourse parts of the Gospel of John.[157]

These documents do not mention evil spirits or demons and the devil is only encountered once:

The Devil is the Source of Sin

1 John 3: 8–10

8.	He who sins is of the devil, for the devil has been sinning from the beginning. To this end the Son of God was revealed, that he might destroy the works of the devil.
9.	Whoever is born of God doesn`t commit sin, because his seed remains in him; and he can`t sin, because he is born of God.
10.	In this the children of God are revealed, and the children of the devil. Whoever doesn`t do righteousness is not of God, neither is he who doesn`t love his brother.

This passage differs from the book of Enoch where it is told that God ordered Michael to arrest the fallen angels and lock them up in the abyss. Here, we are informed that Jesus Christ, the Son of God, had the task of destroying the works of the devil.

The devil is portrayed as the source of evil, sin, and all that is bad and wicked.

[157] Rylaarsdam, "Biblical Lierature".

1 AND 2 PETER

Although the first Letter of Peter claims to have been written by the apostle of Jesus, most scholars are of the opinion that it was only written long after Peter's martyr death in the time of Nero during the sixties AD. Peter was a simple Galilean fisherman and the elegant Greek in this document seems to point to another author.

The second Letter of Peter is an expanded version of the earlier Letter of Jude. It was certainly not written by the apostle, but it is impossible to determine who wrote it and when.[158]

These letters seem to have been influenced indirectly by Enoch with a few references to the devil and fallen angels.

The Devil a Roaring Lion

1 Pet 5: 8–9

8.	Be sober and self-controlled. Be watchful. Your adversary the devil, walks about like a roaring lion, seeking whom he may devour.
9.	Withstand him steadfast in your faith, knowing that your brothers who are in the world are undergoing the same sufferings.

This passage tells us that the devil is dangerous, just like a lion in search of a prey. He must be withstood in faith – presumably by avoiding temptations and serving God more fervently.

Jesus Christ Overcame Evil Powers

1 Pet 3: 21–22

[158] Rylaarsdam, "Biblical Literature"; Enc Brit, "Peter, Letters of".

21.	This is a symbol of baptism, which now saves you - not the putting away of the filth of the flesh, but the answer of a good conscience toward God, through the resurrection of Jesus Christ,
22.	who is at the right hand of God, having gone into heaven, angels and authorities and powers being made subject to him.

The "angels and authorities and powers" are certainly references to fallen angels who have been defeated by Christ through his resurrection and ascension after having been crucified.

The Fallen Angels

2 Pet 2: 4–5

4.	For if God didn`t spare angels when they sinned, but cast them down to Tartarus, and committed them to pits of darkness, to be reserved to judgment;
5.	and didn`t spare the ancient world, but preserved Noah with seven others, a preacher of righteousness, when he brought a flood on the world of the ungodly;

As has been pointed out previously, this passage clearly refers to the account in Enoch of how the fallen angels were banished to the abyss – called "Tartarus" here.

REVELATION

The most puzzling book in the Bible, Revelation, has confused and confounded Bible students through the centuries. However, two recent scholars, Bruce Malina and Adelbert Scholtz, seem to have found the key for understanding Revelation.

Both demonstrated that the visions seen by the author, John of Patmos, were simply descriptions of the astrological constellations and planets in the night sky, as well as the description of natural phenomena, such as a volcanic outburst and a swarm of locusts. Scholtz was even able to date most visions with the help of the computerized recreation of the night sky during AD 96.[159]

Satan and his demons and other allies as the enemies of God and the saints play an important role in the book of Revelation – more than in any other biblical book. It will be worthwhile to investigate how these characters are dealt with in this book. No detailed attention will be given to explanations of the astrological phenomena that John saw – only his message regarding the victory of Jesus Christ over Satan and the demons will be argued.

The Swarm of Locusts

Rev 9: 1–21

1.	The fifth angel sounded, and I saw a star from the sky fallen to the earth. The key to the pit of the abyss was given to him.
2.	He opened the pit of the abyss, and smoke went up out of the pit, like the smoke from a great furnace. The sun and the air were darkened because of the smoke from the pit.

[159] Malina, *On the Genre and Message of Revelation;* Malina and Pilch, *Social-Science Commentary*; Scholtz, *Revelation.*

3.	Then out of the smoke came forth locusts on the earth, and power was given to them, as the scorpions of the earth have power.
4.	They were told that they should not hurt the grass of the earth, neither any green thing, neither any tree, but only those men who don`t have God`s seal on their foreheads.
5.	They were given power not to kill them, but to torment them for five months. Their torment was like the torment of a scorpion, when it strikes a man.
6.	In those days men will seek death, and will in no way find it. They will desire to die, and death will flee from them.
7.	The shapes of the locusts were like horses prepared for war. On their heads were something like gold crowns, and their faces were like men`s faces.
8.	They had hair like women`s hair, and their teeth were like those of lions.
9.	They had breastplates, like breastplates of iron. The sound of their wings was like the sound of chariots, or of many horses rushing to war.
10.	They have tails like those of scorpions, and stings. In their tails is their power to harm men for five months.
11.	They have over them as king the angel of the abyss. His name in Hebrew is "Abaddon," but in Greek, he has the name "Apollyon."
12.	The first woe is past. Behold, there are still two woes coming after this.
13.	The sixth angel sounded. I heard a voice from the horns of the golden altar which is before God,

14.	saying to the sixth angel who had one trumpet, "Free the four angels who are bound at the great river Euphrates."
15.	The four angels were freed who had been prepared for that hour and day and month and year, so that they would kill one third of mankind.
16.	The number of the armies of the horsemen was two hundred million. I heard the number of them.
17.	Thus I saw the horses in the vision, and those who sat on them, having breastplates of fiery red, hyacinth blue, and sulfur yellow; and the heads of lions. Out of their mouths proceed fire, smoke, and sulfur.
18.	By these three plagues were one third of mankind killed: by the fire, the smoke, and the sulfur, which proceeded out of their mouths.
19.	For the power of the horses is in their mouths, and in their tails. For their tails are like serpents, and have heads, and with them they harm.
20.	The rest of mankind, who were not killed with these plagues, didn`t repent of the works of their hands, that they wouldn`t worship demons, and the idols of gold, and of silver, and of brass, and of stone, and of wood; which can neither see, nor hear, nor walk.
21.	They didn`t repent of their murders, nor of their sorceries, nor of their sexual immorality, nor of their thefts.

The previous chapter in Revelation described a volcano that erupted – most likely the volcano on the island of Nisyros to the south of Patmos where John was staying as an exile (Rev 1: 9). Out of the smoke rising from the volcano, a swarm of locusts appeared – most likely blown over from Africa by a strong southerly wind. It was not an unknown phenomenon.

John interpreted the volcano with its flying blobs of glowing lava as the entrance to the abyss and he got the impression that the locusts flew out of this abyss.[160]

This locust plague had a catastrophic impact upon the small island of Patmos and, therefore, John described these insects in superlative and exaggerated terms.

John wrote that the king of the locusts was called Abaddon (Greek: 'Αβαδδών). This is the Greek rendering of a Hebrew name אֲבַדּוֹן – *Abaddon*), which is encountered in Job 26: 6; Job 28: 22; Prov 15: 11; and Prov 27: 20. It denotes the ruling angel of the underworld, the abode of the dead and it means "destroyer". John translated this Hebrew word with Apollyon (Greek: 'Απολλύων), with which he meant the angel of the bottomless pit. The Greek word also means "destroyer" or "killer". In other words: John was under the impression that the locusts came forth from the abyss (the volcano).

The fifth trumpet heralded a star falling to the earth – probably a blazing lump of lava shot out fron the volcano. That must have been a symbol of Satan who was expelled from heaven (Rev 11: 7; Rev 17: 8; Rev 20: 1-3; Luke 10: 18; 1 Tim 3: 6; 2 Pet 2: 4; Jud 1: 6). He was thrown into the abyss and the angel with the fifth trumpet received the key to open the abyss.

---

[160] Scholtz, *Revelation,* 159–63.

Angel with the Key to the Bottomless Pit – Albrecht Dürer, 1498

This abyss or pit is not hell and Satan will only be banished to hell after Judgment Day. In the time between Jesus' resurrection and his second coming, Satan is only bound – not annihilated.

Since the angel of the abyss, Apollyon or Satan, was the king of the locusts, John saw these insects as demons or evil spirits. God allowed them to torment humans as a warning that they should turn away from their evil ways, idolatry, and paganism.

Where the first four trumpets unleashed horrors onto the world at large, the fifth and sixth trumpets targeted human beings – especially those who were guilty of the following six sins:

- The worship of demons (i e astrological signs);
- The worship of inanimate idols made of gold, silver, brass, stone, and wood;
- Murder;
- Sorceriy;
- Sexual promiscuity; and
- Theft.

The number of six sins is a symbolic number pointing to sinful man who strives unsuccessfully to reach the holy number of seven. Man was also created on the sixth day of creation, according to Genesis 1. The intention is to convey the message that every conceivable human sin was covered by the list. Five of these six sins are explicitly forbidden in the Ten Commandments.[161]

The Pregnant Woman and the Red Dragon

Rev 12: 1–17

1.	A great sign was seen in heaven: a woman clothed with the sun, and the moon under her feet, and on her head a crown of twelve stars.
2.	She was with child. She cried out, laboring and in pain, giving birth.

[161] Scholtz, *Revelation,* 158–165.

3.	Another sign was seen in heaven. Behold, a great red dragon, having seven heads and ten horns, and on his heads seven crowns.
4.	His tail drew one third of the stars of the sky, and threw them to the earth. The dragon stood before the woman who was about to give birth, so that when she gave birth he might devour her child.
5.	She gave birth to a son, a male child, who is to rule all the nations with a rod of iron. Her child was caught up to God, and to his throne.
6.	The woman fled into the wilderness, where she has a place prepared by God, that there they may nourish her one thousand two hundred sixty days.
7.	There was war in the sky. Michael and his angels made war on the dragon. The dragon and his angels made war.
8.	They didn`t prevail, neither was a place found for him any more in heaven.
9.	The great dragon was thrown down, the old serpent, he who is called the Devil and Satan, the deceiver of the whole world. He was thrown down to the earth, and his angels were thrown down with him.
10.	I heard a loud voice in heaven, saying, "Now is come the salvation, the power, and the kingdom of our God, and the authority of his Christ; for the accuser of our brothers has been thrown down, who accuses them before our God day and night.

11.	They overcame him because of the Lamb`s blood, and because of the word of their testimony. They didn`t love their life, even to death.
12.	Therefore rejoice, heavens, and you who dwell in them. Woe for the earth and for the sea, because the devil has gone down to you, having great wrath, knowing that he has but a short time."
13.	When the dragon saw that he was thrown down to the earth, he persecuted the woman who gave birth to the male child.
14.	Two wings of the great eagle were given to the woman, that she might fly into the wilderness to her place, where she was nourished for a time, and times, and half a time, from the face of the serpent.
15.	The serpent spewed water out of his mouth after the woman like a river, that he might cause her to be carried away by the stream.
16.	The earth helped the woman, and the earth opened its mouth and swallowed up the river which the dragon spewed out of his mouth.
17.	The dragon grew angry with the woman, and went away to make war with the rest of her seed, who keep God`s commandments and hold Jesus` testimony.

The following astrological phenomena were observed by John during the night of 17 June AD 96:

- Virgo (the Virgin – a symbol of Israel), with the last rays of the sun as a cloak:
- The moon (64% of its surface illuminated) at the feet of Virgo;

- The planet Jupiter, also at the feet of Virgo – a symbol for Jesus Christ who was born in Israel;
- The planet Saturn, the planet connected to Saturday, the Israelite holy day, inside Virgo, and emphasizing the connection between Virgo and Israel;
- Scorpius (the Scorpion), symbolizing Satan;
- Ophiuchus (the Serpent Catcher) – the archangel Michael;
- Coma Berenices (the Crown or Hair of Berenice), the crown of twelve stars on top of Virgo;
- Serpens (the Serpent) – another symbol of Satan;
- Corvus (the Crow), the wings given to the woman; and
- Hydra (the Water Snake) – the stream of water sent by Satan.

Chapter 12 contains a brief biography of Jesus Christ, written in symbolic language. Jesus was born as a member of the nation of Israel and destined to become a king, since his mother had a royal status with her crown of twelve stars, representing the twelve tribes of Israel.

The people of Israel were called the wife of God in the Old Testament. In Isa 54: 5–6 one reads:

> "For your Maker is your husband; Yahweh of Hosts is his name: and the Holy One of Israel is your Redeemer; the God of the whole earth shall he be called. For Yahweh has called you as a wife forsaken and grieved in spirit, even a wife of youth, when she is cast off, says your God."

The male child – Jesus Christ – was destined to rule the nations with a rod of iron – a reference to Ps 2: 9.

The dragon threw one third of the stars from the sky with his tail (there is indeed a dark spot in the Milky Way next to the tail of Scorpius). That is a reference to the fact that Satan managed to recruit angels to support his rebellion against God and that they were thrown out of heaven and were turned into evil spirits or demons. This thought is repeated in Jud 1: 6 – "Angels who didn`t keep their first domain, but deserted their own dwelling place, He [God] has kept in everlasting bonds under darkness for the judgment of the great day" (see also 2 Pet 2: 4).

Albrecht Dürer: The Virgin on the Crescent

The woman of Rev 12 was often seen as the Virgin Mary, the mother of Jesus. She was depicted with a crown consisting of twelve stars and a crescent moon at her feet. This identification does not fit into the bigger picture of this chapter.

Satan did his best to destroy Jesus, which happened when Herod the Great had all the male children below two years of age killed in Bethlehem, but also when Jesus was crucified and his life blood flowed away. However, Jesus was resurrected and taken up into heaven. This was traditionally regarded as a fulfilment of the first prophecy in the Bible, namely Gen 3: 15, where God told the snake: "I will put enmity between you and the woman, and between your offspring and her offspring. He will bruise your head, and you will bruise his heel."

This amounted to a victory over the powers of darkness and Satan and his angels were defeated by the Archangel Michael and his army of angels. The evil spirits were forced out of heaven – although they were not totally annihilated. This is certainly a reference to the events described in the book of Enoch.

The woman, symbolizing all the faithful from Israel, as well as the New Testament, had to flee to the desert – a harsh and difficult environment. The faithful were persecuted by the dark powers, but God looked after his children, even though they had to endure hardship. Satan tried to persecute all her offspring.[162]

The Beast from the Sea and the Beast from the Earth

Rev 13: 1–18.

1. Then I stood on the sand of the sea. I saw a beast coming up out of the sea, having ten horns and seven heads. On his horns were ten crowns, and on his heads, blasphemous names.
2. The beast which I saw was like a leopard, and his feet were like those of a bear, and his mouth like the mouth of a lion. The dragon gave him his power, his throne, and great authority.
3. One of his heads looked like it had been wounded fatally. His fatal wound was healed, and the whole earth marveled at the beast.

[162] Scholtz, *Revelation,* 191–96.

4.	They worshipped the dragon, because he gave his authority to the beast, and they worshipped the beast, saying, "Who is like the beast? Who is able to make war with him?"
5.	A mouth speaking great things and blasphemy was given to him. Authority to continue for forty-two months was given to him.
6.	He opened his mouth for blasphemy against God, to blaspheme his name, and his tent, those who dwell in heaven.
7.	It was given to him to make war with the saints, and to overcome them. Authority over every tribe, people, language, and nation was given to him.
8.	All who dwell on the earth will worship him, everyone whose name has not been written from the foundation of the world in the book of life of the Lamb who has been killed.
9.	If anyone has an ear, let him hear.
10.	If anyone gathers into captivity, into captivity he goes. If anyone will kill with the sword, with the sword he must be killed. Here is the patience and the faith of the saints.
11.	I saw another beast coming up out of the earth. He had two horns like a lamb, and he spoke like a dragon.
12.	He exercises all the authority of the first beast in his presence. He makes the earth and those who dwell in it to worship the first beast, whose fatal wound was healed.
13.	He performs great signs, even making fire come down out of the sky on the earth in the sight of men.
14.	He deceives my own people who dwell on the earth because of the signs which it was given him to do in front of the beast; saying to those who dwell on the earth, that they

	should make an image to the beast who had the sword wound and lived.
15.	It was given to him to give breath to it, to the image of the beast, that the image of the beast should both speak, and cause as many as wouldn`t worship the image of the beast to be killed.
16.	He causes all, the small and the great, the rich and the poor, and the free and the slave, to be given a mark on their right hand, or on their forehead;
17.	and that no one would be able to buy or to sell, unless he has that mark, the name of the beast or the number of his name.
18.	Here is wisdom. He who has understanding, let him calculate the number of the beast, for it is the number of a man. His number is six hundred sixty-six.

While standing on one of the beaches on Patmos, John watched the stars in the sky and saw two beasts, the constellations of Cetus (the Sea Monster) and Capricornus (the Goat with the tail of a fish). They symbolized for him the two most important allies of the devil, namely the Antichrist (1 John 2: 18-22) and the False Prophet (Matt 7: 15; 24: 11 & 24).

The Antichrist must be seen as Satan's agent on earth. It is the personification of all antichristian forces in the world, but it also signifies a figure that is expected to appear in the period before Christ's second coming. This monster received a deadly wound from which he recovered – in imitation of Christ who died on the cross and was resurrected. The Antichrist is, therefore, a personage or figure who imitates Christ and who gains power over the world.

John said that the Antichrist's activities would only be for a limited time, namely 42 months. This period of time also occurs in

Rev 11: 2–3 and Rev 12: 6 where it is given as three-and-a-half years or 1 260 days. This period of 42 months is the product of 7 X 6.

Seven, the sacred number, symbolizes God's work; there were seven days of creation, for instance. Six symbolizes sinful and godless man's unsuccessful endeavor to deify himself and also to reach the perfect number of seven. The creation of man took place on the sixth day of creation, according to Gen 1: 26–31. This period of 42 months is therefore the time in which God is busy with a godless mankind until the final Judgment arrives – a limited time that is sure to end but which is characterized by man's rebellion and blasphemy against God.

The monster from the earth is called the "False Prophet" in Rev 19: 20. We may see him as the chief of the propaganda department of the Antichrist. He had two horns like a lamb, but he spoke like the dragon, like Satan. He made the impression of being Christ-like but he actually served the forces of evil. It was his object of controlling all financial and economic resources by allowing only his followers to participate in the business world. This figure may be seen as an allegory or personification of paganism and all false religions in the world.

The beast from the sea, the Antichrist, had a secret sign and a number, namely "six hundred sixty-six" or 666. His followers were to receive his sign or mark on their foreheads or their right hands and only people with this mark would be allowed to do business. That this number was associated with the beast from the sea and not the beast from the earth is clear from Rev 15: 2 where John mentioned "the beast, and his image, and the number of his name, standing on the sea". This sign or number represented a specific man's name.

Various explanations have been given through the centuries for this mysterious number. Malina correctly pointed out that the number 666 is a triangular number. It is the sum of all the numbers between 1 and 36 (6 X 6 or 6^2). These numbers can be arranged in the form of a triangle with only the 1 in the first row, 2 and 3 in the second row, 4, 5, and 6 in the third row and so forth until the last row between 29 and 36 is reached.[163] This triangle can be seen as the Greek letter delta (Δ).[164].

There is the very distinct possibility that John had the Roman Emperor Domitian, whose full name and title in Latin was Caesar Domitianus Augustus, in mind with the number of 666, which was another way of reaching a triangle, which formed the Greek letter delta (Δ). After all, the spelling of the emperor's name in Greek is Δομετιανὸς (*Dometianos*) – a name that starts with the Δ.[165] That this conclusion is warranted is confirmed by Rev 17: 11 where the beast was identified as the eighth king or emperor. Domitian was indeed the eighth emperor of the Roman Empire.[166]

When the rest of Rev 13 is investigated it turns out that the description of the Antichrist by John of Patmos fits Domitian very well. First of all, it must be remembered that John did not focus on

---

[163] The triangle of numbers that gives a total of 666 is as follows:

1+
2+ 3+
4+ 5+ 6+
7+ 8+ 9+ 10+
11+ 12+ 13+ 14+ 15+
16+ 17+ 18+ 19+ 20+ 21+
22+ 23+ 24+ 25+ 26+ 27+ 28+
29+ 30+ 31+ 32+ 33+ 34+ 35+ 36 =
666

[164] Malina, *On the Genre and Message of Revelation,* 185–87.

[165] See Eusebius: Liber III/XVIII/1–5 for the Greek spelling of the emperor's name.

[166] Wikipedia, "List of Roman Emperors". The predecessors of Doamitian were Augustus, Tiberius, Caligula, Claudius, Nero, Vespasian, and Titus.

the far future as other authors of the New Testament may have done; his book dealt with his own time and the immediate future (Rev 1: 1-3 & 19; Rev 4: 1; Rev 22: 6 & 10). One has, therefore, to look for a figure from his own time. This figure had authority over "every tribe, people, language, and nation" and that could only apply to the emperor in Rome who ruled over an empire stretching from the British Isles to North Africa to Mesopotamia. He was the ultimate antichrist of those times by persecuting Christians like John.

John wrote that this beast had received a deadly wound from which he recovered (Rev 13: 3). That must be an allusion to military setbacks that Domitian's army had suffered when he lost more than two whole legions along the Danube during the eighties, a conspiracy by some senators in September AD 87, and a rebellion by the governor of Upper Germany in AD 89.[167]

Domitian insisted on being worshipped as a living god and to be addressed as "dominus et deus" (master and god). John confirmed this by writing that "the whole earth... worshipped the beast, saying, 'Who is like the beast? Who is able to make war with him?'" (Rev 13: 3–4). John added: "All who dwell on the earth will worship him" (Rev 13: 8).

The beast from the sea had an ally, the beast from the earth, the False Prophet or the personification of paganism and all false religions. According to John, this beast made images of the first beast for the people to worship (Rev 13: 14). This happened when temples for the cult of the emperors, including Domitian, were also erected in cities in Asia Minor, such as Smyrna and Pargamum (see Rev 2 and 3).

The False Prophet also performed "great signs" (or "miracles" – Rev 13: 13). It is known that pagan religions in the Roman Empire widely used magic or what passed for magic to

---

167 Chilver, "Domitian"; Wasson, "Domitian",

impress the masses. Soothsayers, oracles, sorcerers, magicians, and witches were widely active throughout the Roman-Greek world.[168]

We find an unholy and evil trinity in Rev 12 and 13 – the dragon, the beast from the sea and the beast from the earth. That is, the unholy alliance of Satan, the Antichrist, and the False Prophet – in other words, the partnership of the devil, Emperor Domitian, and paganism. Although they had political, military, and religious power, John was convinced that they would eventually be conquered and condemned to eternal damnation (Rev 20: 11–15).

We may safely conclude that John felt vindicated that his prophecies were accurate after Domitian had been assassinated on 18 September AD 96 and John was allowed to return home when he edited his notes on his visions and completed the final edition of his prophetic book.[169]

The Seven Bowls of God's Anger

Rev 16: 1–16

1.	I heard a loud voice out of the temple, saying to the seven angels, "Go and pour out the seven bowls of the wrath of God on the earth!"
2.	The first went, and poured out his bowl into the earth, and it became a harmful and evil sore on the men that had the mark of the beast, and that worshipped his image.
3.	The second angel poured out his bowl into the sea, and it became blood as of a dead man. Every living thing in the sea died.

[168] Greenwood & Airey, *Encyclopaedia of Witchcraft*: 24–25 – see also Acts 8: 9, 18–24; 13: 6-8; 16: 16 & 19: 13–19; Gal 5: 20.
[169] Scholtz, *Revelation,* 199–210.

4.	The third poured out his bowl into the rivers and springs of water, and it became blood.
5.	I heard the angel of the waters saying, "You are righteous, who are and who were, you Holy One, because you judged this way.
6.	For they poured out the blood of the saints and the prophets, and you have given them blood to drink. They deserve this."
7.	I heard the altar saying, "Yes, Lord God, the Almighty, true and righteous are your judgments."
8.	The fourth poured out his bowl on the sun, and it was given to him to scorch men with fire.
9.	Men were scorched with great heat, and they blasphemed the name of God who has the power over these plagues. They didn`t repent and give him glory.
10.	The fifth poured out his bowl on the throne of the beast, and his kingdom was darkened. They gnawed their tongues because of the pain,
11.	and they blasphemed the God of heaven because of their pains and their sores. They didn`t repent of their works.
12.	The sixth poured out his bowl on the great river, the Euphrates. Its water was dried up, that the way might be made ready for the kings that come from the sunrise.
13.	I saw coming out of the mouth of the dragon, and out of the mouth of the beast, and out of the mouth of the false prophet, three unclean spirits, something like frogs;
14.	for they are spirits of demons, performing signs; which go forth to the kings of the whole world, to gather them together for the war of the great day of God, the Almighty.

15.	"Behold, I come like a thief. Blessed is he who watches, and keeps his clothes, so that he doesn`t walk naked, and they see his shame."
16.	He gathered them together into the place which is called in Hebrew, "Har-magedon."

The seven plagues, represented by the seven stars of Ursa Major (the Big Bear), and dispatched by the seven angels/stars in front of God's throne at the northern celestial pole, are as follows:

- Terrible and painful sores on unbelievers
- The water of sea turned into blood and the marine creatures died
- The water supplies on land turned into undrinkable blood
- The sun shone with all its power and caused a heat wave
- Darkness fell on the sea beast's kingdom and people felt pain
- The river Euphrates dried up, enabling the kings of the East (literally: from the rising sun) to advance with their armies to do battle at Armageddon, while unclean spirits like frogs came forth from the two beasts
- Thunder, sounds, an earthquake and hail stones.

Before the final judgment could take place, cosmic battles had to be fought between the forces of darkness (Satan) and the forces of light (the Lamb, that is, the exalted Jesus Christ). During these battles all sorts of woes were to hit the earth and these could be seen as cloak repetitions for the final judgment of God. God sent these woes through his angels or messengers to warn a godless world, as well as the adulterous city of Jerusalem (presented here as Babylon) that rejected Jesus Christ, that He could not tolerate conditions as they were, and that the final judgement would come unexpectedly as a thief in the night. For John, just as for his contemporaries, earthquakes, thunder, lightning, and other natural phenomena were regarded as supernatural events and it is no surprise that he incorporated these into his visions and pictured them as direct acts of God to warn an evil world.

John added that “men blasphemed God” on account of all the disasters. That meant that mankind in general did not heed all God’s warnings. It may also mean that John interpreted the volcano, earthquakes, and other disastrous events as acts of God to the people of Patmos in an effort to convince them to denounce paganism but that it had the opposite effect; instead of repenting, these people cursed John’s God for causing all these difficulties.

Nevertheless, John was convinced that God stayed in control of events on earth and that He placed constraints on the kingdom of Satan so that he and his allies could not do what they wanted. Satan and all evil forces, demons and pagans included, would be totally squashed and wiped out at the symbolic battle of Armageddon, followed by the Day of Judgment.[170]

The Great Prostitute

Rev 17: 1–18

1.	One of the seven angels who had the seven bowls came and spoke with me, saying, "Come here. I will show you the judgment of the great prostitute who sits on many waters,
2.	with whom the kings of the earth committed sexual immorality, and those who dwell in the earth were made drunken with the wine of her sexual immorality."
3.	He carried me away in the Spirit into a wilderness. I saw a woman sitting on a scarlet-colored animal, full of blasphemous names, having seven heads and ten horns.

[170] Scholtz, *Revelation,* 226–33.

4.	The woman was dressed in purple and scarlet, and decked with gold and precious stones and pearls, having in her hand a golden cup full of abominations, even the unclean things of her sexual immorality,
5.	and on her forehead a name written, "MYSTERY, BABYLON THE GREAT, THE MOTHER OF THE PROSTITUTES AND OF THE ABOMINATIONS OF THE EARTH."
6.	I saw the woman drunken with the blood of the saints, and with the blood of the martyrs of Jesus. When I saw her, I wondered with great amazement.
7.	The angel said to me, "Why do you wonder? I will tell you the mystery of the woman, and of the beast that carries her, which has the seven heads and the ten horns.
8.	The beast that you saw was, and is not; and is about to come up out of the abyss, and to go into destruction. Those who dwell on the earth will wonder, whose name has not been written in the book of life from the foundation of the world, when they see the beast, how that he was, and is not, and will come.
9.	Here is the mind that has wisdom. The seven heads are seven mountains, on which the woman sits.
10.	They are seven kings. Five have fallen, the one is, the other is not yet come. When he comes, he must continue a little while.
11.	The beast that was, and is not, is himself also an eighth, and is of the seven; and he goes to destruction.
12.	The ten horns that you saw are ten kings, who have received no kingdom as yet, but they receive authority as kings, with the beast, for one hour.

13.	These have one mind, and they give their power and authority to the beast.
14.	These will war against the Lamb, and the Lamb will overcome them, for he is Lord of lords, and King of kings. They also will overcome who are with him, called and chosen and faithful."
15.	He said to me, "The waters which you saw, where the prostitute sits, are peoples, multitudes, nations, and languages.
16.	The ten horns which you saw, and the beast, these will hate the prostitute, and will make her desolate and naked, and will eat her flesh, and will burn her utterly with fire.
17.	For God has put in their hearts to do what he has in mind, and to come to unity of mind, and to give their kingdom to the beast, until the words of God should be accomplished.
18.	The woman whom you saw is the great city, which reigns over the kings of the earth."

The prophet John was amazed when the angel showed him this vision since it was, in a certain sense, a replay of the vision he had described in chapter 12, a few weeks earlier. On that occasion, he saw a pregnant woman, clothed with the sun, with a crown of twelve stars on her head and with the moon at her feet. She brought a male child into the world while she was attacked by a red dragon. She managed to flee to the desert. Her child was taken to God's throne and the archangel Michael fought the dragon with its seven heads and ten horns.

This previous vision occurred when the constellation Virgo was setting in the west, with the last rays of the sun over her head and the moon at her feet. Her crown of twelve stars consisted of the constellation of Coma Berenices, the Crown or Hair of Berenice. Her male child was the planet Jupiter – a symbol for Jesus Christ. Virgo was a symbol for Israel, the people from which Jesus Christ was born. The red dragon was the constellation of Scorpius with its prominent red star, Antares – a symbol for Satan. The archangel Michael was to be found in Ophiuchus, the Snake Catcher.

John saw a similar scene a few weeks later, most probably on 10 August. There was again this woman – the constellation of Virgo and now called a harlot – who sat on a red or scarlet animal or beast with its seven heads and ten horns. She was also seated "on many waters" – the Aegean Sea towards the west. She was covered with gold ornaments and precious stones. These consisted of the bright planets of Venus, Jupiter, and Saturn, together with a crown in the constellation of Coma Berenices. The crescent moon with 15% of its surface illuminated lay next to her. This constellation was again a representation of Israel. The red beast was again the constellation of Scorpius – the dragon of Rev 12 – which was to be seen adjacent to the constellation of Virgo.

It is no small wonder that John was amazed when he saw this scene, because it was the same woman from Rev 12 who had switched sides.

Where she was pursued by the dragon in the previous scene, she allied herself with this monster in the present scene. John saw her in the "wilderness" – the same spot where she fled in Rev 12: 14 after having been pursued by the dragon.

She was called a prostitute. In the Old Testament, the people of Israel were often accused of prostitution when they worshipped pagan gods and forgot their special relationship with their God, YHWH (Isa 57: 3; Nah 3: 4-5).

The beast is a symbol of Satan with blasphemous names written all over him. He seduced the woman to change her allegiance. She must again be seen as a symbol of Israel, the people who brought forth the Messiah, Jesus Christ – but who also rejected him in the end and demanded that the Roman governor, Pontius Pilate, order his crucifixion. For John, this amounted to prostitution.

The name Babylon was given to this woman. This name carries negative connotations in the Bible. In Genesis 11 one finds the Tower of Babel (Babylon) as a sign of man's rebellion against God. Babylon was also the place where the Judeans were taken into exile after Jerusalem was destroyed by the Babylonians. By giving the name of Babylon to this woman, John conveyed the idea that the woman symbolized something bad and godless.

It is clear from various passages that John had little sympathy for the Jews who did not accept Jesus Christ as their Messiah (Rev 2: 8; Rev 3: 9). He saw that as adultery and prostitution since Israel was supposed to be God's beloved wife on earth according to the Hebrew Scriptures. By rejecting Jesus as Messiah, the Jews became allies of the devil.

In the following chapter, Rev 18, John described the fall of Babylon – his secret name for Jerusalem:

> "After these things, I saw another angel coming down out of the sky, having great authority. The earth was illuminated with his glory. He cried with a mighty voice, saying, "Fallen, fallen is Babylon the great, and has become a habitation of demons, and a prison of every unclean spirit, and a prison of every unclean and hateful bird!" (Rev 18: 1–2).

The rest of this chapter is a description of God's judgment over Jerusalem when the city fell to the Roman legions at the end of the Jewish War of AD 66–70. All that remained was a destroyed city with dreadful demons and septic spirits as only inhabitants.

The Rider on the White Horse

Rev 19: 11–21

11..	I saw the heaven opened, and behold, a white horse, and he who sat on it is called Faithful and True. In righteousness he judges and makes war.
12.	His eyes are a flame of fire, and on his head are many crowns. He has names written and a name written which no one knows but he himself.
13.	He is clothed in a garment sprinkled with blood. His name is called "The Word of God."
14.	The armies which are in heaven followed him on white horses, clothed in white, pure, fine linen.
15.	Out of his mouth proceeds a sharp, two-edged sword, that with it he should strike the nations. He will rule them with a rod of iron. He treads the winepress of the fierceness of the wrath of God, the Almighty.
16.	He has on his garment and on his thigh a name written, "KING OF KINGS, AND LORD OF LORDS."
17.	I saw an angel standing in the sun. He cried with a loud voice, saying to all the birds that fly in the sky, "Come! Be gathered together to the great supper of God,
18.	that you may eat the flesh of kings, the flesh of captains, the flesh of mighty men, and the flesh of horses and of those who sit on them, and the flesh of all men, both free and slave, and small and great."
19.	I saw the beast, and the kings of the earth, and their armies, gathered together to make war against him who sat on the horse, and against his army.

20.	The beast was taken, and with him the false prophet who worked the signs in his sight, with which he deceived those who had received the mark of the beast and those who worshipped his image. They two were thrown alive into the lake of fire that burns with sulfur.
21.	The rest were killed with the sword of him who sat on the horse, the sword which came forth out of his mouth. All the birds were filled with their flesh.

This passage contains a description of the battle of Armageddon. The rider on the white horse, the commander of a huge army, is Jesus Christ. The outcome of the battle is a foregone conclusion: the forces of darkness and evil, the two beasts who are the allies of Satan, will be crushed and they will be hurled into the fires of hell. This will mean that the power of Satan will be broken.

The battle of Armageddon is usually seen as a big event just before Judgment Day, in the unknown future. John, though, described this battle as being fought in his own time and it will only end with Judgment Day and the return of Christ. It is the perpetual war between the forces of light and the forces of darkness.

Satan Bound for a Thousand Years

Rev 20: 1–15

1.	I saw an angel coming down out of heaven, having the key of the abyss and a great chain in his hand.
2.	He seized the dragon, the old serpent, which is the Devil and Satan, and bound him for one thousand years,
3.	and cast him into the abyss, and shut it, and sealed it over him, that he should deceive the nations no more, until the

	thousand years were finished. After this, he must be freed for a short time.
4.	I saw thrones, and they sat on them, and judgment was given to them. I saw the souls of those who had been beheaded for the testimony of Jesus, and for the word of God, and such as didn`t worship the beast nor his image, and didn`t receive the mark on their forehead and on their hand. They lived, and reigned with Christ one thousand years.
5.	The rest of the dead didn`t live until the thousand years were finished. This is the first resurrection.
6.	Blessed and holy is he who has part in the first resurrection. Over these, the second death has no power, but they will be priests of God and of Christ, and will reign with him one thousand years.
7.	And after the thousand years, Satan will be freed out of his prison,
8.	and will come forth to deceive the nations which are in the four corners of the earth, Gog and Magog, to gather them together to the war; the number of whom is as the sand of the sea.
9.	They went up over the breadth of the earth, and surrounded the camp of the saints, and the beloved city. Fire came down out of heaven, and devoured them.
10.	The devil who deceived them was thrown into the lake of fire and sulfur, where are also the beast and the false prophet. They will be tormented day and night forever and ever.

11.	I saw a great white throne, and him who sat on it, from whose face the earth and the heaven fled away. There was found no place for them.
12.	I saw the dead, the great and the small, standing before the throne. Books were opened. Another book was opened, which is the book of life. The dead were judged out of the things which were written in the books, according to their works.
13.	The sea gave up the dead who were in it. Death and Hades gave up the dead who were in them. They were judged, each one according to his works.
14.	Death and Hades were thrown into the lake of fire. This is the second death, the lake of fire.
15.	If anyone was not found written in the book of life, he was cast into the lake of fire

A popular explanation of this chapter sees in it a prophecy of a millennium, a kingdom on earth of Christ with the faithful, during which time Satan will be bound. At the end of this wonderful time, Satan will again be given his freedom. After a final battle, he will be tossed into the flames of hell. However, this explanation cannot be reconciled with all aspects of the text.

It must be stressed, first of all, that the book of Revelation does not deal with the far future, but with events of the present and the immediate future as seen from the perspective of John during the nineties of the first century AD (Rev 1: 1–3, 19; 22: 10).

This explanation presupposes that Christ will return twice – at the start of the millennium, and again for the final annihilation of Satan and all evil forces. The idea that Christ is to return twice is found nowhere else in the New Testament and it cannot be the case in this chapter either.

The thousand years must be seen as a symbolic number. It consists of 10 X 10 X 10 or 10^3. Ten is the number of God's work – just as there were ten plagues in Egypt and Ten Commandments given to Moses. The number of three points to the divine Trinity. This period of thousand years is, therefore, the time between Christ's resurrection and his second coming on Judgment Day.

Through his resurrection and ascension, he overpowered Satan and banished him to the abyss, the space below the earth where he was to be kept, while awaiting Judgment Day – a thought found in Enoch, the Book of Jubilees, and other parts of the New Testament (Matt 28: 18; Luke 10: 18; Joh 12: 31; Joh 16: 11; Col 2: 15; Heb 2: 14; 1 Joh 3: 8; 2 Pet 2: 4; Jud 1: 6). Collossians 2: 15, especially, compares this overpowering of Satan with a Roman general who held a triumphal parade through Rome with his prisoners-of-war as part of the procession.[171]

The first three verses of Rev 20 give a terrestrial perspective. Verses 4–6, on the other hand, describe alternatively a heavenly and a terrestrial scene. The thrones on which deceased martyrs were sitting can only be in heaven and in God's eternity, where time does not exist as on earth (Ps 90: 4 and 2 Pet 3: 8). It is affirmed that these dead people will only be resurrected at the end of the 1 000 years.

We cannot say that those who die are waiting somewhere until Judgment Day arrives and that they are then to be admitted into heaven. There are various biblical pronouncements that those who die are immediately taken up into heaven with spiritual bodies (Luke 16: 22, 23; Luke 23: 34; 2 Cor 5: 1; 2 Tim 4: 18 & Heb 9: 27) – although we, who are still alive on earth and bound to the passage of time, have to await Judgment Day, Resurrection Day, and the second coming of Christ sometime in the unknown future (Matt 25:

---

[171] Scholtz, *Revelation,* 270–73,

31– 46; 1 Cor 15: 23-24 & 1 Pet 1: 5).

The deceased martyrs of Rev 20: 4 are, therefore, in heaven. From a terrestrial perspective, this is still in the unknown future. Those who have died and have left the restraints of time, however, arrive at their eternal destinations immediately after they have died. These martyrs do not sit on thrones on earth during the symbolic period of 1 000 years; they are already experiencing heavenly bliss, together with Christ, while those who are still living on earth are experiencing the symbolic millennium, the period between Jesus' ascension and his expected second coming.[172]

Thrones on which the saints are to be seated are mentioned elsewhere in Revelation (Rev 3: 21; 4: 1–6; 4: 10–11; and 5: 8–9). In all these cases, these thrones are in heaven and that must also be the case with the thrones mentioned in Rev 20: 4.

Where Rev 20: 5 states that the rest of the dead were not resurrected until the end of the 1000 years, one has to realize that this is being said from a terrestrial point of view. When viewed from the dimension of time, Resurrection Day are still somewhere in the unknown future. The rest of the dead are, therefore, the people who were still alive in John's day and awaiting Judgment Day.

We also read of a "first resurrection" and a "second death". It is important to note that a *second resurrection* and a *first death* are nowhere mentioned and one cannot read those into the text.

In Rev 20: 14–15 the "second death" is called the "lake of fire" (hell). The "second death" is, therefore, eternal punishment and death. According to Rev 20: 4–5 the "first resurrection" is the resurrection into heavenly glory.

We must understand that these two strange ideas are somehow connected. They are, after all, mentioned in the same breath.

---

[172] Scholtz, *Revelation,* 274–76.

John, whose Greek was not quite up to standard, struggled to express himself and he tried to convey the idea that the resurrection of the blessed (the first resurrection) was far more desirable than eternal death (the second death). The (first) resurrection is, therefore, number one and (the second) eternal death is placed on number two in order of preference or desirability.[173]

Satan, together with all antichristian forces and false religions, will come with a final assault on the church and the faithful before the end. They will, however, not be successful because they will be dropped into hell ("the lake of fire and sulphur") at Christ's expected second coming – just as important prisoners-of-war were ritually executed at the end of a triumphal parade in the city of Rome. John quoted Enoch 10: 5 in this regard: "And on the day of the great judgment he [Azazel] shall be cast into the fire."[174]

Satan in the Abyss by Gustave Doré

IN A NUTSHELL

According to the Q Document, a substantial part of Jesus' ministry was devoted to the healing of sick people and to help them to get rid of sickening spirits. He had an encounter with the devil while fasting

[173] Scholtz, *Revelation,* 276.

[174] Scholtz, *Revelation,* 281

in the desert, but that was probably on account of hallucinations. Jealous Jews accused him of being an ally of the devil.

Although the early Proto-gospel of John describes seven "signs" or miracles by Jesus,[175] it is noticeable that Satan and demons are almost absent – in contrast with the later gospels where Satan and demons make abundant appearances. This may be an indication that the Proto-gospel of John, which was probably written by the apostle John himself or by somebody to whom he told his experiences with Jesus, may be more trustworthy regarding Jesus' attitude towards the devil and his assistants.[176] That means that the other gospels, written several decades after Jesus' time, may have exaggerated the role of demons and unclean spirits in cases where Jesus healed people from afflictions, maladies, and diseases.

Paul was a child of his time. As a young Jewish man, he studied the Scriptures in Jerusalem. He must have been familiar with Enoch and the Book of Jubilees – or, at least, have had contact with the ideas in those books. He believed in the existence of Satan as an unsavory character and an anarchistic angel, as well as demons as malignant monsters. Their fate was sealed and they would be finally vanquished on Judgment Day, although Christ had already broken their power.

He was certainly familiar with the pagan Greek world, but his Jewish abhorrence of paganism forced him to view pagan deities and idols as detestable demons.

A bad health issues – his thorn in the flesh – was caused by one of Satan's angry angels.

The devil, as God's abominable adversary, endeavored to lure Christians away from Christ or to make them disobedient towards God's directives. Christians could, though, rely on God and

[175] Pretorius, *Gospels,* 179.

[176] Pretorius, *Gospels,* 180–83.

the armament he provided to survive the spiritual war against Satan and his damnable demonic forces.

The Gospel of Mark contains ten reports about Jesus who healed people of their diseases by chasing away evil spirits. The idea that illness was caused by demons was part of the Jewish folk-lore during Jesus' time, first recorded in the Book of Jubilees.

This belief was, however, also wide-spread in the Hellenistic world. Many magical papyri from this period with formulae for dealing with sicknesses, demons, and other frightful forces are known. The practice of magic attempted to manipulate and control the world with its disastrous diseases and deceptive demons.[177]

It has already been shown that Enoch and the Book of Jubilees were held in high regard by the Essenes or Nazoreans, of which sect Jesus was a prominent member. This sect was also known as practitioners of the healing arts. It is, therefore, not a surprise that Jesus was often portrayed as healing the sick of their afflictions and ailments. Suffering from a sickness and being infested by a dirty demon were regarded as two sides of the same coin and, therefore, the evangelists often linked these two activities.

Satan was mentioned a few times in the Gospel of Mark, but he only appeared in person when Jesus was tempted in the desert after his baptism.

Matthew's unique parts contain a few references to evil spirits and the devil with his angels. One must conclude that Jesus and the people who witnessed his ministry were convinced that illness and disorders were caused by demons. They had no other explanations for these conditions with their lack of knowledge of medicine. Evil spirits were a reality because the unwelcome and unpleasant symptoms of various diseases proved that they existed.

---

[177] Rylaarsdam, "Biblical Literature".

The sources from which Luke took the passages quoted above clearly shared in the prevalent belief that maladies and afflictions were caused by invisible and ungraspable evil and horrible spirits. No other explanation was possible and nobody had any inkling of the role played by bacteria, viruses, toxic substances, malnutrition, or genetic deviations. Satan and his angels, the demons, were a frightening part of reality.

The book of Acts, which contains the story of the deeds of the apostles and the ministry of Paul, paid much less attention to the devil and evil spirits than the Synoptic Gospels. It appears, nevertheless, that Satan was seen as the deceiver who persuaded people to tell lies. The belief in the reality of demons was widespread and they were seen as the cause of disease.

It is noticeable that John's Gospel and letters paid much less attention to Satan and evil spirits. They were, nevertheless, a reality.

Satan is a major role player in the apocalyptic book of Revelation. Evil spirits also appear from time to time, inter alia in the form of a locust plague. Satan is the great enemy of God and he did his best to prevent the baby Jesus from growing up. The abyss, which was his abode, became a physical reality when a volcano spewed glowing lumps of lava into the sky.

While the Old Testament doesn't contain anything resembling the devil and where evil spirits were God's servants, the New Testament provides a radically different picture. That forces one to ask: How much of the numerous episodes where Satan and unclean spirits appear in the New Testament can be regarded as reliable and accurate descriptions of what had happened, or how much of these descriptions must be explained as primitive and pre-scientific superstition? Answers to this question will be suggested in the last chapter. Before that, the Qur'an must be scrutinized for the convictions of Muslims regarding Satan and evil spirits.

Chapter 8
SATAN IN THE MUSLIM SCRIPTURES

THE QUR'AN

The ideal situation would be if this discussion of the Muslim concept of Satan and evil spirits could have been presented with quotations in Arabic from the Qur'an. Unfortunately, the present author is not at all proficient in that language and he is totally dependent upon an English translation. The translation by the Muslim scholar MaulawI Sher 'AlI will be used.

This translation contains a comprehensive index of topics and a glossary at the end of the publication and that was invaluable in finding key texts regarding Satan and evil spirits in the Qur'an.

Iblis Banned from Heaven

Surah 7: 10 - 18

10. And as for those whose scales are light, it is they who shall have ruined their souls because of their being unjust to Our Signs.
11. And We have established you in the earth and provided for you therein the means of subsistence. How little thanks you give!
12. And We did create you *and* then We gave you shape; then said We to the angels, 'Submit to Adam;' and they *all* submitted but Iblis *did not;* he would not be of those who submit.
13. *God* said, 'What prevented thee from submitting when I commanded thee?' He said, 'I am better than he. Thou hast

	created me of fire while him hast Thou created of clay.'
14.	God said, 'Then go down hence; it is not for thee to be arrogant here. Get out; thou art certainly of those who are abased.'
15.	He said, 'Grant me respite till the day when they will be raised up.'
16.	*God* said, 'Thou shalt be of those who are given respite.'
17.	He said: 'Now, since Thou hast adjudged me as lost, I will assuredly lie in wait for them on Thy straight path.
18.	Then will I surely come upon them from before them and from behind them and from their right

Surah 17: 62–65

62.	And *remember the time* when We said to the angels, 'Submit to Adam,' and they *all* submitted, except Iblis. He said, 'Shall I submit to one whom Thou hast created of clay?'
63.	*And* he said, 'What thinkest Thou? *Can* this whom Thou hast honoured above me *be my superior'?* If Thou wilt grant me respite till the Day of Resurrection, I will most surely bring his descendants under my sway except a few.'
64.	He said, 'Begone! and whoso shall follow thee from among them, Hell shall surely be the recompense of you all- an ample recompense.
65.	'And entice whomsoever of them thou canst, with thy voice, and urge against them thy horsemen and thy footmen and be their partner.

Surah 18: 51–52

51.	*And remember the time* when We said to the angels, 'Submit to Adam,' and they *all* submitted except Iblis. He was one of

	the Jinn; and he disobeyed the command of his Lord. Will you then take him and his offspring for friends instead of Me while they are your enemies? Evil is the exchange for the wrongdoers.
52.	I did not make them witness the creation of the heavens and the earth, nor their own creation; nor could I take as helpers those who lead *people* astray.

Surah 38: 72–78

72.	When thy Lord said to the angels, 'I am about to create man from clay,
73.	'And so when I have fashioned him *in perfection,* and have breathed into him of My
74.	So the angels submitted, all of them together.
75.	But Iblis *did* not. He behaved proudly, and was of those who disbelieved. Spirit, fall ye down in submission to him.'
16.	*God* said, 'O Iblis, what hindered thee from submitting to what I had created with My two hands? Is it that thou art *too* proud or art thou *really* of the exalted ones?'
77.	He said, 'I am better than he. Thou hast created me of fire and him hast Thou created of clay.'
78.	*God* said, 'Then get out hence, for, surely thou art rejected.

There are four accounts in the Qur'an about the origin of Satan. Short descriptions to this episode appear in Surah 2: 35; Surah 15: 32–35; and Surah 20: 117.

Satan's initial name was Iblis and it is not quite clear what type of creature he was. In Surah 7: 10–18, where God addressed Adam, the first human, Iblis was one of the angels in his entourage. The same is to be found in Surah 17: 62–65 and Surah 38: 72–78.

However, in Surah 18: 51–52 he is explicitly called "one of the jinn". According to the list of definitions given in this translation of the Qur'an, the jinn are "evil spirits which inspire evil thoughts in the minds of men. They are the agents of Satan". Therefore, the angels and the jinn must not be confused with each other.

The confusion and even contradiction regarding the nature of Iblis led to much speculation and debate within Islamic scholarship. Angels are deemed to have been created of light and are incapable of sin, while jinn are created of fire and can sin. It is certainly no easy matter to solve this dilemma.[178]

When God created Adam, he ordered the angels to prostate themselves before this new creature. Iblis refused with the argument that he was created from fire (the same as the jinn), while Adam was of a lower order in creation, having been created from clay.

The idea that Adam was created from clay comes from Gen 2: 7 –

> "YHWH God formed man from the dust of the ground, and breathed into his nostrils the breath of life; and man became a living soul."

The disobedience of Iblis forced God to banish him from heaven. He got, though, some respite before being consigned to hell, by being allowed to tempt the offspring of Adam to sin and deny God.

Creation of the Jinn and Man

Surah 15: 27–28

27. And, surely, We created man from dry ringing clay, from black mud wrought into shape.
28. And the Jinn We had created before from the fire of hot wind.

---

[178] NW Enc, "Iblis"; End Brit, "Iblis".

Surah 55: 15–16

15.	He created man from dry ringing clay which is like baked pottery.
16.	And the Jinn He created from the flame of fire.

The jinn or evil spirits were created by God from the flames of fire and from hot wind. Man was formed from clay.

Reason for the Creation of Jinn and Men

Surah 51: 57–58

57.	And I have not created the Jinn and the men but that they may worship Me.
58.	I desire no sustenance from them, nor do I desire that they should feed Me.

God created creatures with a mind, jinn and humans, to be worshipped by them. He doesn't need sacrifices or gifts from them.

The Temptation of Adam and Eve

Surah 2: 37

37.	But Satan caused them both to slip by means of it and drove them out of the state in which they were. And We said: 'Go forth; some of you are enemies of others, and for you there is an abode in the earth and a provision for a time.'

The fall of man was attributed to the temptation by Satan, the fallen angel (or jinn) who was previously called Iblis.

The Power of Satan

Surah 16: 99–101

99.	And when thou recitest the Qur'an, seek refuge with Allah from Satan the rejected.
100.	Surely, he has no power over those who believe and who put their trust in their Lord.
101.	His power is only over those who make friends with him and who set up equals to Him.

Satan has no power over believers – only over those who befriended him and chose to commit evil.

Satan's Goals

Surah 4: 117–122

117.	Allah will not forgive that anything be associated with Him as partner, but He will forgive what is short of that to whomsoever He pleases. And whoso associates anything as partner with Allah has indeed strayed far away.
118.	They invoke beside Him none but lifeless objects; and they invoke none but Satan, the rebellious,
119.	Whom Allah has cursed. And he said, 'I will assuredly take a fixed portion from Thy servants;
120.	And assuredly I will lead them astray and assuredly I will ,:, excite in them vain desires, and assuredly I will incite them and they will cut the ears of cattle; and assuredly I will incite them and they will alter Allah's creation.' And he who takes Satan for a friend beside Allah has certainly suffered a manifest loss.
121.	He holds out promises to them and raises vain desires in them, and Satan promises them nothing but vain things.
122.	These are they whose abode shall be Hell and they shall find no way of escape from it.

Anybody who worships anything besides God is actually serving

Satan, whose goal is to lead people astray and away from obedience to God. Their fate is punishment in hell.

Jinn Inspired False Beliefs

Surah 6: 101

10 I.	And they hold the Jinn to be partners with Allah, although He created them; and they falsely ascribe to Him sons and daughters without any knowledge. Holy is He and exalted far above what they attribute to Him!

The false belief of Christians that God could have offspring, was thought out by the jinn.

Virgins in Heaven

Surah 55: 56–57

56.	Which, then, of the favours of your Lord will you twain deny?
57.	Therein will also be chaste maidens of modest gaze, whom neither man nor Jinn will have touched before them

The faithful may expect the company of virgins in heaven. It appears that the jinn are able to have intercourse with human women (as described in Enoch and the Book of Jubilees).

Men and Jinn Headed for Hell

Surah 7: 180

180.	Verily, We have created many of the Jinn and men whose end shall be Hell! They have hearts but they understand not .therewith, and they have eyes but they see not therewith, and.they have ears but they hear not therewith. They are like cattle; nay, they are even more astray. They are indeed quite heedless.

Surah 32: 14

14.	And if We had enforced Our will, We could have given every soul its guidance, but the word from Me has come true: 'I will fill Hell with Jinn and men all together.'

It seems that jinn, just as men, have minds, can see and hear, but can also sin against God. Their final destination is in hell.

SUMMARY

Depiction of a *shaitan* by Siyah Qalam, c. 14th/15th century.

The Qur'an, however, gave quite another reason for Satan's rebellion, namely that Iblis declined to bow before Adam, the first human being. He was the only angel or jinn to be dismissed from heaven.

The jinn are creatures of God, made from fire, and they chose to become evil on their own, without any reason. They are allied with Satan. Although the Qur'an copied or repeated many ideas from the Christian Bible, including the concept of Satan, the description of the origin of Satan differs fundamentally from the relevant descriptions in the Bible.

The New Testament doesn't supply the reason why Satan and his angels became disobedient and rebelled against God before they were banished from heaven. The extra-biblical book of Enoch explained that some angels, the Watchers, were filled with lust for human women and begat giants as their offspring.

Chapter 9
DEDUCTIONS AND INTERPRETATIONS

SERIOUS QUESTIONS

The title of this book, To Hell with the Devil, can be interpreted in any one of two ways:

- It may mean that we must agree with the Scriptures that Satan, a real spiritual being, indeed deserves to be roasted and toasted for all eternity in the flames of hell after Judgment Day; or –
- It may also be seen as an impolite and even rude call to get rid of the concept of an imaginary, surreal, and mythological character that caused much unnecessary misery and mishaps and misfortune in the history of this world.

These two possibilities lead to the following big questions that must be answered at the end of this quest and analysis of the Scriptures:

- Is Satan a real, yet invisible, character as presented in the Hebrew, Christian, and Muslim Scriptures? Does he indeed exist in the spirit world and does he exert an influence upon the minds of human beings to persuade them to commit wrong and bad actions? Does he cause accidents, criminal actts, disaasters, and tragedies? Or –
- Is he only a mythological, fictitious, and concocted personage, borrowed from the Persian religion and molded into a non-existing, fabricated, and imaginary enemy of almighty God?

It is also necessary to ask:

- Are there really demons, namely malicious, malevolent, malignant, and mischievous ethereal beings that torment, traumatize, and torture people and cause all sorts of diseases, disorders, dissent, and disasters? Or –
- Are these deranged and disobedient and diabolical demons merely imaginary, unreal, and fanciful entities, the products of superstitious and even hallucinatory minds?

The answers to these questions depend, furthermore, on the following questions:

- How far can we trust the Scriptures to provide us with reliable and trustworthy information about the world, ourselves, and the universe? And –
- How far must we proceed with the process of demythologizing the Scriptures to fit our current established scientific insights?

Answers to all these questions will be sought in the following paragraphs.

CONTRADICTIONS IN THE SCRIPTURES

Traditional Christians are convinced that the Bible contains a single and unified message and that the Old Testament and the New Testament do not contradict each other, but complement each other.

That is, however, not the case when these two parts of the Bible are compared and investigated thoroughly, honestly, and with an open mind, especially regarding the different biblical views regarding the devil and evil spirits. The analysis of the Scriptures in the previous chapters found the following:

Satan

In the Old Testament, Satan was a member of God's entourage and he had access to God on his throne in heaven as one of he sons of Gd. He had to obey God's commands and constraints, and he merely acted as the accuser of certain people, such as Job or the high priest. He had no power to act independently and he was certainly not the source of all evil. God took full responsibility for all the tragedies that Job had to endure, according to the last part of the book of Job.

In contrast, the New Testament pictures Satan as an evil enemy of God, a fallen angel who was flung out of heaven and who does his best to destroy or undermine God's authority.

No other book in the New Testament shows the influence of the books of Enoch and Jubilees as much as Revelation. John of Patmos, the author, described how the Serpent or the Dragon, Satan, tried to prevent the birth of Jesus Christ and how the archangel Michael overpowered him. He had two powerful allies, namely the Antichrist and the False Prophet. The Jews, who rejected Jesus as their Messiah, were described as having an alliance with the devilish Dragon.

What are we to believe about Satan? It is not possible to reconcile the views found in the Old Testament with the New Testament. These inconsistencies and contradictions mean that either the Old Testament, or the New Testament, or both, cannot be trusted or relied upon where information about Satan is concerned.

Unclean Spirits

The same type of confusion can be found between the two testaments when descriptions of evil or unclean spirits are found.

According to the Old Testament, evil spirits are God's servants. They caused people to behave in a bizarre manner or to tell lies to achieve God's purposes.

The New Testament, on the other hand, describe Satan as the prince of the demons. They are presented as Satan's angels or messengers. They are seen as the cause of diseases and disorders and disabilities, and they had to be exorcized to heal sick people.

Sickness is often mentioned in the Old Testament (Gen 48: 1 & 10; Prov 13: 12; Hos 7: 5; Mic6: 13; Dan 8: 27; *etcetera*). The only case in the Old Testament where a health complaint had a supernatural cause was in the case of Job where God allowed Satan to torture Job with painful boils (Jon 2: 7). No other cases of people who suffered ill health were plagued by degenerate demons, sordid spirits, or diminutive devils as in the New Testament.

Jesus admitted in Luke 11: 24–26 and Matt 12: 43–45 that his expulsion of evil spirits did not always work. It happened that a sick parson was liberated from his demons, but those demons just returned with some friends and caused even more havoc and heartache. That forces us to ask: can sick people really be cured through exorcism?

Paul mentioned in 2 Cor 12: 7–9 a painful "thorn in the flesh" when an angel of Satan struck him with the fist. God was unwilling – or even unable – to remove this affliction and agony.

The stark contrast and difference between the sick and sinful spirits of the Old Testament and of the New Testament cannot be overlooked. It also seems as if the New Testament authors were not quite sure how to deal with these slippery and slimy specters.

These confusions and contradictions must lead to the deduction that the teachings of the Bible regarding damnable and dirty demonic spirits are anything but clear. One must ask: how much of the information about evil spirits in the Bible is credible?

Confused Confessional Creeds

The same type of confusion seems to be found in the Belgic Confession and the Heidelberg Catechism. It has already been shown that they contain discrepancies and contradictions. The Belgic Confession even admits that its presentation of God's providence and management of his creation is at odds with the reality of evil and suffering. These aspects cannot be reconciled and it is declared that this contradiction must be the result of a monumental mystery.

All these contradictions and disagreements must necessarily lead one to conclude that the way the Bible and the confessional creeds treat the devil and evil spirits cannot be accepted or trusted.

More or less the same situation applies to the Qur'an. It is simply stated that the angel (or jinn) Iblis flatly refused to bow before Adam with the excuse that Adam was of a lower order in creation than he. However, what his real motive was for defying God's direct command cannot be fathomed and his behavior was totally irrational, insane, and in conflict with his nature as a sinless angel.

All these contradictions, confusions, and conflicts regarding Satan and evil spirits forces one to deduce that the it is not possible to rely on the representations and reports of the Scriptures.

THE NEED FOR A DEVIL

A Definition of God

The three monotheistic religious systems, Judaism, Christianity, and Islam, cannot survive without the devil. Their adherents worship an all-powerful, ubiquitous, all-knowing, eternal, perfect, and benevolent God, the designer and creator of the universe. This very concept of God calls for a diabolical figure as his adversary and antithesis. Without such a figure, this concept of God would eventually fall apart and become untenable.

Nobody can deny the reality of evil, wrongdoing, crime, wickedness, malevolence, and calamities of all sorts in this world. This reality has caused unimaginable amounts of misery, suffering, pain, horror, hardship, and unhappiness. One is forced to ask: is it possible to reconcile this undeniable reality with the concept of a perfectly good, loving, and righteous God who micromanages his creation as outlined above? Many people nowadays think the answer is "No".

The history of philosophy and theology contains various efforts to exonerate this good, caring, benevolent, and almighty God by finding reasons why this horrible state of affairs exists, without blaming God for it all. Such an exercise is known as a "theodicy" – the doctrine or theory to reconcile the idea of a good, well-meaning, and almighty God with all the evil and wickedness and distress in the world that He had created and still manages.

The most widely-accepted solution to this dilemma is to be found, amongst others, in the definition of God in the Belgic Confession. Although this definition is contained in a Christian creed, most Judaists and Muslims will find most of this definition acceptable:

"Article 1: The Only God

We all believe in our hearts and confess with our mouths that there is a single and simple spiritual being, whom we call God – eternal, incomprehensible, invisible, unchangeable, infinite, almighty; completely wise, just, and good, and the overflowing source of all good.

This definition of God must be augmented with the following:

Article 13: God's Providence

We believe that this good God, after he created all things, did not abandon them to chance or fortune but leads and governs them according to his holy will, in such a way that nothing happens in this world without his orderly arrangement.

Yet God is not the author of, nor can he be charged with, the sin that occurs. For his power and goodness are so great and incomprehensible that he arranges and does his work very well and justly even when the devils and wicked men act unjustly.

We do not wish to inquire with undue curiosity into what he does that surpasses human understanding and is beyond our ability to comprehend. But in all humility and reverence we adore the just judgments of God, which are hidden from us, being content to be Christ's disciples, so as to learn only what he shows us in his Word, without going beyond those limits.

This doctrine gives us unspeakable comfort since it teaches us that nothing can happen to us by chance but only by the arrangement of our gracious heavenly Father. He watches over us with fatherly care, keeping all creatures under his control, so that not one of the hairs on our heads (for they are all numbered) nor even a little bird can fall to the ground without the will of our Father.

In the Catechism, one finds the following descriptions of God, which disagrees with the Belgic Confession in certain respects:

Question 26: What believest thou when thou sayest, 'I believe in God the Father, Almighty, Maker of heaven and earth'?

Answer: That the eternal Father of our Lord Jesus Christ (who of nothing made heaven and earth, with all that is in them; who likewise upholds and governs the same by his eternal counsel and providence) is for the sake of Christ his Son, my God and my Father; on whom I rely so entirely, that I have no doubt, but he will provide me with all things necessary for soul and body and further, that he will make whatever evils he sends upon me, in this valley of tears turn out to my advantage; for he is able to do it, being Almighty God, and willing, being a faithful Father.

Question 27: What dost thou mean by the providence of God?
Answer: The almighty and everywhere present power of God; whereby, as it were by his hand, he upholds and governs heaven, earth, and all creatures; so that herbs and grass, rain and drought, fruitful and barren years, meat and drink, health and sickness, riches and poverty, yea, and all things come, not by chance, but by his fatherly hand.

Question 28: What advantage is it to us to know that God has created, and by his providence does still uphold all things?
Answer: That we may be patient in adversity; thankful in prosperity; and that in all things, which may hereafter befall us, we place our firm trust in our faithful God and Father, that nothing shall separate us from his love; since all creatures are so in his hand, that without his will they cannot so much as move.

According to the Catechism, Christians claim that there is a perfect, omnipotent, omniscient, and omnipresent spiritual being who created everything and is still in control of everything – even the bad things that happen to us. We have no choice but to accept all these bad things with patience because that is the way God governs his creation. He is supposed to be totally good, wise, just, infinite, unchanging, eternal, merciful, loving, and caring – despite all the bad and horrible things that He allows or causes to overcome us.

This definition does not agree with the Belgic Confession where it is denied that this omniscient, omnipresent, almighty, and caring God causes bad things to happen. This discrepancy needs to be illuminated further.

Difficulties with these Definitions

The definition of God in the Belgic Confession states the following:

- God created the universe and still micromanages it. Everything that happens is the result of how He organizes and arranges it.
- Bad things do happen, but that cannot be blamed on God.

The author of the Belgic Confession realized that these two statements cannot be reconciled and, therefore, he declared that this discrepancy and disagreement is the result of an unfathomable and insoluble mystery – too big for our limited human minds to grasp.

To this must be added that Article 12 of the Confession rejects the idea of human free will since all man's actions are controlled by the omnipotent, ubiquitous, and omniscient God. Yet, man decided on his own to fall into sin and that he, therefore, deserves punishment. This is another glaring contradiction.

The definition or description of God in the Belgic Confession is also at odds with the oldest parts of the Hebrew Scriptures. It has already been shown that the Old Testament ascribes all calamities, accidents, misfortune, crimes, bad or irrational behavior, and wrongdoing of humans to the influence or guidance of God. This is also the message of the Catechism.

For instance: King Saul's strange actions and inexplicable psychiatric problems were blamed on evil spirits dispatched by God. The song of Hannah (1 Sam 2: 1–10) specifically ascribes poverty, famine, humiliation, and death to the actions of YHWH.

The following texts tell the same story: Exod 4: 21, Deut 28: 59, Jos 11: 20, 1 Kgs 9: 7, Isa 45: 7, and Amos 3: 6. The ten plagues that harassed and horrified the poor Egyptians were all caused or sent by the God of the Israelites.

Special mention must be made of Exod 4: 21 – "YHWH said to Moses, 'When you go back into Egypt, see that you do before

Pharaoh all the wonders which I have put in your hand, but I will harden his heart and he will not let the people go.'" In other words: God promised to make Pharaoh stubborn, hardheaded, and obstinate, which did happen repeatedly (Exod 7: 3; 9: 12; 10: 1; and 14: 8).

In the book of Job, written in the post-exilic period, the emphasis has shifted somewhat. Satan was introduced and he was described as the agent who wrought all the catastrophes in Job's life, but it was still under the control, command, and consent of God.

The author of Chronicles deliberately switched the blame for King David's sinful and boastful census from God to Satan (I Chron 21: 1–2 and 2 Sam 24: 1–2). This is the only instance where the Old Testament exonerated God for wrongs perpetrated by people. This author just could not imagine that the righteous and perfect God would or could cause somebody like David to do something wrong or bad.

The authors of Enoch and the Book of Jubilees found a very handy scapegoat to blame for all the horrible, unacceptable, wretched, and wrong events or actions in the world, namely Satan, a fallen angel. This figure was discovered in the Persian religion and he was gratefully incorporated into a new Jewish mythology – which was also wholeheartedly adopted by the New Testament authors. Jesus, for instance, also thought that the devil tried to sabotage his work.

There was a definite need for the invention or adoption of Satan to exonerate and justify God and to rescue his reputation as the source of all that is good, perfect, praiseworthy, excellent, and right.

The same is to be found in the Qur'an. An original mythology was created to explain the existence of Satan – an undisciplined and rebellious angel (or jinn) who would not obey

God to bow before Adam. He was blamed for all the wrongdoing, crimes, godlessness, and evil doctrines in mankind – leaving God blameless.

It must be concluded, therefore, that the three monotheistic religions – Judaism, Christianity, and Islam – needed to invent or embrace a diabolical being to remove the blame or guilt from God for all the wrongs, woes, wretchedness, sadness, suffering, and sins on earth.

A Crisis of Faith

The position taken by the Heidelberg Catechism, mainly on account of the Old Testament belief that all catastrophes, calamities, chaos, and crime are ultimately the work of God – without invoking the destructions wrought by Satan and his evil spirits – may lead to one of two possible reactions:

- People may argue that their bad circumstances, ill health, misfortune, and unhappiness must be the will of God, which they have to endure with patience and fortitude. To do anything to alter these circumstances will amount to a rejection of God's will; or –
- People may experience a crisis of faith when they experience bad times, which have to be blamed on God. That causes them to become angry at God, to become bitter, or even to lose their fath altogether.

A good example of somebody who experienced a serious crisis of faith was the poet who wrote the book of Lamentations. When reading this gripping testimony of a survivor of the destruction of Jerusalem by the Babylonian army in 587 BC, followed by the captivity and deportation of the Jewish elite, one can easily detect a wide range of negative emotions and reactions towards God. The following emotional reactions can be spotted:

- *Anger towards God for causing all the hardship, poverty, and loss of life*: "The Lord is become as an enemy, he has swallowed up Israel; He has swallowed up all her palaces, he has destroyed his strongholds; He has multiplied in the daughter of Judah mourning and lamentation" (Lam 2: 5). "Look, YHWH, and see to whom you have done thus! Shall the women eat their fruit, the children that are dandled in the hands? Shall the priest and the prophet be killed in the sanctuary of the Lord?" (Lam 2: 20).
- *Sadness and alienation from God*: "Yes, when I cry, and call for help, he shuts out my prayer" (Lam 3: 8).
- *Horror*: "The hands of the pitiful women have boiled their own children; they were their food in the destruction of the daughter of my people. YHWH has accomplished his wrath, he has poured out his fierce anger; He has kindled a fire in Zion, which has devoured the foundations of it" (Lam 4: 10–11).
- *Disappointment*: "He has led me and caused me to walk in darkness, and not in light. Surely against me he turns his hand again and again all the day. My flesh and my skin has he made old; he has broken my bones" (Lam 3: 2–4).
- *Depression*: "For these things I weep; my eye, my eye runs down with water; because the comforter who should refresh my soul is far from me: My children are desolate, because the enemy has prevailed. Zion spreads forth her hands; there is none to comfort her" (Lam 1: 16 – 17).
- *Helplessness*: "Servants rule over us: There is none to deliver us out of their hand" (Lam 5: 8).

- *Bitterness*: "He has filled me with bitterness, he has sated me with wormwood. He has also broken my teeth with gravel stones; he has covered me with ashes" (Lam 3: 15–16).
- *Doubt in God*: "You have covered with anger and pursued us; you have killed, you have not pitied. You have covered yourself with a cloud, so that no prayer can pass through" (Lam 3: 43–44).
- *Fellings of guilt and self-blame:* "The yoke of my transgressions is bound by his hand; they are knit together, they are come up on my neck; he has made my strength to fail: The Lord has delivered me into their hands, against whom I am not able to stand" (Lam 1: 14). "YHWH is righteous; for I have rebelled against his commandment" (Lam 1: 18).
- *Resignation*: "Who is he who says, and it comes to pass, when the Lord doesn`t command it? Doesn`t evil and good come out of the mouth of the Most High?" (Lam 3: 37–38).
- *A plea that God would help him to get rid of his doubts*: "See, YHWH; for I am in distress; my heart is troubled; My heart is turned within me" (Lam 1: 20). "Why do you forget us forever, [and] forsake us so long time? Turn you us to you, YHWH, and we shall be turned; Renew our days as of old (Lam 5: 20–21).

This suffering and destitute poet evidently felt very confused. On the one hand, he felt angry and bitter towards God for bringing about all the destruction, death, and disasters. On the other hand, he did not want to give up his faith in God and cried out in anguish and agony that God would not forget him.

Who is to be Blamed?

Many people who have gone through bad times experienced the same type of existential crisis and the resulting turmoil in their faith as the poet of Lamentations. They blamed God for their misfortune and misery, but they also tried their best not to lose faith in this God. They also blamed themselves and convinced themselves that they had deserved the rough treatment from God. If there are no disgusting devils or despicable demons, only God and themselves can be blamed.

It is, however, difficult to blame God who is supposed to be the source of all goodness, blessings, benevolence, and happiness. People experiencing a crisis of faith and becoming angry at God, may easily feel guilty about this sacrilegious and sinful reaction. For this reason, the devil simply had to be invented, as happened in the books of Enoch and Jubilees, and eagerly and gratefully copied by the New Testament and the Qur'an.

All this forces one to ask: can we continue having faith in this type of God who tortures and torments people? Isn't it time to revise our views of God?

The Need for Salvation

A constant theme in the sermons of Christian preachers is that sinners have to repent, turn to God, and believe in Jesus to be "saved" from the horrors of hell in the afterlife.

Hell was, of course, invented by Enoch and the Book of Jubilees as the eventual fate of Satan and his evil spirits – as has been shown previously. The authors of the New Testament followed them in this regard.

Christians have, accordingly, to be grateful that Jesus endured hell when he died on the cross and took their place in hell, although only for a limited time before he was resurrected. However, the concept of hell only makes sense when it is seen as the ultimate fate of a devised devil and demons, as well as of damnable and depraved sinners.

Preachers would have little to tell their congregations if the devil and delinquent demons didn't enter the picture. The doctrine of salvation simply needs Satan to make sense.

According to the Qur'an, man faces only one of two possible fates after death: paradise in heaven or torture in hell together with Satan. One can avoid this horrible fate of eternal damnation by become a Muslim, which means to submit to God. Therefore, Islam needs the concept of Satan to convince people to convert to this religion.

GETTING RID OF MYTHS

Ancient Mythology

The Hebrew and early Christian mythologies regarding the composition of the cosmos were described in Chapter 3. The next chapter briefly explained current scientific theories and insights. It was also pointed out that educated Christians of our time had to adjust their views regarding the cosmos, our world, God as creator, and ourselves drastically in the light of solid and substantiated scientific findings in the fields of astronomy, biology, chemistry, medicine, physics, and psychology.

Educated Jews, Christians, and Muslims accept that God's residence, heaven, cannot be located just beyond the visible stars. They argue that God, as creator, cannot be part of his creation and He must reside somewhere outside the observable universe, supposedly in other spatial and temporal dimensions.

The cosmology and astrology of the Bible contain many ideas taken from Babylonian, Egyptian, Persian, and Greek mythologies, with the difference that the multitudes of pagan deities were transformed into angels and demons – which amounts to pretty much the same state of affairs. Educated people of our time, including believers, cannot accept this cosmology and astrology anymore. They have exchanged these mythologies with more scientific and rational views of the universe.

There can be no doubt that the defiant devil and his angelic assistants, the delinquent demons, are an integral part of the ancient Hebrew, early Christian, and Muslim cosmologies and mythologies.

Less sophisticated societies of our time tend to see the world in a similar way as the ancients and they still live in a spirit-filled and demon-infested world. Buys, an expert on Christianity in Africa, reported that indigenous African Christians often combine elements of their ancestral religions with ideas from the Bible. They experience the world inter alia as a place filled with mysterious spiritual forces, just as the ancients.[179]

It may be expected of ultra-conservative and fundamentalist believers to still adhere to the ancient pre-scientific world-view. That is, after all, what they find in the Scriptures that were supposedly inspired or given by God. No amount of scientific evidence will move them away from their entrenched convictions.

If educated and informed believers of our time, on the other hand, reject the ancient mythologies, it must inevitably also lead to a rejection of the belief in the existence and reality of Satan and other evil and malicious spiritual beings that cause physical and mental problems in people.

Joseph Pierre quoted opinion polls that showed that between 50% and 60% of Americans do not believe in something like demonic possession anymore.[180] This trend exists most likely in most Western societies.

Texts such as 1 Enoch 10: 12–15; Luke 8: 30–31; Rom 10: 7; 2 Pet 2: 4; Rev 1: 18; Rev 11: 7; Rev 17: 8; and Rev 20: 1–3 tell us that Satan and the unholy spirits were exiled to the “abyss” or

---

[179] Buys, “The Relevance of a Reformed Perspective”.

[180] Pierre, “Demonic Possession”.

"Tartarus" until they can face Judgment Day, after which they will be dumped into hell with its everlasting flames. This "abyss" was thought of as part of the realm of the dead, somewhere beneath the surface of the flat earth. Revelation even mistook the outburst of a volcano to the south of Patmos, where the author lived as an exile, which threw glowing blobs of lava into the air, to be an opening into the abyss and hell.[181]

A similar train of thought is to be found in the Qur'an (Surah 4: 121–122; 7: 41; 8: 11; and 101: 9).

More enlightened and informed believers of our cen-tury cannot accept this aspect of the ancient mythologies either. Their solution is to think of the abode of these spiritual beings as outside the visible universe, per-haps in another (undiscovered or inaccessible) dimension.

However, this idea that a sly Satan and his monstruous mates are being kept locked up somewhere in a spot called the abyss, is also part and parcel of an ancient mythology, which may and even must be discarded.

It must be repeated that the biblical authors thought of concepts such as "spirit" or "soul" in a very concrete manner. These concepts were seen as simply a person's breath, life force, personality, or even as the blowing wind. When more sophisticated believers of our time conceptualize of spirits or souls, they think of totally immaterial entities – an idea foreign to the ancient biblical way of thinking. That means that believers of our time have totally demythologized the scriptural teachings about angels, evil spirits, demons, and jinn. The biblical authors did not visualize of spirits as immaterial entities, as we tend to do today and that means that

---

[181] Schltz, *Revelation,* 129–137.

believers of our time have departed from the biblical concepts and, as it were, "modernized" these concepts.

The process of demythologizing that started with the rejection of the ancient world-view, namely that the earth is the center of the universe, must necessarily also lead to an abandonment of a belief in angry angels, devious demons, and a dangerous devil.

Satan, as drawn by Gustave Doré

Some more serious questions emerge. For instance: we are repeatedly told in Genesis 1 that God created a perfectly good creation, consisting of heaven and earth. The angels were, therefore, supposed to be part of this perfectly good creation. How was it then possible for some of these perfectly good spirits to become rebels and foes of God? What could they conceivably gain by challenging the Almighty? It just does not make any sense.

We may furthermore ask: If God is omniscient and he knows the future, why did he bother to create perfectly good beings that would, in any case, later fall into sin and cause so much trouble in his creation? He must have known what would happen when he created Lucifer and the other angels who would turn against him.

Why didn't he just desist or refrain from creating them?

Our views about evil, criminality, immorality, wickedness, and depravity must be revised, with the exclusion and expulsion of diabolical spiritual beings. We may say with conviction: To Hell with the Devil! We may well get rid of this useless, unnecessary, nonsensical, and outdated piece of superstition without feeling guilty about rejecting a scriptural concept – just as we don't feel bad anymore about rejecting the notion of a flat earth.

Parapsychology, Supernatural Phenomena, and Spiritualism

There is a discipline called parapsychology, which endeavors to investigate abnormal and supernatural phenomena, such as clairvoyance, telepathy, telekinesis, reincarnation, and the possible influence of spiritual beings on human beings and earthly events. Although the first investigations of this sort already started during the 1880's, no real progress has been made since then, despite thousands of attempts to prove the reality of psychic phenomena.

The scientific community is very skeptical regarding the purported findings of the practitioners of parapsychology and criticize their lack of rigorous scientific methods to reach their findings, their biased way of interpreting vague and ambiguous data and their lack of acceptable or convincing theories to explain the data they are supposed to gather. No known and accepted scientific theories can explain the so-called findings of these investigations.

Parapsychology must, therefore, be regarded as a pseudoscience – comparable with quackeries such as palmistry, astrology, and phrenology[182]. Many people felt the need to establish communication with deceased loved ones. All sorts of charlatans, called clairvoyants and mediums, provide in this need. During sessions in dark rooms, called "seances", contact is purportedly made with the dead. Rigorous scientific investigations have unmasked these practices as fraudulent. No real contact with the spirits of the deceased could ever be attained.[183]

---

[182] Stenger, *The New Atheism,* 182–83; Enc Brit, "Parapsychological phenomenon".

[183] Enc Brit, "Spiritualism".

All this amounts to the conclusion that there is no scientific proof for the purported contact with ethereal beings such as spirits, angels, or demons.

Exorcism

Unfortunately, grievous harm is often being done when people with genuine medical and psychological disorders are subjected to exorcism, a serious form of mental torture and even physical abuse. They get the promise from these exorcists that their problems and pains will vanish if the demons causing these conditions are driven away – and when no lasting cure is effected, their arthritis, bipolar disorder, cancer, depression, epilepsy, fibromyalgia, and gout just get worse.

Exorcists usually claim positive results with their rituals. That may be due to the placebo effect. In other cases, the victims may fall into a hypnotic trance, which may have had some therapeutic value, especially if that person is deeply religious and has faith in the skills of the exorcist. However, cases are known of people who were so seriously injured during a session of exorcism to try to get rid of destructive demons that they were seriously injured and even died.[184]

THE CONCEPT OF GOD NEEDS REVISION

God is Needed to Explain the Existence of the World

It was argued at length that concepts such as a devil, demons, and demonic possession must be discarded as untenable, useless, and unsubstantiated. It may also be argued that our concept of God, as formulated in the quotations from the Belgic Confession and the Heidelberg Catechism, ought to be revised, as well.

[184] Villines, "Exorcism and Psychology".

The reason for that is that the idea of an intelligent, omniscient, omnipresent, almighty, and benevolent creator and manager of the universe, contains certain inner contradictions and absurd implications if taken to its ultimate logical conclusions and deductions.[185]

A very basic question that has been asked many times, runs like this: why is there anything and not nothing? Why do the world and the universe exist, instead of not existing?

Human beings are organisms with sophisticated brains as thinking organs and they have the urge or the need to understand the world in which they live. They are curious and inquisitive and seek the meaning of it all.

The three monotheistic religions have a simple answer: there is a creator who thought everything out and called it all into existence. This explanation satisfies believers and they do not think any further about the ultimate implications of this belief.

Is God Really Omnipotent?

We must ask: is the God of the Scriptures really all-powerful? Are there limitations to his power and authority? These questions may be broken up into the following points:

- Did God have any choice in designing and creating the universe as it is with all its laws of nature that guide and govern all physical and chemical processes? Is it in any way conceivable that another set of laws of nature could exist in another universe? After all, the set of laws we have discovered, form a coherent, unified, elegant, and rational whole and no other systeem seems to be possible.

---

[185] See my book Who, Where, and What is God? for a more detailed exploration of some absurd consequences of the belief in the biblical God.

- Did God have any choice in formulating all the laws of nature by using another system of mathematics that forms the basis of all the laws of nature? Mathematics, as we know it, forms a unified, coherent, elegant, and rational whole. Is it conceivable that it can ever be replaced by any other mathematical system?
- Did God have any choice in formulating any other rules of ethics, the rules that regulate moral, decent, and acceptable behavior between sentient and intelligent creatures? Is it in any way possible to have any set of moral rules that excludes or disregards values such as accountability, concern for fellow creatures, forgiveness, honesty, integrity, responsibility and tolerance?
- Did God have any choice in formulating any other laws of natural justice and rules of human rights that are universally accepted by informed and well-meaning people on earth?
- Did God have any choice in formulating any other rules for the discipline of logics that guides all the communication of accurate and credible information between people and between people and machines? Can the rules of logic ever be changed?

The emphatic answer to all these questions must be in all cases: "No, certainly not."

That means that God, the supposed omnipotent designer, creator, and manager of the universe, cannot be the ultimate authority. If He designed and created the universe, He was powerless to design it in any other fashion and He had no choice but to adhere to the laws of nature and to the system of mathematics on which these laws rest. He was powerless to formulate any other rules or laws for the proper interaction of human beings.

In other words: God – if He is the intelligent designer and creator of all – just cannot be omnipotent and the highest authority in the universe. If He drew up the designs for his creation, He was bound by the rules of mathematics and logic, the values of ethics, and the laws of natural justice – which severely limited his purported omnipotence and supposed position of highest authority in his creation.

The concept of a devil also casts doubt upon the idea that God is all-powerful and micromanages his creation. If God really organizes and rules everything, even the minutest event, then the actions of Satan must also be under his control and direction, as depicted in the story of Job – which removes all guilt from Satan for all his supposedly wicked workings and evil enterprises. If God does not control the devil and Satan can do whatever he likes – although he is bound and incarcerated in a mythological "abyss" – then God is not totally in command and control of his creation. That means that his power is limited and He cannot be all-powerful or omnipotent.

Whatever the case, the introduction of the devil into religious thought casts a huge shadow over the idea that God must be all-powerful or omnipotent. If so, then He cannot be the God worshipped by Jews, Christians, and Muslims.

Is God Really Omniscient?

The God worshipped by believers is deemed to be omniscient. That means that He is supposed to know everything that is to be known. He must have full information about everybody on earth, as well as about everything else in the unlimited and unbounded universe, including any intelligent inhabitants of planets in other star systems..

That implies that He must also be aware of the properties, position and movement of each and every galaxy cluster, individual galaxy, star, planet, meteorite, comet, living organism, molecule, atom, and subatomic particle. The problem is that all molecules and atoms of a certain chemical substance and all sub-atomic particles lack individuality. There is no way to identify a certain molecule, atom, neutron, or electron and distinguish it from any other molecules, atoms, or particles. It is, therefore, impossible to know how each and every one of these entities behaves. Not even God can do it, because that is just the way the universe was designed and constructed.

Therefore, the God of the Scriptures just cannot be omniscient and know all that is to be known.

In Other Words

In other words: the universe and humanity are being ruled by the laws of nature, by a set of systems of mathematics, logic, rules of natural justice, human rights, and morals. The underlying principle of all these systems is the principle of rationality. All these rules and laws complement each other in a rational way without any contradictions or clashes. No rules of logic are broken when these systems are investigated and described and compared or coordinated with each other.

Of course, every scientist will acknowledge that we haven't yet discovered all the laws of nature, all the axioms of mathematics, the mechanisms in operation in the mysterious wide universe, and the brains and minds of intelligent members of the species homo sapiens.

We may regard God as the personification or embodiment of all these eternal and universal laws, systems, and rules – just as Satan can be regarded as the personification or embodiment of all that is wrong, wicked, wayward, or wanton.

It is an impersonal God who cannot be blamed for treating human beings unjustly, unfairly, and unfeelingly. It is more or less the God of Plato who thought that the unifying principle in the universe was the Idea of the One or the Idea of the Good, situated in the realm of ideas, which realm transcends the physical universe.

When children are taught that God created the world and the universe, they often ask: "But who created God?" The answer usually is that nobody created God and that He just exists from eternity to eternity. This type of answer does not really satisfy or explain anything because we still want to know where God came from. However, if we accept this concept of an impersonal God, consisting of all the laws and rules described above, one can truly say that these rules and laws are eternal, divine. They always existed and nobody thought them out. They simply exist of necessity and they rule the universe and the human world. They just could not have been any different.

If we embrace this type of impersonal God, the need for a devil or an evil spiritual personage disappears. We can banish the idea of such a creature and declare with confidence: To Hell with the Devil! We don't need him.

We can no longer blame God or Satan for all the woes, wickedness, or wrongdoing in the world. We, human beings, must take responsibility for all our crimes, corruption, and cruelty.

We cannot blame God or Satan for all the natural catastrophes and calamities and chaos that befall us. We live in a universe that is ruled by the laws of nature and we must accept that there is a natural explanation for every event, however disastrous or mysterious.

Value of the Scriptures

The Scriptures must be seen as a record of man's struggle to find meaning in life and to understand where he came from, how the world works, and how human societies must be managed fairly, justly, and decently.

There is certainly much of value in these Scriptures, but educated people of our time have outgrown the superstitions and mythologic elements found in them, while retaining respect for the moral rules and practical wisdom in these documents, as well as receiving inspiration from biblical figures who stood firmly on certain principles and values, despite opposition and other limitations.

FINAL OUTCOME

The final result of all the evidence presented and all the arguments formulated is simply as follows: the belief in the devil and demons must be classified as merely an outdated superstition, with no basis in reality. There are certainly no diabolic demons, satanic spirits, or a desperate devil who conspire against all that is acceptable, beautiful, commendable, decent, ethical, fitting, and good.

a”

We may live happy, meaningful, enlightened, and productive lives without being plagued or terrorized by ancient, archaic, and anachronistic myths and delusions. The devil and his demons may be regarded as nothing but fictitious beings, just as the infamous Darth Vader who fought on the side of the “Dark Side.”

BIBLIOGRAPHY

Editions of the Bible

Passages from the Bible are quoted from the *World English Bible* as found on a CD with the title *The Bible Collection, Deluxe Edition*, and published by ValuSoft, a division of THQ Inc, Waconia MN, 2002.

The above-mentioned CD also contains the Hebrew text of the Old Testament and the Greek text of the New Testament, as well as *Strong's Complete Greek & Hebrew Lexicon*. Other lexica utilized are mentioned under the heading of Other Publications.

The text of the Q Document, containing parts of the Gospel of Luke, were taken from the New Revised Standard Version, as corrected by Funk and Miller.

In addition, the following editions of the biblical text in the original languages were consulted:

Elliger, K. and W. Rudolph, eds. *Biblia Hebraica Stuttgartensia.* Stuttgart: Deutsche Bibelgesellschaft, 1997.

Nestle, E. and E. Nestle, eds. *Novum Testamentum Graece*. Stuttgart: Deutsche Bibelstiftung, 1981.

The Qur'an

Quotations from the Qur'an were taken from the translation by MaulawI Sher 'Ali: *The Holy Qur'an, Arabic Text and English Translation*. Tilford, Surry: Islam International Publications Limited, 2021. It is published on the following website:

chrome-extension://efaidnbmnnnibpcajpcglclefindmkaj/https://www.alislam.org/quran/Holy-Quran-English.pdf

Another translation that was consulted:

Rodwell,, J.M. and Alan Jones. *The Koran.* London: Phoenix, 1994.

Other Literature

Alexander, Denis. *Creation or Evolution, Do we Have to Choose?* Oxford: Monarch, 2008.

Allen, R.H. *Star Names: Their Lore and Meaning*. New York: Dover, 1963.

Anonymous. *The First Book of Enoch.* Translated by R H Charles. From: The Apocrypha and Pseudepigrapha of the Old Testament. Oxford: The Clarendon Press. https://www.ccel.org/c/charles/otpseudepig/enoch/ENOCH_1.HTM

Anonymous. *The Book of Jubilees.* Translated by R.H. Charles. *The Apocrypha and Pseudepigrapha of the Old Testament*, Oxford: Clarendon Press, 1913. Scanned and Edited by Joshua Williams, Northwest Nazarene College. http://www.pseudepigrapha.com/jubilees/index.htm

American Psychiatric Associatio. *Diagnostic and Statistical Manual of Mental Dirsorder, Fifth Edition, DSM-5.* Arlington: American Psychiatric Association, 2013.

Aristotle: On The Heavens. Translated by J. L. Stocks. http://classics.mit.edu/Aristotle/heavens.html

Armstrong, Karen. *The Bible: The Biography.* London: Atlantic, 2007.

-----. *Islam: A Short History.* London: Phoenix, 2009.

Ayala, F.J. "Evolution". In *Encyclopaedia Britannica*, 2010.

Aziz, Hasan. "Did Prophet Mohammad (PBUH) have epilepsy? A neurological analysis". *Epilepsy Behav*. 2020 Feb;103(Pt A) :106654. doi: 10.1016/j.yebeh.2019.106654. Epub 2019 Dec 9. https://pubmed.ncbi.nlm.nih.gov/31822396/#:~:text=Similarly%2C%20The%20Prophet's%20peri%2Drevelation,Prophet%20did%20not%20have%20epilepsy.

Barnes, J. "Plato". Chicago: Encyclopaedia Britannica, 2010.

Ben-Daniel, John." The Parables of Enoch (1 Enoch 37-71): Provenance and Social Setting". https://www.academia.edu/50310427/The_Parables_of_Enoch_1Enoch_37_71_Provenance_and_Social_Setting

Biography.com Editors, "Pope Francis Biography".

Bless, Claire *et al. Fundamentals of Social Research Methods: An African Perspective* . Cape Town: Juta, 2013

Boshoff, Willem *et al. Geskiedenis en Geskrifte: die Literatuur van ou Israel.* Pretria: Protea, 2008.

Buys, P.J. "The Relevance of Reformed Perspectives on Demonology for Africa." *In die Skriflig* (Online) vol.53 no.4m Pretoria, 2019 https://www.scielo.org.za/scielo.php?script=sci_arttext&pid=S2305-08532019000400006

Carter, Rira. *Mapping the Mind.* London: Phoenix, 1998.

Chilver, G.E.F. "Domitian". Chicago: Encyclopædia Britannica, 2010.

Clark, Stuart. *The Big Questions: The Universe*. London: Quercus, 2010.

Collins, Francis. *The Language of God : a ScientistPresents Evidence for Belief.* London: Pocket Books, 2007.

Conversi, Leonard W. "Tragedy". Chicago: Encyclopaedia Brittanica, 2010.

Cornelius, F. *Geistesgeschichte der Frühzeit II/1*. Leiden: Brill, 1962.

Cunningham, G.C. *Decoding the Language of God.* New York: Prometheus, 2010.

Dawkins, Richard. *The Greatest Show on Earth : the Evidence for Evolution.* London: Bantam, 2009.

Dennis, G. "Jewish Myth, Magic, and Mysticism". https://ejmmm2007.blogspot.com/2012/06/jews-and-zodiac-pt-1-good-sign.html.

Denova, Rebecca. "The Origin of Satan". World History Encyclopedia. https://www.worldhistory.org/article/1685/the-origin-of-satan/

Dolansky, S. "How the Serpent Became Satan : Adam, Eve and the Serpent in the Garden of Eden". *Biblical Archaeology*, 04.08.2016. http://www.biblicalarchaeology.org/daily/biblical-topics/bible-interpretation/how-the-serpent-became-satan/

Duchesne-Guillemin, Jacques, Ed. "Zoroastrianism". Chicago: Encyclopaedia Brittanica, 2010.

Encyclopaedia Brittaniua. "Atom". Chicago: Encyclopaedia Brittanica, 2010.

——— "Babylonian Exile". .". Chicago: Encyclopaedia Brittanica, 2010.

——— "Chaos". Chicago: Encyclopaedia Brittanica, 2010.

——— "Empedocles". Chicago: Encyclopaedia Brittanica, 2010.

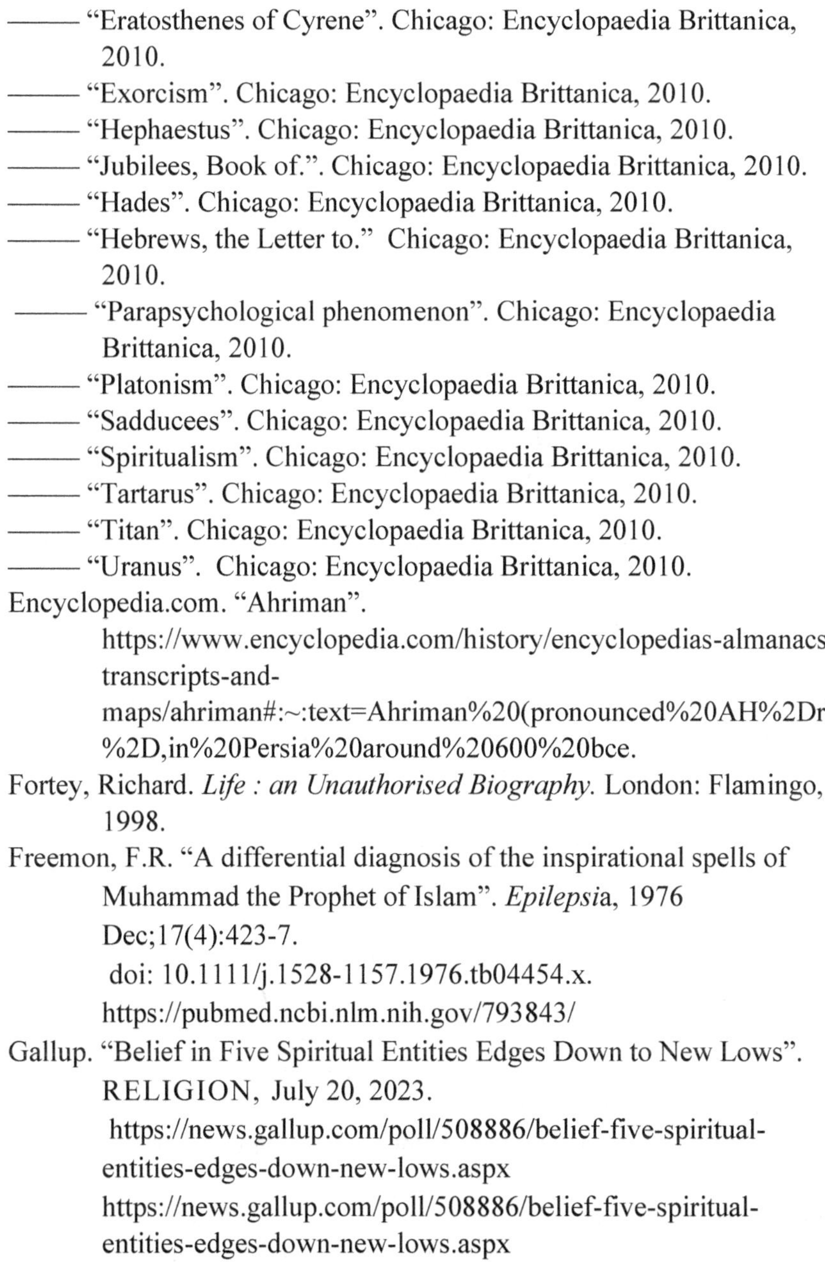

——— "Eratosthenes of Cyrene". Chicago: Encyclopaedia Brittanica, 2010.

——— "Exorcism". Chicago: Encyclopaedia Brittanica, 2010.

——— "Hephaestus". Chicago: Encyclopaedia Brittanica, 2010.

——— "Jubilees, Book of.". Chicago: Encyclopaedia Brittanica, 2010.

——— "Hades". Chicago: Encyclopaedia Brittanica, 2010.

——— "Hebrews, the Letter to." Chicago: Encyclopaedia Brittanica, 2010.

——— "Parapsychological phenomenon". Chicago: Encyclopaedia Brittanica, 2010.

——— "Platonism". Chicago: Encyclopaedia Brittanica, 2010.

——— "Sadducees". Chicago: Encyclopaedia Brittanica, 2010.

——— "Spiritualism". Chicago: Encyclopaedia Brittanica, 2010.

——— "Tartarus". Chicago: Encyclopaedia Brittanica, 2010.

——— "Titan". Chicago: Encyclopaedia Brittanica, 2010.

——— "Uranus". Chicago: Encyclopaedia Brittanica, 2010.

Encyclopedia.com. "Ahriman". https://www.encyclopedia.com/history/encyclopedias-almanacs-transcripts-and-maps/ahriman#:~:text=Ahriman%20(pronounced%20AH%2Dri%2D,in%20Persia%20around%20600%20bce.

Fortey, Richard. *Life : an Unauthorised Biography.* London: Flamingo, 1998.

Freemon, F.R. "A differential diagnosis of the inspirational spells of Muhammad the Prophet of Islam". *Epilepsia*, 1976 Dec;17(4):423-7. doi: 10.1111/j.1528-1157.1976.tb04454.x. https://pubmed.ncbi.nlm.nih.gov/793843/

Gallup. "Belief in Five Spiritual Entities Edges Down to New Lows". RELIGION, July 20, 2023. https://news.gallup.com/poll/508886/belief-five-spiritual-entities-edges-down-new-lows.aspx
https://news.gallup.com/poll/508886/belief-five-spiritual-entities-edges-down-new-lows.aspx

----- "Fewer in U.S. Now See Bible as Literal Word of God". RELIGION. July 6, 2022. https://news.gallup.com/poll/394262/fewer-bible-literal-word-god.aspx

Galileo Galilei, *Dialogue Concerning the two Chief World Systems – Ptolemaic and Copernican,* 1630. Translated by Stillman Drake. Berkeley: University of California Press, 1967.

Gauquelin, Michel. *Astrology and Science.* London: P. Davies, 1972.

Glick, T.F. 2010. "Intelligent Design (ID)". In *Encyclopædia Britannica*, 2010.

Gottheil, Richard, and Enno Litmann. "Enoch, Books of (Ethiopic and Slavonic). *Jewish Encyclopedia..* https://www.jewishencyclopedia.com/articles/5773-enoch-books-of-ethiopic-and-slavonic

Graham, Billy. Angels: God's Secret Agents. Nashville: Thomas Nelson, 1995.

Graffin, Greg. and S. Olson. *Anarchy Evolution: Faith, Science and Bad Religion*. New York: Harper Collins, 2010.

Greenwood, S. & Airey, R. *The complete Illustrated Encyclopaedia of Witchcraft & Magic*. London: Hermes House, 2007.

Hawking, Stephen. *The Grand Design.* London: Bantam, 2011.

Hengel, M. *Judentum und Hellenismus, Studien zu Ihrer Begegnung unter Besonderer Berücksichtigung Palästinas Bis zur Mitte des 2. Jh.s v. Chr*. Tübingen: Mohr Siebeck, 1973.

Heyns, Johan Adam and Willie D. Jonker. *Op Weg met die Teologie*. Pretoria: N.G. Kerkboekhandel, 1974.

Jacobs, Joseph, and Ludwig Blau. "Satan". In: *Jewish Encyclopedia.* https://www.jewishencyclopedia.com/articles/13219-satan

Jacobus, H.R. "The Zodiac Sign Names in the Dead Sea Scrolls (4q318): Features and Questions." *Aram*, 24 (2012) 311–31. file:///c:/users/user/downloads/the_zodiac_sign_names_in_the_dead_sea_sc.pdf.

Josephus, Flavius. *The Wars of the Jews, or History of the Destruction of Jerusalem*. Translated by W Whiston. Project Gutenberg E-Book, 2009. ` https://www.gutenberg.org/files/2850/2850-h/2850- h.htm#link6noteref-20 Kaye, E.M. and J. Herskowitz. "

Joubert, Gideon. *Die Groot Gedagte. Abstrakte Weefels van die Kosmos.* Cape Town: Tafelberg, 1997.

Kenny, A.J.P. "Aristotle". Chicago : Encyclopaedia Britannica, 2010.

Kent, William. "Devil." The Catholic Encyclopedia. Vol. 4. New York: Robert Appleton Company, 1908. http://www.newadvent.org/cathen/04764a.htm.

Kolb, Bryan, and Ian Q. Wishaw. *Fundamentals of Human Neuropsychology.* New York: Worth, 2009.

König, Adrio. *Die Groot Geloofswoordeboek. Vereeniging: Christelike Uitgewersmaatskappy, 2006.*

Lezak, Muriel Deutsch, et al. *Neuropsychological Assessment.* New York: Oxford University Press, 2012.

Malina, Bruce. *On the Genre and Message of Revelation: Star Visions ans Sky Journeys.* Peabody, Ms, 1995.

Malina, B.J & Pilch, J.J. *Social-Science Commentary on the Book of Revelation.* Minneapolis: Fortress, 2000.

McGregor, G.H.C. and A.C. Purdy. *Jew and Greek: Tutors unto Christ, the Jewish and Hellenistic Background of the New Testament.* London: Saint Andrew, 1959.

Miller, Robert J. ed. *The Complete Gospels: Annotated Scholars Version.* Sonoma, CA: Polebridge, 1992.

Mills, D. *Atheist Universe: The Thinking Person's Answer to Christian Fundamentalism.* Berkeley, CA: Ulysses, 2000.

Oakes, L. and L. Gahlin. *Ancient Egypt: An Illustrated Reference to the Myths, Religions, Pyramids and Temples of the Land of the Pharaohs.* London: Hermes, 2004.

Olby, Robert. "Mendel, Gregor". Chicago: Encyclopedia Brittanica, 2010.

Oosthuizen, J.L. "Galilei, Galileo". In: Gaum, Frits, *Christelike Kern-Ensiklopedie.* Wellington: Lux Verbi, 2008.

Papineau, David, and Howard Selina. *Introducing Consciousness.* Cambridge: Icon. 2005.

Perrin, N. "Bultmann, Rudof (Karl)". Chicago: Encyclopaedia Britannica, 2010.

Peters, F.E. *The Harvest of Hellenism, a History of the Near East from Alexander the Great to the Triumph of Christianity.* London: Barnes and Noble, 1972.

Philo of Alexandria. On The Giants. Translated by Charles Duke Yonge. http://www.earlychristianwritings.com/yonge/book9.html.

Pierre, Josph M. "A Differential Diagnosis of Demonic Possession: Psychological explanations for an enduring phenomenon that may be on the rise. *Psychology Today,* 5 December 2023. https://www.psychologytoday.com/za/blog/psych-unseen/202305/a-differential-diagnosis-of-demonic-possession

Plato. *Timaeus*. Translated by Benjamin Jowett http://classics.mit.edu/plato/timaeus.html

Pretorius, Albertus. *Jesus f Nazareth: A Deluded Messiah.* Eugenem OR: Wipf & Stock, 2022.

———. *The Gospels Explained.* Eugene, OR: Wipf & Stock, 2024.

———. *Who, Where, and What is God?* Eugene OR: Wipf & Stock, 2022.

Ratzinger, Joseph. "Schöpfungsglaube und Evolutionstheorie". In: *Dogma und Verkündigung*, München 1977, 143–156.

Reichert, Ben. "What Is Demonology and Why is it Important For Christians to Understand it?" Christianity.com, 3 October 2023.https://www.christianity.com/wiki/angels-and-demons/what-demonology-important-christians-understand-it.html

Rodwell, J.M. and A. Jones, eds. *The Koran.* London: Phoenix, 1994.

Rousseau, Leon. *Die Grot Avontuur : Wondere van die Lewe opAarde.* CapeTown: Human & Rousseau, 2006.

Rylaarsdam, J. Coert, *et al.* "Biblical Literature". Chicago: Encyclopaedia Brittanica, 2010.

Sandeen, E.R. "Fundamentalism, Christian". In *Encyclopædia Britannica*, 2010.

Scholtz, Adelbert. "Einstein, Albert". In: Gaum, Frits, *Christelike Kern-Ensiklopedie.* Wellington: Lux Verbi, 2008.

———. "Freud, Sigmund". In: Gaum, Frits, *Christelike Kern-Ensiklopedie.* Wellington: Lux Verbi, 2008.

———. *The Theory and Practice of Pastoral Care. Mauritius:*Lambert Academic, 2018.

———. *The Prophecies of Revelation : a Reconstruction of the Visions of John of Patmos.* Mauritius: Lambert Academic Publishing, 2017.

Shanks, Hershel. "An Interview with John Strugnell". Biblical Archaeology Review. July–August 1994. https://www.bib-arch.org/online-exclusives/dead-sea-scrolls-12.asp

Gustave Doré: Satan cast out by the archangel Michael

Steinhardt, Paul J. and Neil Turok. *Endless Universe : Beyond the Big Bang.* London: Phoenix, 2008.

Stenger, Viktor. *The New Atheism: Taking a Stand for Science and Reason.* New York: Prometheus, 2009.

Stoker, H.G. *Beginsels en Metodes in die Wetenskap.* Johannesburg: Boekhandel De Jong, 1969.

Taylor, J.E. and D. Hay. "Astrology in Philo of Alexandria's De Vita Contemplativa: Paper Read at Aram Society for Syro-Mesopotamian Studies 29th International Conference on the Theme of Astrology in the Ancient Near East, Held at The University of Oxford, 08-10 July 2010". file:///c:/users/user/downloads/astrology_in_philo_of_alexandrias_de_vit.pdf

Thiel, R. *And then There was Light.* New York: Knopf, 1958.

Transman (Pty) Ltd v Dick and Another 2009 (4) SA 22 (SCA).

Toy, Crawford Howell, and Kaufmann Kohler. "Jubilees, Book of". *Jewish Encyclopedia.* https://www.jewishencyclopedia.com/articles/8944-jubilees-book-of#:~:text=The%20Book%20of%20Jubilees%2C%20presenting,Angel%20of%20the%20Presence%20(i.

Van Aarde, A.G. "A Commemoration of the Legacy of Rudolf Bultmann, Born 130 Years Ago". *Studia Historiae Ecclesiasticae*, Vol 40, No 1, 2014. https://uir.unisa.ac.za/handle/10500/13710

Van der Toorn, K., Becking, Bob, and van der Horst, Pieter Willem, eds. *Dictionary of Deities and Demons in the Bible*. Grand Rapids: Wm. B. Eerdmans, 1999.

Van Helden, A. "Galileo". Chicago: Encyclopaedia Britannica, 2010.

Van Lill, "Darwin, Charles Robert." In: Gaum, Frits, *Christelike Kern-Ensiklopedie.* Wellington: Lux Verbi, 2008.

Veronelli, Laura *et al*. "Geschwind Syndrome in frontotemporal lobar degeneration: Neuroanatomical and neuropsychological features over 9 years". *Cortex*. . 2017 Sep:94:27-38. doi: 10.1016/j.cortex.2017.06.003. Epub 2017 Jun 27. https://pubmed.ncbi.nlm.nih.gov/28711815/

Villines, Zawn. "Exorcism and Psychology: What's Really Going on?". *Good Therapy, 8 March 2013.* https://www.goodtherapy.org/blog/psychology-exorcism-demonic-possession-0308137

Visser, A.J. *De Openbaring aan Johannes*. Nijkerk: Callenbach, 1962.

Wasson, D.L. "Domitian". *Ancient History Encyclopedia, 25 April 2013)* http://www.ancient.eu/domitian/

White, Ethan Doyle. "Satanism: Occult Practice. Britannica, 2024. https://www.britannica.com/topic/Satanism

Wikipedia. "List of Roman Emperors". https://en.wikipedia.org/wiki/List_of_Roman_emperors

———. "List of the Dead Sea Scrolls". https://en.wikipedia.org/wiki/List_of_the_Dead_Sea_Scrolls

Zimmer, Carl. *Evolution*. London: Arrow, 2003.

LIST OF ILLUSTRATIONS

Frontispiece
Albrecht Dürer: St Michael Overcoming the Devil
https://www.mutualart.com/Artwork/Saint-Michael-overcoming-the-devil/31B5300010234B9F5BDB22DFFD32A172

Contents
Albrecht Dürer: St Michael and his Angels fight the Dragon
https://www.albrecht-durer.org/St.michael-And-His-Angels-Fight-The-Dragon.html

Chapter 1
Darth Vader
https://i.pinimg.com/originals/42/13/96/421396f1cbf4ba0eef01ba9f65a552bc.jpg

Chapter 2
Pan – Greco-Roman Antioch Floor Mosaic, 3rd Century A.D. (Hatay Archaeology Museum, Antakya
https://www.theoi.com/Gallery/Z22.1.html

Tomas de Torquemada
https://www.avilaturismo.com/en/tomas-de-torquemada

Chapter 3
The Beit Alpha mosaic with Hebrew names for the different constellations of the Zodiac. The seasons are depicted on the corners.
https://www.israelinphotos.com/2012/12/beit-alfa-synagogue-national-park.html

The Hebrew conception of the cosmos.

https://www.quora.com/Do-creationists-generally-accept-the-heliocentric-model-and-is-this-model-in-accordance-with-the-Bible

The Aristotelian worldview, as adapted by Christian theologians.
https://en.wikipedia.org/wiki/Aristotelian_physics

Lucifer, King of Hell, by Paul Gustave Doré.
https://en.wikipedia.org/wiki/Dante%27s_Satan#/media/File:DVinfernoLuciferKingOfHell_m.jp

Chapter 4

Frontispiece to Galileo's Dialogo Sopra di Due Massimi Sistemi del Mondo, Tolemaico e Copernicano
https://en.m.wikipedia.org/wiki/File:Galileos_Dialogue_Title_Page.png

Albert Einstein
https://tvtropes.org/pmwiki/pmwiki.php/UsefulNotes/AlbertEinstein

How our Solar System fits into the bigger picture of the Universe
https://www.pinterest.com/pin/522558362987375677/visual-search/?x=0&y=0&w=362&h=894.

Charles Darwin
https://www.smithsonianmag.com/science-nature/what-darwin-didnt-know-45637001/

Chapter 6

Albrecht Dürer: Adam and Eve
https://www.britannica.com/topic/Fall-of-Man

Albrecht Dürer: Job and Satanhttps://picryl.com/media/job-op-de-mestvaalt-ab5912

Gustave Doré: The Fallen Angel (engraving — 1866)
https://smecsundaymorningforum.org/tag/the-fallen-angel/

Gustave Dore: Satan at the Gates of Hell
https://www.art.com/gallery/id--b184935/satan-posters.htm

Chapter 7
The apostle Paul (ceiling mosaic, Archiepiscopal Chapel of St. Andrew, Ravenna, Italy)
https://www.biblegateway.com/blog/2016/05/our-letters-to-the-church-series-is-complete-whats-next/paul-mosaic-ravenna-275x272x72/

Angel with the Key to the Bottomless Pit – Albrecht Dürer, 1498
https://www.metmuseum.org/art/collection/search/397142

Albrecht Dürer: The Virgin on the Crescent
https://www.metmuseum.org/art/collection/search/391039

Satan in the Abyss by Gustave Doré
https://www.wikiart.org/en/gustave-dore/satan-s-flight-through-chaos

Chapter 8
Depiction of a *shaitan* by Siyah Qalam, c. 14th/15th century.
https://en.wikipedia.org/wiki/Shaitan#:~:text=The%20Quran%20speaks%20of%20various,%22)%2C%20is%20their%20leader.

Chapter 9
Satan, as drawn by Gustave Doré
https://en.m.wikipedia.org/wiki/File:GustaveDoreParadiseLostSatanProfile.jpg

Darth Vader
https://za.pinterest.com/pin/326511041725746889/

Bibliography

Gustave Doré: Satan cast out by the archangel Michael
https://www.britannica.com/topic/Satanism

The Knight, Death, and the Devil by Albrecht Dürer (1513)
https://victorianweb.org/graphics/durer/2.html

\

www.ingramcontent.com/pod-product-compliance
Lightning Source LLC
LaVergne TN
LVHW020536100826
845148LV00010B/1495

9798385219308